Julius Rodenberg

England, literary and social

From a German point of view

Julius Rodenberg

England, literary and social
From a German point of view

ISBN/EAN: 9783744715171

Printed in Europe, USA, Canada, Australia, Japan

Cover: Foto ©Suzi / pixelio.de

More available books at **www.hansebooks.com**

ENGLAND,

LITERARY AND SOCIAL,

FROM A

GERMAN POINT OF VIEW.

ENGLAND,

LITERARY AND SOCIAL,

FROM A

GERMAN POINT OF VIEW.

BY

JULIUS RODENBERG.

LONDON:

RICHARD BENTLEY & SON, NEW BURLINGTON STREET,

Publishers in Ordinary to Her Majesty.

1875.

LONDON :

PRINTED BY WILLIAM CLOWES AND SONS,

STAMFORD STREET AND CHARING CROSS.

AUTHOR'S PREFACE.

THE following Essays were written at various times, after long and often repeated residences in England. They not only reproduce impressions, but also recapitulate the studies to which such residences gave rise. Published originally in periodicals for the most part, they have been enlarged, revised, and are here for the first time presented in a complete form. Unity of place, object, and tone, if I may be allowed the expression, lends them a certain esoteric connection, justifying their appearance in their present form; although they cannot claim to be considered in a systematic sense as a perfect whole.

Everywhere starting from some important point in the history of literature and education, the Author of these Sketches has endeavoured to seize, here and there, out of the isolated periods

of England's development in both these provinces, a moment, not indeed arbitrarily, but
always guided by the idea of making it the central
point of a picture, which from the concrete offers
a perspective of the abstract: the people, and the
country of England.

Nor, if the Author has rightly delineated persons and conditions, is the merit his, but rather
that of English and German inquirers, in whose
track he has followed: all that out of his
own observation he has added is simply a background to the landscape, some local colour, some
reference to the ground itself, out of which these
persons and conditions grew. An inexhaustible
pleasure has it been to him to seek out those
places which stood in any local connection with
the objects of his interest, and to mark the vicis-
situdes they have undergone in the lapse of centuries. No track or corner relating to these
objects has he left untrodden; the whole day
long in the midst of the budding life of the
present has he sought out the traces of the
past; in old cathedrals, and in houses blackened with smoke; in castle and in city, by land

and by sea, in many a street and on many a shore.

The Ocean, which from England's coasts carries the eye into an apparent infinitude, and the City, which gives the impression of the strongest and most strictly-defined peculiarity—the church-tower, beyond which a thousand lives have never looked, the immeasurable sea in which another thousand lie cradled—this opposition and this interchange of the old time-hallowed, fast-rooted, yea, pedantic, on one side, and on the other, ever-varying, fantastic, and strange, runs from its natural beginning through the life, the history, the poetry of England; and I should be glad if the present book reflected any of the manifold lights which spring from the method of consideration I have mentioned.

This work was already finished in its several parts when the war of 1870 delayed further completion. It may be allowed to this, as to many other labours of peace, to refer to the period when the war interrupted them. The sickly *trait* which the German cosmopolitism wore, almost compulsorily, is eradicated—the echo of it we would cherish. It is not the German way to shut one-self up in one's own self-complacency. We would progress, busy ourselves with the external world, and recognise all that is great therein. But the effect will be other than it once was. To us also, in the widest measure, is this recognition assigned, but the genius of the German people will prevent us losing our senses in the contemplation of our own grandeur. With the consciousness that we are what we now are, of our own strength alone; with the happy feeling of creation and action around us, we will never deny the friend-ship of earlier years, and we would see with deep regret enmities prolong themselves, whose first germ lay but in the fault which Germany, with God's help, will avoid, in self-conceit, and the want of a generous recognition of that which is not German!

JULIUS RODENBERG.

EISENACH, *September* 1872.

TRANSLATOR'S PREFACE.

A NOTICE of this work, which appeared in the 'Times,' in December 1872, speaks of it as one of many efforts of the Author to endeavour " to make his countrymen know and love England."

It appeared to the Translator that an interest would be evoked in this country to read the opinion which an impartial foreigner had formed of some of our social and literary characteristics. The papers are partly historical, partly the result of personal impressions of the Author whilst a tourist in England.

The Translator has left a few occasional foreign modes of expression where he deemed that a certain character and freshness would be lost by a too literal English rendering.

TEMPLE, 1875.

CONTENTS.

———◆◆◆———

KENT,

AND

THE CANTERBURY TALES.

B

I.

THE German traveller in England is least likely to forget his first view of Albion's earliest charms, the white cliffs of Dover rising out of a fresh green sea.

He treads the land of Kent with the feeling that he is here treading a new land apart from all he has yet seen. Other faces, other houses, other landscapes, another sky, and another mode of life, suddenly come before him, but withal an echo, as from the distant years, brings him home. He remembers that his own past greets him here, thinking of those words in Camden's 'Britannia': "Here was the first Saxon rule established in Britain A.C. 456, and from them it was called Cantwararŷc." (Edit. Francof., p. 242.)

Where now the red banner with the blue cross waves, there fluttered once the Saxon flag with the white horse—the horse whose figure adorned the Saxon ships as it adorns the straw roofs of peasants' houses in Lower Saxony at the present day, the white steed which Hengist and Horsa bore on their shield, and which, through the

B 2

Hanoverian succession, has entered the blazon of the three United Kingdoms. Removed since the accession of Victoria, it has yet remained in the county of Kent from time immemorial, and there in the old Saxon kingdom, once the kingdom of the men of Cantium, it tells the history of the past to the wanderer in the sunshine on its land.

A fair land it is, this England's garden, blest with all which makes the heart glad; with fruit and corn and hops, with meadows and woods of stately oaks and elms, with rivers filled with fish, and wayside villages. Between these here and there, surrounded by its park and timber, a hundred years old, rises one of those baronial halls in which no other county is so rich as Kent, or one of those old-fashioned manor houses in the style of the Tudors, the ancient seat of the landed gentry. What a charm of homeliness, honour, and trust, broods over the red brick walls of these residences, rising among towns filled with the hum of labour, out of a crown of trees by the wayside—pictures of distinguished rest, of secure possession, of constancy and duration in the midst of that ceaseless change to which we are all subject! Old, and yet not in decay—closed, yet not hostile—proud, yet not insolent—they stand there unhurt by the storms which have ruined

the castles in France and threatened those in
Germany, seats of courage, plenty, hospitality,
the old brothers of the city, the remains of good
Old England. Landed proprietors lived here—
squires, so called—people who were not noble,
though they had a long line of ancestors and
a splendid coat-of-arms. A mean between the
nobility and the peasantry, they were the famed
old gentry, the land's substance, the might of the
realm, the real kernel of the English nation, representing its wealth and independence, strength-
ened by Cromwell's iron regiment when he smashed
the heads of the nobles. The conceptions of
"squire," "gentry," and its correlative "gentleman," are so thoroughly English, that they can
only be made plain to a Continental understanding
by description.* The moral meaning of gentleman
we know, and have adopted it in our own German
language. But this is only one side of the con-

* "I am styled 'gentleman' by Act of Parliament," says
Mr. Sampson Brass in the 'Old Curiosity Shop,' though no
English reader would take him really to be a "gentleman."
The conventional has nothing in common with the legal
term. Washington Irving says there is "an indescribable
something which always distinguishes the gentleman, which
dwells in a man's air and deportment, and not in his clothes."
—'Tales of a Traveller,' p. 116, Bohn's Edition.

ception, by no means all. The squire—an antiquated title, in the place of which is now the country gentleman, one of the most enviable personalities in modern English life—was originally a knight's son before receiving knighthood. Every holder of a fee-simple of more than 20*l.* sterling, was then entitled to knighthood : more and more, however, men withdrew themselves from this costly honour, and after the 46th year of Edward III., 1373, the title "squire" was accorded to every large landowner, without consideration of knighthood or fee. The squire, or lord of the manor, has been defined as a landowner of the lower nobility : but he is more and less; less, since he has no *legal* status, as the nobleman has—more, since he may be of more aristocratic descent, and possess a local influence which is not to be referred to any law, but is inherited with the land itself, often through centuries, from father to son. "Nobilis fit," the English Peer is *made,* under the old title is often a new family; but "nascitur generosus," a man must be *born* of this kind, as is plain from the notable reply put in the mouth of James I., who, after his succession, was asked by his nurse to make her son a gentleman, "My good woman, I can make him a Lord, but it is beyond my power to make him a gentleman." Even Selden, the famous jurist, whose 'Treatise on Titles of Honour,' published in 1614, is still an authority on the respective ranks of the nobility and gentry, goes so far as to say that not even God Almighty can make a gentleman. The matter is made clear by considering the gentry as corresponding to the German nobility, The gentry is divided into the *titled* and the *non-titled.* The first class is made up of baronets and knights. This class, compared with the nobles, is known as the lesser or lower nobility. But neither knight nor baronet has, beyond his title and precedence in order of rank, the slightest privilege over the old squire or untitled gentleman; they rather represented and still represent the gentry which may be elected only for the Lower House, while the nobility is admitted by law to the Upper.

But the nobility of England can, as far as regards age, scarcely be compared with that of Germany, still less with that of France. This is owing to its political nature, which, as before remarked, is most nearly related to the Upper House: a Lord is always also a Peer; he thus preserves the mark of his origin better than the nobility of any other land in Christendom. All nobility is and can only be originally a nobility of merit; but through the unlimited inheritance of a distinction in its essence personal, this character is in most other lands almost lost. In England it has not only remained in principle; but the tendency of modern time is to cause it, in fact, to assume greater importance. Though inheritance still exists, it is narrowed; the children of great families return, after a time, back into the people, whence their ancestors sprung. A Peer's eldest son, succeeding to the title at his father's death, is during his life only conventionally a Lord, and is therefore eligible for the Lower House. Changed in England, more than elsewhere, is the usage of conferring nobility on merit as such, by giving it a seat in the House of Lords. Twenty of the greatest families have been founded by City merchants, and seventy Peers owe their elevation to a successful career as advocates or administrative functionaries. The English nobility is an institution with a living organism, in which the blood, through assimilation, and rejection of used up elements, is continually renewed; instead of separating itself from the people, it has always drawn its greatest strength from its connection with them, and thus, though with fewer ancestors than Continental nobility, it possesses greater riches and popularity.

A "title without means"* is not of much value

---

* Cf. 'The Act of Attainder against the Duke of Oldford.' —'Saturday Review,' March, 1873, p. 379.

in England, and bankruptcy is looked on as a sufficient ground for degradation. A dozen profligate Peers might be mentioned, who, after running through their property, were either not called to the Upper House or had their names taken out from the list of members. In earlier centuries wars, in later revolutions and treasonable conspiracies, have made great gaps among them. The war between the Red and White Roses asked for whole hecatombs of noble victims : it was strictly commanded before the battle that the nobles should be killed, the commoners alone spared. Thus in thirteen engagements, from St. Alban's day, in the year 1455, to the day of Bosworth, in 1485, two kings, four princes, ten dukes, two marquises, twenty-one counts, two viscounts, and twenty-seven barons fell, either on the field of battle or afterwards by assassination. Attainder, too, since the time of the Conqueror, has considerably thinned the ranks of the nobles : no less, indeed, than eighty lords have died under the hands of the executioner or common hangman.

Little trace now exists of the great Norman nobility of William, as little of the creations of Lackland. Among England's oldest titled families, three can trace their genealogy to the time of Henry III., and three to that of the first Edward ;

but these, strangely enough, are in the lowest ranks
of the English Peerage, while its higher dignities
point back invariably to a more modern origin.
Scarce a sixth of the present sitters in the Upper
House held their titles at the time of the Revolution in 1688, and in thirty years the list of the
Peers has been increased by over sixty names.
Out of twenty dukedoms, one only comes from the
fifteenth century, and the oldest marquisate is not
older than the sixteenth. Of 108 earldoms, two
only came from the fifteenth century, thirty-one
from the eighteenth, and fifty-four from the nineteenth. Only one viscount dates from the sixteenth century. Baronies go back as far as the
thirteenth century, of which there are six, and
four from the fourteenth : of the former, three are
Peeresses in their own right. One of these,
Baroness Boscawen, represents the Barony of
Despencer; she and the Baroness de Ros are of
the two oldest noble families of England, created in
the year 1264. Beyond this can none of the Upper
House trace their descent, whilst the name and
family of many of the gentry is in the ' Doomsday
Book,' as that of the famous Millais, the painter of
the 'Bride of the Huguenot.' But the squire was
quite a different being from his descendant the
country gentleman, yet not more so than the life

of the present from that of the past. He who
would know him in his rough, sometimes too
rough, yet always genial humour, must read some
romance of the last century, as, for instance, ' Tom
Jones,' where Fielding has given us so delightful
a picture of the two worthy neighbours, Squires
Western and Allworthy, of whom the last does
nothing but make others happy, while the first—a
far truer picture of his time—does nothing but
hunt, curse, and become fuddled with—the parson.

Not less ancient than the dwellings of the
landed proprietors in Kent are its towns. Dover
claims precedence, as being the first entered by
any one landing in that county, with its old Norman castle, *clavis et repagulum totius regni*, as Matthew Paris describes it. As Kent was the nearest
point to the Continent, so all England's conquerors
landed here. Julius Cæsar and the Romans at
Dover ; the Saxons at the Isle of Thanet, now no
more an isle; and lastly the Danes. So these
coasts were strictly watched in the time of the
Normans, and the Cinque Ports especially constructed for their defence, of which, however, some,
like Sandwich, for more than a hundred years have
been part of the mainland. The governor of these
five havens is called Lord Warden, a post which,
since the havens disappeared, has become a sinecure,

and is given to deserving statesmen, as last to the
Duke of Wellington and Lord Palmerston. The
residence of the Lord Warden is Walmer Castle,
an old castle by the sea, not far from the village
of the same name, in which I, in the beginning of
1860, lived, and saw the then Lord Warden
Palmerston riding merrily with his groom behind
him. It is a lovely residence : the perfume of the
fields mixes itself with the salt breeze of the sea ; on
the left lies the little picturesque village of Deal,
and opposite in the sea the dangerous Goodwins,
" that fearful sandbank where the skeletons of so
many stately ships lie buried " (' Merchant of
Venice,' iii. 1), once, in far back days, the possession of the Earl of Goodwin, father of that Harold
whom William conquered at Hastings. So has the
sea, ever labouring—here washing away, there
adding—buried in its deeps part of the mainland,
and elsewhere made islands, as that of Thanet,
or havens, as that of Sandwich, part of the present
Continent.

Sandwich, now a quiet little rustic town, lies
not far from the ocean, which, however, can only
be seen from the top of the old crumbling tower
of the church, surrounded by its graves. To the
stranger who passes through its empty streets it
must seem a city of the dead, a realm reigned

over by sleep and dream; there are few traces to
remind him that active life once dominated here.
Three hundred years ago Sandwich was the object of
a peculiar invasion, friendly, however, and welcome
—that of the Protestant Flemings, who sought
a refuge here, when, flying from Alba, they determined rather to give up their home than their
creed. The exodus of Belgium's richest merchants,
most excellent fabricators and most diligent manufacturers, lasted for a year. They wandered in all
directions, but those who turned to England and
greeted its coast as *Asylum Christi* first settled in
Sandwich, where we find a great number of them
in the year 1561. Their artistic knowledge, and
their love of freedom, they brought with them
wherever they went; and well might one say of
them here in England as later was said in the
Mark Brandenburg, that "those towns in which
they dwelt were happy, for God followed them
with His blessing." In spite of Papal Bulls,
Queen Elizabeth secured them a hospitable reception. The mayor and council of Sandwich were
advised to receive them in a friendly manner, and
to give them especially every assistance in the
prosecution of their trade, linen and cloth weaving, which they brought with them to our shores.
This was done. Two weekly markets were or-

dained in Sandwich for the selling of their goods, which were soon sought out of all parts of England. They had a church and churchyard, as they had desired on landing, a place to worship their God, a place to bury their dead, and liberty to practise their trade. Sandwich, which shortly before, through the fact of its haven becoming covered with sand, was sunken from its former greatness, attained new altitude and reputation. Well might Schiller make his Marquis Posa cry to the tyrant Philip II.—" Thousands fled from their fatherland, poor and happy. Elizabeth received the fugitives with open arms, and Britain blossomed and bore fruit through our country's handiwork."

Others soon followed the colony of Sandwich. Samuel Smiles, whose story of the settling of the Flemish in Kent we here recapitulate, tells us that in the very first years of Elizabeth's reign a troop of eighteen Walloon families, under the guidance of their rector Hector Hammon, *Minister verbi Dei*, came to Canterbury, where they were received with no less friendliness. Here they set up their looms, hitherto unknown in England, for brocade, Orleans silk, and half-silk produce. The high-spirited and liberal Matthew Parker, Archbishop of Canterbury, gave them for their religious service a crypt of the Cathedral once consecrated

to the Holy Virgin, and in this crypt—out of whose
former wealth in gold, purple, jewels, and costly
stones Henry VIII. only left the rings on which the
silver lamps hung—these refugees assembled themselves for prayer and preaching. The community
which here flourished during the seventeenth century became afterwards smaller from year to year;
at the beginning of the last century the greater
number, together with the Huguenots, had gone
to London, where their posterity are still extant
among the Spitalfields' weavers. The remainder,
however, is still in Canterbury; and although the
community consists but of twenty members, out of
which are two elders and four deacons, it still
holds in the so-called " French Church," which is
the present name of the old crypt, its Calvinistic
service, while above in the Cathedral all the pomp
of the High Church of England displays itself.

A deeper impression was left by the Flemish
colony in Sandwich. Here, not long after their
landing, they constituted a third part of the
people. Though cloth-weaving was their speciality, they by no means confined themselves to
this. Many of the branches of that industry in
which England beyond doubt takes precedence,
and which is the fountain of its national wealth,
as, for instance, that of the cloth and wool manufac-

ture, these Flemish introduced, and helped to perfect others. They built the first Dutch windmills on the coast of Kent ; they fabricated porcelain ; above all, they tended garden and field after the fashion of their former home. " Till the time of these settlers," says Smiles, " the art of gardening was almost unknown in. England ; cabbages, radishes, turnips, and other vegetables were scarcely to be had : indeed, one scarcely knows how to cook them even at the present day." The Spanish Catharine, Henry VIII.'s first wife, accustomed as she was to salad in her southern home, could scarcely procure one in all England, and was obliged to import it from the Netherlands. All this, and more, the Flemish brought : they changed the fair Kent into that garden, in which all is green and bloom to the edge of the ocean ; and though Sandwich has long since become a quiet town, which gives no more any information as to its second elevation, yet the gardens which surround the houses like a voluptuous crown, and recommend themselves as much by their neatness as by their fertility, remind us still of the days of those settlers from the Netherlands. But these have long since ceased to be a separate people, though, mixed with the general, numberless families still retain their Dutch names. A direct descend-

ant of the Bouveries—the original Bouverie being
a great wool-manufacturer, who in the year 1567
escaped to Sandwich from the Inquisition of Alba
—sits now in the House of Lords as Earl Radnor;
and the Right Hon. E. H. Knatchbull-Hugessen,
an offshoot of the Flemish Hugessen, a weaver,
represents in the House of Commons the town
which once received as an asylum his ancestors.

The town, however, which more than any other
in Kent preserves recollections of bygone time,
and tells those who care to hear such voices of the
past a whole history of old English life and poetry,
is Canterbury, lying inland halfway between
London and the sea.

II.

There it stands, the old archiepiscopal town, the Cantuaria of the Saxons, the metropolis of the men of Kent, the "Kantelburg" of the German students of theology—there it stands before me, with its old cathedral, with its old churches, asylums, cloisters, old streets, and old gabled houses. A feeling steals over me as on that morning, when I stood under the shadows of its houses, not as if I were myself old, but as if the old time were again young; such rest lies over it, as out of past centuries. The sun shines on its grey slate roofs and towers with another light, as if less colour were there, paler, fainter, more dreamy; like the sunshine on old sacred paintings. All round is the old wall, in some places fallen, but everywhere overgrown with ivy and wild flowers, which smell strong in the midday sun. Quiet gardens lie under the walls; in the still streets are old inns, with dark, cool, arched chambers; and in the darkest corner stands "mine host," who has lost nothing of the redness of his nose from wearing a fashionable white cravat, and properly

is no more called "host," but "waiter;" and the
"butler," who, alas! has lost his leathern apron,
brings me a pewter pot and tumbler; and the
"ostler" sits in the yard on the shafts of a waggon,
polishing the silver garnishing of his harness, and
humming part of a harvest-song, with the beautiful refrain,

> "Over, over, over and over,
> Let every man drink off his can,
> And toss it over and over."

Again I go into the streets and bye-lanes,
which are full of the warm August sunshine and
shadows, of crowds of men, and the gay bustle of
the morning market; and amongst all the other
old houses also that "very old house bulging
out over the road, a house with long, low lattice-
windows, bulging out still farther, and beams with
carved heads on the ends bulging out too, so that
I fancied the whole house was leaning forwards,
trying to see who was passing on the narrow
pavement below."

Every reader of Dickens's masterpiece, 'David
Copperfield,' knows that in this house, with its
old-fashioned brass knocker, its low-arched door
and corners, its angles and carvings, and its quaint
little panes of glass, and yet quainter little windows, as old as the hills, yet as pure as any snow

that ever fell on them, the fair Agnes lived; that
angel of a wife with whom poor David was blessed,
when he, sick of the joys and the sorrows of the
world, returned home to this old town of his youth,
to find in its familiar obscurity peace, and in the
forgotten playmaiden the good, true, forgiving
friend and helpmate whom he could never forget.

A thousand remembrances awake as I walk
along through the High Street of the town (so
is called regularly in every English provincial
town the old "Heerstrasse"). Here is a small
street, "Mercery Lane," which seems more anti-
quated than all the other antiquated streets; and
here is an open space, and on it stands, in all
its mediæval splendour and magnificence, the
Cathedral.

The Cathedral is the prominent trait in the features of Canterbury, and wherever one may stand,
in the streets or in the environs of the town, it
remains present to him, like an earnest and solemn
thought. So long as one can see Canterbury, its
quadrangular towers are conspicuous in the wide
plain to the traveller who passes in the railway,
a last reminiscence of monkish, as the Castle at
Dover of feudal England.

The ground-stone of this building was laid by
William the Conqueror; but the individual parts

date from the most various periods of those centuries which, for the West of Europe, have become the classical age of architecture. Hence the whole has a character of variety, intimately connected through the transcendental spirit which formerly loved to celebrate the Highest in poems of stone, which for the princes and great of this world made dark fast castles, but for the King of kings that light dome—whose towers stretch full of longing towards Heaven.

The choir of the Cathedral has an imposing effect when one first sees its pillars, its arches, and, walking under its vaults, thinks he beholds above him the arches of an oak-wood turned into stone, from which the German spirit obtained its first architectural inspiration. It is the Anglo-Norman style which does not essentially differ from our Gothic, for the same German rudiments are in both. Upon the north side of the Cathedral are the cloisters, the chapter-house, and the remains of the archiepiscopal palace. The treasure-chamber is in a quadrangular Norman tower at the east end, and here were kept, before the abolition of the Catholic religion in England, the numerous relics of which Erasmus has written. In the nave, in the aisles, and the crypt, in the twilight which falls through the stained-

glass windows, lie buried a king of England, a
queen, a prince, many cardinals, and all the archbishops of Canterbury who in the four hundred
years from 1161 to 1502 here lived and died.
Their stone figures, with the mitre on their heads,
the crosier in their hands, and with faces as if
they slept, repose on their stone sarcophagi. What
a row of coffins and of remembrances! Yet only
two of them have preserved for us, over so long
a time, their romantic or historical charm—

> " Black Edward's helm and Becket's bloody stone."
> —*Don Juan*, x. 73.

The Black Prince! Edward III.'s heroic son,
who does not know him? The favourite of ancient
folk-lore, gay, full of animal spirits, the intrepid
conqueror of Cressy, who yet was destined in
early manhood to suffer and to die! To this day
that little book which, under the title 'History of
Edward the Black Prince, together with the Conquest of France,' represents his military exploits,
his love adventures, and his early death, forms
a chief ingredient of that flying literature that
one so often meets in London's old quarters in
the form of a long pamphlet, with innumerable
leaves and pictures therein. How happy the
readers of this history are still at the thought
that the king's son at last loves and marries a

daughter of the people, the beautiful maid of Kent, "an overflowing young thing!" and how little care they that historical criticism has long ago informed us that the beautiful maid of Kent, this "overflowing young thing," was really a widow with four children; and might have been the exact ideal of that other Prince of Wales, whom our older contemporaries remember as the "finest gentleman in Europe," the famous Prince Regent, and subsequent George IV., whose device in reference to the fair sex was "fair, fat, and forty."

There the Black Prince of Canterbury lies in the Cathedral, buried in the land which he loved, in the town in which he willingly tarried, and in the place which he appointed in his will for his resting-place. Upon his sarcophagus is his figure in gilt brass, fully armed—with the halo and the German legend "Ich Dien," which this prince won, together with the ostrich feathers, in the battle of Cressy, and the arms which all following Princes of Wales inherit to this day—with the locked hands, out of which, however, Cromwell took the sword. "The miscreant," says my guide-book,—which might well have been written by a strong High Churchman,—who broke the precious stone out of the crown of the dead Prince

my author does not say, but I conjecture it was
his own friends, the High Churchmen in Henry
the Eighth's time. His other treasures have been
left to him, namely, his old glove, his rusty helmet,
his torn shirt of mail, and his self-composed Norman-
French epitaph, of which this is a literal translation :—

" I had gold, silver, splendid cloth,
  Great treasures, horses, houses, land ;
  Yet now a poor ragamuffin,
  Lie I buried under the ground ;
  And couldst thou see me, once so proud and awful,
  I believe thou wouldst not know me more ;
  And wouldst never suppose, without reading it,
  That I was once a man, to say nothing of a prince."

Is not the English moralist right when he says
that one may take fire (and even diamonds, as the
example before us shows) out of the past, but
never ashes ?

Such a fire out of the past glimmers brightly
about the other great trophy of Canterbury—the
stone of Thomas à Becket.

Here in his own Cathedral was he murdered at
the altar, upon the stone slab which shows to this
day the stains of his blood. A City boy of very
humble origin, but of most brilliant talents, he soon
knew how to make himself noticed. After the

completion of his studies in Oxford, Paris, and
Bologna, he was in 1154 made Archdeacon of the
Archbishop of Canterbury. From here he came to
the Court of Henry II., the first Plantagenet, who
himself, a man of great importance, had a sharp
eye for the importance of others. In three
years had Thomas à Becket, through the favour
of the King, climbed the highest secular steps
in the kingdom. He was Chancellor in 1157,
a title which in its signification, that of a first
minister, is now known as that of the Premier,
and in the English language has still maintained
itself, if not with the same sense, still with the
same word as " Lord Chancellor." He was a
worldly man; kept a good table, a brilliant retinue,
numberless servants, fine horses, and supported
his King in his endeavours against the hierarchy
until he obtained the highest spiritual rule, became,
that is, Archbishop of Canterbury, and Primus
Regni, " Primate of all England." Then he
turned his point suddenly against the King, and
a hard antagonist the King had in him—hard
as he was himself. The State and the Church
had never, perhaps, during the whole of the
Middle Ages, been pitted against each other in
like bold individualities. Becket, who as Chancellor had shown himself the thoroughly worldly-

minded executor of his sovereign's commands, says Pauli, in his 'Pictures of Old England,' strove with zeal, as soon as he attained the primacy, to carry out in England the consequences of the pseudo-Isidorian decretals, the sum of the exaggerated pretensions of Gregory VII., and the recently published doctrines of canonical law of Gratian; while in Becket's own trial, the first peer of the realm for the first time employed that insti-. tution which may be described as a trial by jury.

Becket fled, but he continued the battle, supported by the authority of the Pope; so that when he at length returned he had by no means the intention of yielding his position; but his purpose was, says Pauli, to endure shame and infamy, and at the worst to die in that consecrated place where he had acted as pontiff, and to secure a victory by the death of a martyr. And so the catastrophe happened in the year 1170, which Fitzstephen, the historian of the Archbishop, and after him Hume, relates in the following manner :—

"And the King himself, being vehemently agitated, burst forth into an exclamation against his servants, whose want of zeal, he said, had so long left him exposed to enterprises of that ungrateful and imperious prelate. Four gentlemen of his household—Reginald Fitz-Urst, William de Tracy, Hugh de Moreville, and Richard Brito—taking these passionate expressions to be a hint for Becket's death, immediately communicated their thoughts to each other; and swearing to avenge their prince's quarrel, secretly withdrew from Court (which at the time was held, as in those times very often happened, within the French possessions of Bayeux, in Normandy). Some menacing expressions which they had dropped gave a suspicion of their design; and the King despatched a messenger after them, charging them to attempt nothing against the person of the Primate; but these orders arrived too late to prevent their fatal purpose. The four murderers, though they took different roads to England, arrived nearly about the same time at Saltwoode, near Canterbury; and being there joined by some assistance, they proceeded in great haste to the archiepiscopal palace. They found the Primate, who trusted entirely to the sacredness of his character, very slenderly attended; and though they threw out many menaces and reproaches against him, he was so incapable of fear that, without using any precautions against their violence, he immediately went to St. Benedict's Church to hear vespers. They followed him thither, attacked him before the altar, and having cloven his head with many blows, retired without meeting any opposition. This was," so concludes the chronologist, "the tragical end of Thomas à Becket."

But only his worldly end; the Church had another fate in preparation for him, for he was to her as a fallen martyr; therefore she made him a saint, and constrained the monarch who was not able to conquer him whilst living to make a pilgrimage to his grave when dead.

In the year 1172 Becket became canonized amongst the saints of the first rank as " Martyr

of the Faith;" and on the 7th of July, 1220, his
remains were interred with great solemnity in the
chapel built by the successor of Henry II., which
henceforth was dedicated to him, and until the
Reformation remained " the chapel of St. Thomas
the Martyr." The papal legate and the Archbishops of Canterbury and Rheims bore the coffin
upon their shoulders. Of all the saints in England he was the most popular; and your true
Briton swears only by St. Thomas of Canterbury. But out of Britain, also, the popularity of
St. Thomas so quickly spread that, as early as
1194, only twenty-four years after his murder, in
the Blasiusdom, founded by Henry the Lion at
Brunswick, the history of the death and martyrdom
of the new saint was represented upon the painted
walls of the choir, which were probably at the
time of the Reformation covered with whitewash,
and have been only lately again brought to light.
Legend availed itself of the welcome circumstance. It relates to us that the murderers, to be
sure, escaped, but the dogs refused to eat the
crumbs which fell from their table; and that they
themselves at last threw their arms and coats of
mail to the ground, unable any longer to bear the
burden. One of the knights put to death his own
son. All four sought the Holy Land; three of

them reached it, and were, after they had confessed under the cross and received absolution,
buried over against the Holy Sepulchre. The
fourth, Tracy, was driven back by a storm, and
died a miserable death.

But history knows nothing of all this; less
moral than legend, it informs us that all four murderers within the next two years showed themselves at Court, well pleased with their deed,
rode out hunting with the King, and otherwise
stood on the best footing with him. Instead of
'having,' according to the legend, 'the wind
against him,' Tracy was immediately after the
murder made Chief Justice of Normandy, and
lived later in Devonshire; Fitz-Urse settled over
in Ireland; and traces of the Morevilles were long
preserved in England.

Again, legend adds to the circumstance that the
day of Becket's murder, the 29th of December,
1170, was a Friday; now one remembers that
it was likewise a Friday on which he was born,
a Friday on which he was christened, on which
he left England as a fugitive, on which he was,
through a vision, warned of his death, and on
which he, notwithstanding, came back, in order to
suffer on a Friday the death of a martyr. Throughout the Middle Ages, therefore, we find Friday as

a day set apart consecrated to St. Thomas. The day
of his burial, the 7th of July, was the day of the
" Translatio D. Thomæ " in the calendar, and was
until the 16th century celebrated with festive bon-
fires throughout all England. During the whole
of the Middle Ages the worship of the saint continued, and culminated in the Canterbury processions. These were held every year in spring, and
were days of universal rejoicing ; from the most
distant countries came pilgrims to Canterbury
to worship at the shrine of St. Thomas. Here
kings made donations; here the people brought
their savings; and out of the rich treasures
which were thus collected succeeding archbishops
completed that lordly work which otherwise,
perhaps, might have remained uncompleted, the
Cathedral, which they raised over the now empty
tomb of the last British martyr.

All this, however, was altered under Henry VIII.
After his separation from the Romish Church he
not only seized the immense accumulated riches in
Becket's chapel, but also caused the saint himself to
be summoned before his court of justice, and, "when
he remained absent," condemned him as a person
guilty of high treason. Henceforward we find the
former St. Thomas of Canterbury called always
" Thomas Becket the Traytor;" his name was

struck out of the calendar, his festive fires forbidden, his bones were burnt, his ashes strewn in the wind, and only his blood upon the stone, the last surviving trace of the saint, remained.

At this time also ceased the pilgrimages, which had through the thirteenth, fourteenth, and fifteenth centuries preserved the character of a public feast ; but it is to these that we owe that great poem of Geoffrey Chaucer, the 'Canterbury Tales,' which in its kind claims, not less than the Cathedral itself, a monumental significance, for it shows the beginning of a national literature, and has procured for its creator the respected title of " The Father of English Poetry."

Geoffrey Chaucer was a contemporary of Petrarch and Boccaccio. He was born in London, probably in the year 1340. At that time reigned King Edward III., of most glorious memory, the father of the Black Prince. The flood of national life flowed in high and proud waves. Rulers of Norman blood, but fixed firmly through a band of nearly two centuries on the new soil, sat on the throne of England; the oppressed Saxon people for the first time raised its head again, and enriched with the powerful sound of its native idiom, which yet bore the scent of the oak forests and the heathy hills, the elegant dialect of the Norman barons, whose more refined manners and courtly behaviour by degrees also penetrated the long, solitary halls of the rustic Saxon thanes. Out of the hitherto hostile Anglo-Saxon and Norman-French elements grew the one and only English language, and the one and only English people; it was a great time for England, and all had the character of a gay and joyful change. While France, says Macaulay, was wasted by war, till she at length found in her own desolation a miserable defence against invaders, the English gathered in their harvests, adorned their cities, pleaded, traded, and studied in security. Many of our noblest architectural monuments belong to that age. A copious and forcible language, formed by the infusion of French into German, was now the common property of the aristocracy and the people. Nor was it long before genius began to apply that admirable machine to worthy purposes; whilst English battalions, leaving behind them the devastated provinces of France, entered Valladolid in triumph, and spread terror to the gates of Florence, English poets depicted in vivid tints all the wide variety of human manners and fortunes, and English thinkers aspired to know or dared to doubt, where bigots had been content to wonder and believe. The same age which produced the Black Prince and Derby, Chandos and Hawkwood, produced also Geoffrey Chaucer and John Wycliffe.

That was the spring of England, and Geoffrey Chaucer, its poetical herald, its first singer. Yet more; he has something in his appearance which greatly puts me in mind of the " Bible unfolding" Luther. A friend to study, of extensive reading, with various attainments, as free from the superstitions of his age as the condition of natural science allowed him to be—he was at the same time a man of life, the world, and the people; who understood their language, loved it, and if he did not create it, yet formed its national peculiarity and prepared it for literary use.

The life of Chaucer is a varied existence. He plentifully experienced the favour and disfavour of fate, heartily enjoyed the pleasures of this world, and fought with all the irksomeness of existence even to his death. He visited foreign lands, and had intercourse with men of all ranks. With the courtly magnificence of the kings' palaces he was no less familiar than with the daily employments of the citizen and the peasant. Classically educated, he was in succession courtier, soldier, diplomatist, officer, and representative of his country in Parliament. Above all, he knew his own people, and felt himself one with them; he loved his native country in his old age with a still youthful heartiness; until the last the splendour and freshness of the English landscape were reflected by his soul. His good fortune took from him nothing of his amiable modesty, and no adversity was strong enough to strike him to the earth; although his public life was not without storms and clouds, yet his poetical appearance at the commencement of English literature, and of the English people's life, is as a first fair day of spring.

All his biographies written before the year 1866, as, for instance, Hertzberg in his excellent introduction to his translation of the 'Canterbury Tales,' and Pauli in his 'Pictures of Old England,' give as the earliest date in Chaucer's life the autumn of 1359, in which he, under Edward III., joined the expedition against France. Since 1866, our knowledge in this respect has been enriched in a remarkable way. In the above-named year, Mr. Bond found in the British Museum two parchment scrolls, which for three or four hundred years had been glued together in the cover of an old MS. bought by the Museum, and known as "Additional MS., 1862" ('Fortnightly Review,' Aug. 1866, quoted in 'Chaucer's England, by Mr. Browne,' London,

1869; and Lehmann's 'Magazine for Foreign Literature,' No. 17, April 1867). From further communications of Mr. Bond it appears that in the new binding of the above-mentioned MS. these fragments would have been probably cast aside, were it not for a strict regulation of the Museum to preserve carefully all even apparently trifling portions of any old writings. It is to this circumstance we owe one of the most remarkable discoveries in the life of Chaucer. Both these leaves of parchment appear to have belonged to an old household account-book kept for the Countess Elizabeth, the wife of Prince Lionel, Edward III.'s third son. The Countess, the daughter and heiress of William de Burgh, last Earl of Ulster of this name, was, after the election of the King, brought up by his wife; in her ninth year (1341) she was betrothed to the Prince, and was married to him in the year 1352. Among her ancestors on the maternal side was Joan of Acre, the daughter of Edward I., and her mother was Maud, sister of Henry, the first Duke of Lancaster. The strips of parchment which were preserved appear to be out of the Monastery of Amesbury, of which an aunt of the Countess Elizabeth was Abbess, and they contain an index of accounts referring to the years 30–33 of Edward III.—that is, 1357–60. Here it

is that we meet with the name of Geoffrey Chaucer
for the first time. It is in the April of 1357, and
the Countess is in London, in order to make
some purchases for her wardrobe for a visit to
Windsor Castle, where the feast of St. George
was at that time held, at the ceremony in which
the youngest son of Edward III. was invested with
the Order of the Garter with especial pomp.
So we find entered in the account-book, a short
under-coat, a pair of red and black hose, and
a pair of shoes, for Geoffrey Chaucer. The second
time the name occurs is on the 20th of May, when
again an article of clothing was provided for
Chaucer ; and once more at Christmas, when he
was presented with a gift of 3s. 6d. for " neces-
saries." It appears from these, in themselves unimportant, notes that in the year 1357 Chaucer
was probably page in the retinue of Prince
Lionel, or of the Countess Elizabeth ; they can
therefore so far serve to decide a point in Chaucer's
life which before had not been quite clear.
The old English biographies speak with a
certain predilection of his residence in the lordly
park and castle of Woodstock, which existed some
time after the time of Elizabeth, although they
have now long vanished from the face of the
earth. A peculiar glimmer of romance always

shone upon the park of Woodstock, and is even now bound up with its remembrance. Henry I. laid it out as the first park in England ; and here, under the roses of the gardens, ended the sad and sweet romance between Henry II. and his fair love Rosamond, the heroine of Körner's tragedy of the same name. In the beginning of the seventeenth century was shown in the palace of Woodstock " Rosamond's bower," which since that time has not ceased to be an object of English poetry and talk. Here then, right in the heart of the beautiful English landscape, upon the charming hills of Oxfordshire, where the Glyme winds picturesque, one has long loved to imagine the poet in his old age. Hither, we suppose, he withdrew himself from a life of bustle to a quiet house which had been bestowed upon him in the charming neighbourhood of the royal forests, and here he wrote the ' Canterbury Tales '—

> " In a lodge out of the way,
> Beside a well in a forest."

It is a pretty picture ; May, which to his heart and fancy was continually a feast, once more adorns the meadows with white and green ; and while the venerable oaks rustle before his bay window, the spring wind and scent of flowers bear the remembrances of former days into his room, where he, sitting amidst his books, is composing the great poem of his life. They yet show in Woodstock a way where he was wont to walk in the morning, and some of the old trees which lovingly arched over him; even in the days of Elizabeth stood by Woodstock Park a stone house which was known under the name of " Chaucer's house." Only we fear that this way where he in the morning willingly wandered has originated from a poem, 'The Dream,' which, only of late years contested, is ascribed to Chaucer, but which B. Ten Brink (' Chaucer's Studies of the History of his Development') pointed out is not genuine. This song is the only one in which Chaucer apparently painted the landscape scenery of Woodstock, and immortalised his residence therein.

One early morning, with the first dawn of day, he could, he informs us, remain in bed no longer. He rose, and wandered away merrily and alone by a hill-side till he came to a land of white and green, fairer than any he had ever before beholden. The ground was green with maples scattered here and there; flowers and woods of the same altitude; nothing but a wilderness of green and white.

If this poem is not by Chaucer, the testimony is weak, which it is imagined may be found in his writings, for his residence in Woodstock. Nevertheless, the belief therein was so fast rooted, that a poet of the eighteenth century, Mark Akenside, composed an inscription for an imaginary statue of the poet at Woodstock, which contains the lines—

> " Such was old Chaucer. . . . .
> . . . . . . Here he dwelt
> For many a cheerful day. These ancient walls
> Have often heard him, while his legends blithe
> He sang, of love, or knighthood, or the wiles
> Of homely life : through each estate and age,
> The fashions and the follies of the world
> With cunning hand portraying."

But the old Chaucer was never so well off; the authenticated facts do not agree with these pleasing fantastic forms; nay, they speak wholly against them. At the time when the sunshine of Court favour shone upon him, leisure was certainly wanting to him, even if a poetical residence had been bestowed upon him in Woodstock, sixty English miles away from the capital, to sing joyful legends, for his business tied him to London for many years under Edward III. as Custom Inspector of the London harbour ; and later, under Richard II. again, as Bookkeeper of the royal building

in Westminster, and of different parks, among
which Woodstock was not mentioned; yet he himself says, in the 'House of Fame,' which belongs
to the year 1384 :—

> " No tidings commen to thee,
> Not of thy very neighbours,
> That dwellen almost at thy dores;
> Thou hearest neither that ne this,
> For whan thy labour all done is,
> And hast made all thy reckenings
> Instead of rest and of new things,
> Thou goest home to thine house anone,
> And also dombe as a stone,
> Thou sittest at another booke,
> Till," &c.

And on the other hand, when he was dismissed
from his office in disgrace, though he had leisure,
the kingly favour was wanting to him; to which
alone such an asylum could have been due. Shall
we therefore entirely give up the thought of a
joyful and song-stirring stay of Chaucer at Woodstock, who through this has received a certain individuality which we so willingly foster? I think
not. But we must make up our minds to transfer
to his youth what is asserted about his old age,
and to refer to his first song what he says about
his last. So much more sunny and serene was life
to him at the beginning than at the end; all that

fate had for him in failures and dissensions gathered
over him in his last days : then had he no rest to
wander joyfully in the forests of Woodstock. Not
here did he conclude his work as a poet; but it is
possible that he began it here. For that the two
strips of parchment which Mr. Bond discovered
in the British Museum give us welcome support.
The household of the Prince Lionel and of the
Countess Elizabeth at that time seems to have resided in the castle of Hatfield, but numerous were
the journeys and trips they made thence. The two
preserved leaves of the household account-book
name all the places in which the Countess with
her followers stayed during the three years, and
amongst these places is Woodstock. Most likely
Chaucer's poem, 'The Assemble of Foules,' originated at this time, for it refers to the marriage
of John of Gaunt with Lady Blanche of Lancaster, who in the poem delays the marriage for
a year (cf. 'Chaucer's England,' by Mr. Browne,
p. 19). Now the marriage actually took place
in the year 1359; so that we have the year
1358 as the date of a poem written in honour of
an event of a princely family, in which year
Chaucer was himself among the followers of the
Countess.

Out of this early epoch, at that time and place,

originates the circumstance of his inviolable fidelity
to the House of Lancaster, which became for him
decisive, and in a certain measure affected his
destiny. John of Gaunt, Duke of Lancaster, was
the brother of Prince Lionel, in the service of
the wife of one or the other of whom Chaucer
served, and he stayed at Hatfield, during the
three years over which the leaves of the household
account-book extend. Here, therefore, must the
young poet have made the Duke's acquaintance,
whose marriage he sung; just as he afterwards
dedicates to the early death of the Duchess an
expression of sorrow in a poem, ' Book of the
Duchess.' In the year 1359—the year with which
his biographers have hitherto begun as the first
accurate date of his life—Chaucer joined the campaign against France, was taken prisoner, and was
not set free till the peace of the year 1360. After
he returned to London he married Phillippa Roet,
a maid of honour to Queen Philippa, and sister of
the widow, Katherine Swynford, the mistress of
the Duke of Lancaster, whom, after the death of
his second wife, he married.

In the last years of the reign of Edward III.,
especially after the death of the Black Prince, the
influence of the Duke of Lancaster increased; and
befriended by this, even before he became connected

with him, Chaucer enjoyed days and years of
prosperity as great as his heart could desire. He
not only held a lucrative Court employment and
received a kingly pension, but he was several times
sent with diplomatic commissions to foreign countries, *in secretis negotiis Domini regis versus partes
transmarinas;* and the account-roll of the Royal
Exchequer, in which the sums for these missions are
noted, gives him the title of " Armiger Regis,"
which we may nearly translate as gentleman of the
bed-chamber.   Two of these documentary-attested
missions took him to Italy ; one to Genoa, in the
year 1372, the second to Milan, 1377.   There is a
place in the ' Canterbury Tales' in which Chaucer
says that Fraunces Petrarch had himself told him
the tale of the Patient Griselda in Padua ; a personal
meeting and acquaintance with the "Poet Laureate"
of Italy would naturally follow.   Of the two
missions it can only be the first in which the
meeting took place, since Petrarch died in 1374 ;
although it was a long distance from Genoa to
Padua, in which vicinity, upon his estate in
Arqua, the last years of Petrarch's life were
brought to a close.

Perhaps we may here, with Mr. Browne
(' Chaucer's England,' i. 25), once more refer
to the parchment leaves of the British Museum,

and, out of the relation of Chaucer to Prince
Lionel, conclude that he was amongst the followers of that Prince when he, in the year 1369,
went to Milan in order to take Violante, daughter
of the Duke of Galeazzo of Milan, as his second
wife. There is here, as one may understand, no
ground to doubt the fact itself, which, communicated to us by Chaucer in expressions so
little to be misunderstood, and not contradicted by
the accompanying circumstances, at the same time
bears in itself something symbolical—a kind of
knightly homage to the mature beauty and perfection of the Italian poetry offered upon its own classical soil by the youthful genius of the poetry of
England. Not long after Chaucer had seen for the
last time the Italian sky, his darkest days began.
Edward III. died, and was succeeded by his grand-
son Richard II., the son of the Black Prince. At
the first, during the minority of his nephew, the
influence of the Duke of Lancaster asserted itself,
and so long it went well with our poet after the
customary way. But the year 1386 marks the
solstice. In that year the Duke, who was titular
King of Castile, undertook an adventurous expedition into Spain, through which he aspired to gain
the throne; but the undertaking failed lamentably,
and the Duke remained away from England for

three years. During this time a revolution happened in the Government; a party hostile to the
House of Lancaster, led by the Duke of Gloster,
seized the helm of the State under the weak King.

But the year 1386 was also that in which we see
Chaucer as a representative of the County of Kent,
in the Parliament which assembled on the 1st of
October, in Westminster. It may be assumed
that he here, as well as he could, defended the
cause of his friend, his patron for many years, and
his brother-in-law, the Duke of Lancaster. But the
end was not far off. In the December of the same
year he was discharged from all his employments,
and in the year 1388 the payment of his Court
pension was stopped, whilst that of his wife, which
she had held as a Court lady, had been already
lost through her death in the year 1386. Thus
it happened, that the man who had hitherto been
accustomed all his life to a rich income found
himself henceforth continually in pecuniary embar-
rassment.

It is true that his position once more improved
when, in 1389, after the return of Lancaster,
Gloster's regiment was overthrown, and a son of
the former, the Earl of Derby, was minister. But
only for two years Chaucer filled the situation
of Clerk of the King's Works, for which he

was indebted to the favourable turn in political affairs. In the year 1391 we again find him without office and almost without means; and so he remained until the last year of the century and of his life, when the House of Lancaster, to which he once more closely joined his fate, began to be glorious in the history of England, giving it a list of kings, but at the same time also bequeathing to it the bloody feud of the White and Red Roses. All in all, Chaucer passed the thirteen years from 1386–99, if not in misery and poverty, yet with scarcity and privations of every kind, struggling with debts and creditors. But now his God-graced nature, sunny in its deepest depths, showed itself, which no earthly trouble could darken; for in these thirteen years, like the nightingale singing in the night, he produced his great poem, which, borne from century to century, belongs to the world's literature as it opens that of England.

I do not know in what sense or to what extent John Morley is right, when, in his 'English Writers from Dunbar to Chaucer,' he says, that only Englishmen can understand this poet thoroughly. To me, I must confess, this does not appear so difficult. I have always pictured to myself this free, bright, and independent man just as Morley describes him, telling us that when he was rich, he seems to have enjoyed all the good things which his riches could procure without restraint ; and that after he was deprived of his property, he raised no common lamentation, but consoling himself with his own peculiar wealth, ate a worse dinner, and wrote his 'Canterbury Tales.'

48 ENGLAND

III.

The connection of Kent with the 'Canterbury
Tales' is not so accidental as it may at the first
glance appear. Apart from the local relation into
which we almost immediately enter, there exists
a personal one, if we may say so. If we know
no longer the place on which the house where
Chaucer was born once stood, yet it cannot have
been far from the boundaries of Kent, since the
giant town on the Thames at this time covers a
part of it ; and as Chaucer was descended from a
knightly family which was originally settled in
Kent, he must have had an estate there also,
since, as has already been said, in the year 1386
he was sitting as one of the deputies, or knights
of the shire, in Parliament for the county of Kent.
So he was fast rooted in the soil which he has
selected as the scene of his masterpiece.

The poem itself begins in the following manner :—In the first days of April, when with
the sweet spring showers the desire of travel is
aroused, at this time of the year, it happened that
in an inn at Southwark, an old part of London

upon the left bank of the Thames, a gay and distinguished company was assembled, consisting of
twenty-nine persons, who were on a pilgrimage to
Canterbury. Where now is the High Street in
the Borough of Southwark, commonly called High
Street, Borough, to distinguish it from other streets
of the same name, there was at that time the great
highway leading to the south and south-west of
England. The right bank of the Thames, now
peopled by hundreds of thousands, and blackened
by smoke, one of the chief centres of London's
mighty commerce, with numberless manufactories,
chimneys, and warehouses, was at that time open
land, with green fields and gardens. It was only
at the outlet of London Bridge, at Southwark,
that there had, from different causes, arisen in
ancient times a town-like settlement. Two great
priories, the monastery of St. Mary Overies and
the nunnery of Bermondsey, had early given rise
to the activity and busy intercommunication
which naturally resulted from the vicinity of such
ecclesiastical institutions as these. Near to St.
Mary's, and not far from the bridge, there stood,
till the Reformation, the Bishop of Winchester's
magnificent palace, one of the richest prelates,
whose wide jurisdiction included Surrey. The
most important agent in this intercommunication

E

was the high road which ran from the bridge to
Kent, Hampshire, and Cornwall. Here heavily-
laden waggons moved, and here assembled the
motley crowd of pilgrims to the shrine of St.
Thomas of Canterbury.

Immediately behind the houses, as many as
there may have been in that street, the way to
Canterbury began, which was all inclosed with
green hedges, over an arched bridge, named Locks-
bridge, the remains of which were again erected in
1847, and in some of the narrow lanes of Kent
may be traced to this day. The street which ran
out into this high road must have been very lively
with merchants' shops, in which the pilgrims provided themselves for the journey, and with inns, in
which they with their whole troop of servants and
horses lodged. Here still in Stow's time, who wrote
his ' Survey of London' in 1598, were many good
hostelries for the accommodation of travellers;
the oldest being the ' Tabard,' so called from its
shield, a kind of sleeveless frock open at both sides,
with a square collar, now worn by heralds, and
called their coat-of-arms, when they are in service.

Later, probably however not long after Stow
wrote, the name of ' Tabard ' was corrupted into
' Talbot,' and under this sign the old inn, or at
least a part of it, exists to this day on the old spot.

This 'Tabard' is the inn in which the pilgrims of the 'Canterbury Tales' assembled, and amongst its guests we find the Poet. The prologue which describes these, the inn, and the landlord, is the crown of the work. There is so much humour, freshness, colour, and heartiness in it, that we become fond of the Poet before we know his work, and in love with each of his figures before we have their tales. They are taken almost exclusively from the wealthy middle classes of the nation, for the Knight with his son, the "Squire," holds only a kind of middle rank in the English society of the time; whilst the Yeoman who accompanies him is his free, but not knightly, serving-man, possibly his forest verderer or ranger. The "Reeve" belongs to a similar if somewhat higher circle of life, for which we still have the German word "greve;" he is the steward or bailiff of a nobleman in Norfolk. Then there are the representatives of the clergy, the secular as well as the ecclesiastical order of the monks and nuns, a Prioress, a Nun, a Benedictine, a Mendicant Friar, a Seller of Indulgences, a Clergyman, and the Beadle of an ecclesiastical Court of Justice. Science is represented by a Student of Oxford, a Student of the Law, and a Doctor of Medicine; trade and commerce by a Merchant, the Wife of

Bath, that admirable creation full of jovial humour, which alone would suffice to preserve our Poet's name from oblivion; by a Mercer, a Carpenter, a Weaver, a Dyer, a Carpet-Manufacturer, a Cook, a Sailor, and the Steward of a so-called " inn of court." The representatives of the landed population are a Miller, a Ploughman, and a " Franklin," the proprietor of a freehold property of the class of those who, together with the " squires," and since Chaucer's time numbered amongst them, by degrees began to form what we have already described as the landed gentry. All these persons are in their separate individualities described in the most lively manner : they stand forth in their anti-quated costumes, they converse in their wonderful language, and they give altogether such a full and impressive picture of the society of the middle ages in England, that we, if every other source were to be lost to us, out of this poem alone could build it up again. These worthy people are all present in the court and hall of the 'Tabard' in order that they may set out on their journey to Canterbury the next morning, and, as we have said, the Poet is amongst them. "The chambers and the stables were wide, and we were provided with the best," says he; but his first word of tenderness is for the Host. " Mine

Host," indeed, is painted as an ideal and model of
that excellent class which to poets and literary
men has always been so dear. "He accommodated
each of us" (so says and sings Chaucer of him),
"and then invited us to the table. Then he served
us with the best food; the wine was strong, and we
drank willingly of it. A right important man was
our Host; he might have been a marshal in a
noble house: a great man was he, with eyes deep
set in his head; a better citizen was there not
in 'Chepe.'" Cheapside, at this day the chief
vein of the City's traffic, was in the Middle Ages
the residence of London's richest and most respectable burghers. "Straightforward in his speech,
wise, and full of learning, he was not wanting in
manly appearance. He was also a good-natured
fellow, and after supper he began to play and sing,
and speak of sports and other matters. When we
had paid our bills he said, 'See, my masters, you
are heartily welcome; for, by my honour, if I do not
lie, I have not seen this year so merry a company
in my inn. Therefore would I willingly do you
some good if I only knew how, and I am at this
moment thinking over some entertainment which
may amuse you and yet cost nothing. You go to
Canterbury, God be with you! the blessed martyr
reward you for it! Now I know well if you

make the journey that you are prepared on the
way to chatter and sing, for truly there is no
pleasure in travelling and being silent as a stick.
Now I will make a proposal to you, and by the
soul of my father, who is dead, if you are not
pleased with it to-morrow, then strike off my head.
Talk no more about it, but hold up your hands.'"
This simplest of all parliamentary proceedings is
in unanimous favour for the Host, and he says—
" Good : now listen. Each of you shall on this
journey tell four tales, two on the way to Canterbury, two on the way back; he whose story has
most sense and wit, shall, on your return, have a
supper here, in my inn, at the cost of you all. To
make your pleasure more, I will myself ride with
you at my own charges and be your guide and
your umpire."

Brave man, classical pattern of all hospitable
virtue! With acclamations was the proposal of
that disinterested one received, who rode forth
with them at his own cost to arrange afterwards
a supper at the cost of them all. Thereupon wine
was brought, and they drank, and went to rest.
Next morning, in the early grey dawn, "mine
Host" awaked them, gathered them together in a
flock, and away to Canterbury !

And so they ride away beside the Thames bank,

in the splendour of the young sun, between the
hills of Blackheath and Greenwich, where the
heath is green and the zephyr fans them with
sweet airs, and in the tender-leaved trees sing
little birds, which have slept with open eyes the
whole night long. Upon ambler, courser, and beast
of burden, with the pilgrim's scallop-shell on their
trappings and caparisons, we see them pass away,
those Canterbury Pilgrims. We hear the tingling
of the little bells on the harness of their horses;
we see the poor man of God, the Student of Oxen-
ford, whose nag was as lean as a rake, and he
himself not altogether fat; we see the Knight
who in Palestine fought against the heathen,
and his son, the Squire, with sleeves long and
wide, and curls as crisp as though they had been
laid in the press. We see the Yeoman in green
coat and hat, the bow in his hand, the hunting-
horn by his side; the Seller of Indulgences from
Rouncival, without beard but with long flaxen
hair, merry, with all his pockets crammed to
overflowing, full of indulgences from Rome; the
Benedictine, whose fat face drew from the Host
the exclamation, " There must be good pasturage
whence thou comest;" the Mendicant Friar, with
his " tippet ay farsed ful of knives and pinnes," in
order to make presents to beautiful women, who

lisps his English to make it agreeable; then Madame Eglantine, the Prioress, who speaks French after the school of Stratford-atte-Bow; the Good Wife of Bath, who has already been five times married, and therefore is not without experience when she says :

"But never was it given to mortal man,
To lie so boldly as we women can."

We see, further, the Cook, and the Advocate, who rides in a mixed coat with silken sash and small buckles; the Doctor of Medicine in red and sky-blue; the Shipman who has often brought over a cargo of wine from Bordeaux in his bark called " The Magdalene." We see the Miller, a strong fellow with red beard and bagpipes, the Mercer, Carpenter, Weaver, Dyer, and Carpet Manufacturer, brave burghers, every one of them worthy to be an alderman; men of importance, with wives that one would address as "madame;" wise people and considerate, with a Cook amongst their followers who can cook fowls and marrow-bones, and bake tarts in Cyprus wine; in short, we see them all, the immortal nine-and-twenty; the honest Host always in front smoothing quarrels, which, with some significance, at once break out amongst the clerical part of the company.

Owing to the power which was intrusted to him, he obtains silence, and at the second milestone of the old highway to Canterbury, by the well of St. Thomas, decides, through the drawing of straws, whose turn it should be to begin the Tales. The lot fell upon the Knight; he drew, as they had agreed upon, the shortest straw; and now begin the 'Canterbury Tales,' only interrupted by the prologue before each, in which is contained every little amusing merriment of the pilgrims, as well as the endeavours of the Host to keep the same within proper limits. "Ah! sir," cried he once to the Mendicant Friar (for, as we have said, the clergy gave him the most trouble), "you should be courteous and agreeable as becomes a man of your standing; we will have no disputes in this company, relate your tale and leave the Beadle in peace." The Host is perpetually in motion; he sees and hears all. As judge and reporter, he leads the procession, and every one who is called upon, or who himself offers to relate, comes to him out of the number, whilst the remainder group themselves around as well as they can. It is a picture of the English Parliament, already in the fourteenth century a fast-rooted national state and company, a House of Commons on horseback, with the Host as self-chosen Speaker, " our Host hadde the wordes for us alle" (v. 17,361). Unlike the Speaker, however, he continually interfered with the debates. Every tale drew from him an exclamation either of praise or blame; he took part for or against the heroes who appeared in it; and he seems, on the whole, to have liked the merry tales more than the mournful.

When the Doctor of Medicine had ended his relation of the evil deeds of Appius Claudius, and Virginia's death sacrifice, then indeed the Host's gall overflows, and he begins to swear as if he were mad. "Hang him," cries he; "by God's nails and blood, this was a cursed thief, a false judge." Then turning to the Doctor, he blames him for having told such a melancholy story. "I have nearly got a heartache from it," says he, "and I must have some medicine to counteract it, either a pull of moist corny beer, or a merry story. Thou Seller of Indulgences, relate us one, for thou knowest full many." "It shall be done," replied the Seller of Indulgences; "but first, by the sign of this beer-house, I will have something to drink, and will eat a biscuit." Then immediately the "gentils," the respectable people of the company, who have a presentiment of no good, begin to cry, "No; no roguery; relate to us a moral tale from which we may learn something." "Willingly," says the

Seller of Indulgences; "but, by my cup, I will think over a respectable tale whilst I drink."

These little intercalations, full of wit and humour, form, so to say, the frame which incloses the various subjects of the poem ; and they give to the whole its character of variety, and its tone of actual life.

Whilst we listen to the narratives, the picture of the narrators becomes complete in its most tangible reality. Under the hoofs of their gently-stepping horses the road glides along; and as the sun rises during their conversation, now serious, now cheerful, we see village after village emerge and vanish. At Boughton, six (English) miles from Canterbury, we have the surprise of seeing a couple of new pilgrims thrust in among the number of those already known to us; namely, a Canon who seeks the stone of the wise, and his servant, "the Chanouns Yeman," who is, nevertheless, not much edified by the wisdom of his master, since out of all the work which the kindling of the coals causes he has hitherto won nothing whatever, but on the contrary, has lost all, even his red cheeks. These two figures may be considered as adding a very powerful trait to the picture of manners of society at that time, and give the Poet an opportunity of making the deceitful practice of the alchymists, already becoming a public calamity, a subject of his satire, with a boldness and distinctness for those days remarkable.

The Story of the Goldmaker, which Chaucer puts into the mouth of the last individual portrayed, is perhaps the sole Story derived by the Poet from his own immediate time. The material of the others he took without exception as he found it; some from the French Fabliaux, that inexhaustible source of the mediæval " conteurs ;" others from the ' Gesta Romanorum,' probably brought over from Germany to England; others from other collections of a similar kind, written for the most part in Latin ; clothing all these very diverse persons and things, different both in time and place, conformably with the costumes of his century and the local colouring of his country, being therein, even in anachronisms, the model of later poets—Shakspeare not excepted.

IV.

Chaucer's work has in its design, as need scarcely be mentioned, the greatest external resemblance to the work of Boccaccio, who in his 'Decamerone' is known to employ the same means of uniting a series of unconnected tales by a connecting narrative. But this idea is not the special property of Boccaccio. It originates in the East, where we find it, for example, in the 'Thousand and One Nights.' Long before Chaucer as before Boccaccio, it was brought to Europe by the 'Disciplina Clericalis' of Father Alfonsi or Alfonsus, a Spanish Jew converted to Christianity, who lived in the twelfth century, and whose book, a collection of tales and moral meditations in Latin prose, translated later into French verse under the title 'Castoiement d'un père à son fils,' was much in vogue from the thirteenth to the fifteenth century as a work of instruction, and is indeed very often quoted by Chaucer. This style of relating became still more popular through a book with secular contents, which on this ground had numerous patrons, namely, the 'Tales of the Seven

Wise Masters.' From this book, which was much
circulated in England, and of which a new edition
was some years ago prepared by the Percy Society,
the English Poet is more likely to have got
the hint for his work than from Boccaccio. Certainly it is beyond question, not only that he was
acquainted with Italian literature, but also that it
exercised a great influence upon him. He quotes
once (v. 15,946) direct from Dante, "the gret
poet of Itaile, that highte Dante;" he was, as we
have already remarked, on terms of friendship with
Petrarch, and has made good use of Boccaccio's
Latin work, ' De casibus virorum illustrium' in
the tragedies of the Monk, and of his poem ' La
Teseide,' written in Italian, in the Story of the
Knight. But Boccaccio's principal work, the
' Decamerone,' he appears not to have known;
he nowhere makes mention of it; there appears
no trace of his having used it; and of the sole
story, which is found in both, Chaucer remarks
expressly that he had it from Petrarch, to whose
memory he dedicates a few touching lines in the
prologue to the ' Student of Oxford :'—

> " I wol you tell a tale, which that I
> Lerned at Padowe of a worthy clerk,
> As preved by his wordes and his werk.
> He is now ded, and nailed in his cheste,
> I pray to God so geve his soule reste.

Fraunceis Petrark, the laureat poete,
Highte this clerk, whos rethorike swete
Enlumined all Itaille of poetrie."

The story which hereupon follows is that of
Patient Griselda, and the work to which he alludes
is Petrarch's Latin romance, 'De Obedientia et Fide
uxoria Mythologia,' the version of which Chaucer
has almost literally followed, although it flatters
the poetical illusion, and in no way opposes itself
to objective truth to assume that he owed the first
incitement to the words of Petrarch, to the occasion of that fortunate meeting in the summer plain
of Lombardy.

The oral traditions to which Professor Ebert
especially refers in his excellent 'Handbook of
Italian National Literature' (p. 18), contributed
by no means in the smallest degree to make these
materials for stories, in their substance scarcely
anything more than anecdotes, the common property of the mediæval world. Passing from
writing to the mouth of the people, and from this
again anew into writing, they enriched the store
of popular literature of that day with those antique
mythological, knightly, fabulous, and legendary
elements from which Chaucer as well as Boccaccio
drew. Thus there arose from the same causes
and in the same century, but independently of one

another and at opposite points of Europe, under
the blue sky of Italy and in the mist of England,
the two classical models of the modern art of
narrating in prose and rhyme—the ' Decamerone '
and the ' Canterbury Tales.'

A striking resemblance in the way of life
and development of the two poets causes many a
point of inward relationship besides the outer
relationship shown in their works.   Both were
men of letters, of courtly education, clever in
affairs of State ; men who had learnt to know the
world by travelling, and mankind by manifold
changes of circumstances.   There prevails, therefore, in their writings a lively tone of entertainment, full of humour, wit, and *bonhomie*.   By each
of them, with sovereign ease, are the social questions of that time   treated of, and types of the
society of that time depicted ; and therefore, with
respect to the history of culture, the ' Decamerone '
has for the Italy of Boccaccio exactly the same importance which the ' Canterbury Tales' claim for
Chaucer's England.

It can, then, be scarcely needful to remark expressly that his book is as little free as that of
Boccaccio from so-called *anstössigen stellen*.   There
was too much of this in the tone of that time,
of the finer moral cultivation : and the respect

which was paid to women,—the touchstone of the
value of the period, as, I think, Rousseau calls it,—
never indicated any particularly high grade. Never
in the Christian world has woman occupied such
a degraded position as at the time of the *Minne-
sänger* and love courts. Whilst in poetry woman's
favour and the grace of love was the theme re-
·peated, even to tediousness, in reality women were
treated with revolting contempt. But did such a
contradiction really exist between the song and the
life? Where was there to be found in the rhymes
of the Troubadours a word about the soul, the duty,
the worth of woman? Did they not rather celebrate, without exception, merely the charm and
beauty of her body? Deprive their song of its
poetical veil, and scarcely anything else will remain but the woman, whose sole destiny appears
to be to minister to the pleasure of man. What
wonder if woman became by degrees that for which
man took her; if immorality of conduct and shame-
lessness in speech became so very characteristic
of the feminine world of the Middle Ages, that
Chaucer in good earnest, and with the appearance
of a speaking likeness, set forth as woman's representative " the Good Wife of Bath."

This earnestness, if it in no way alters the fact,
increases our sympathy for the Poet. Mature

F

consideration of life and worldly prudence give
something mild even to his ridicule, without
depriving it of its point.　It spares no position,
no class of society ; it lashes with striking conviction their follies, their superstitions, even the perverted aims of literature, as much as might be at
that time.　As precursor of Cervantes, he ridi-
cules in the ' History of Sir Topas' the fabulous ·
poetry, then become common, of the metrical
romances, as centuries later the Spanish poet ridiculed in his costly parody the deteriorated chivalry
of the romance of prose.　But in his scorn and
in his satire Chaucer remains always the " gentleman."　Through each of his words flows the
breath of a free soul, the sympathetic warmth
of a good and great heart.　In his verse is eternal
May, and the scent of the fresh bloom of the
English hawthorn.　So says Alexander Smith.

But while this is, as it were, the spirit that
animates his poetry, we must not forget what was
probably with him the main point, the story itself.
We should do him a great injustice did we regard
him in this respect as either a naturalist or an
empiric.　He has, on the contrary, meditated with
great clearness on the art of a narrator; and in
one place in his work has spoken very positively about it (v. 10,715–19).　Here he lays down

first of all, as a fundamental law of every story,
variety. He says, " the knote why that every tale
is told " must be so drawn and loosened, that the
reader or hearer be not " taryed ;" that his " lust "
may not cool, and that the " savour" of the fable
may not become flat through the " fulsomnes of
the prolixité."

This direction he has himself followed throughout the whole of his work ; not merely in the
single stories, but in their order of succession,
which is excited by the wave of unceasing change.
A sad tale is followed by a lively one. The
reader, still feeling emotion at the tragic fate of
Arcite, is immediately afterwards provoked to irre-
pressible laughter by the comical presentment of
the drunken Miller, and his dispute with the
too sensitive Carpenter. At no moment in this
comprehensive work does a stop occur, or the
action stagnate. As the persons change, so change
also the theme and tone of the discourse : the
Knight and the Advocate, the Seller of Indulgences and the Manorial lord, my Lady Prioress
and the Masters of Trades, all these manifold
callings of the life of the Middle Ages, the
world and the cloister, the university and the
guildhall, the town and the village—all these
furnished the Poet with the wealth of their

varieties, this fulness of life and colour to the picture of his time.

No wonder, therefore, that this model and masterpiece became and continued the favourite book of all following generations. Its popularity is shown in the first place from the great number of manuscripts in which it is preserved to us. In a ballad addressed to him by the French poet, Eustace Deschamps, we have evidence that during his life Chaucer and his poem enjoyed high fame, even on the Continent; whilst the verse in which his friend Gower (†1408) dedicates to him his 'Confessio Amantis,' places it beyond question how much he was valued in his own country.

Another contemporary poet who survived him, Occleve (1420), painted his portrait on the margin of a manuscript, which, preserved and plentifully copied, gives us a true idea of Chaucer's appearance, who describes himself as "in the wast schape, sma and fair of face, elvish by his countenance" (v. 15,113 and 15,114), with a double-pointed beard, after the fashion of the time. When fifty years later Guttenberg's art came to England, the 'Canterbury Tales' was one of the first works which issued from Caxton's printing-press (1475–76). Here also is again shown the remarkable connection between Kent and the

'Canterbury Tales,' already alluded to above; for William Caxton, their first printer, was, as he himself tells us, born in the little Kentish village of Weald.

Six years after the first edition of the Canterbury Tales Caxton published a second; and before the seventeenth century a considerable number of editions existed. Now Chaucer became the source to which England's great poets made pilgrimage. Shakspeare drew from one of his smaller epics 'Troilus and Cressida,' the first principle of his tragi-comedy; and Milton, in his 'Il Penseroso,' summons him up immediately after the great singers of antiquity,

> " Call up him that left half told
> His story of Cambuscan bold,
> Of Camball and of Algarsife,
> And who had Canace to wife;
> That owned the virtuous ring and glass,
> And of the wondrous horse of brass,
> On which the Tartar king did ride."

Nevertheless the Story of the Squire, to which Milton alludes in the above lines, is not the only piece in the 'Canterbury Tales' which the poet has left half told. We must rather regard the whole work as we possess it, as a fragment. Besides the two prose stories, which Chaucer in the prologue

calls 'Treatises,' it contains 17,368 genuine lines
of verse really coming from Chaucer, therefore over 3000 more than the 'Divine Comedy,'
and almost 2000 more than the 'Iliad;' nevertheless the poet carried out scarcely the half of his
original plan.

V.

It is late in the afternoon, and the sun is already setting, when the order of the story comes to the Manciple, the economist of a London law court. The Cook has fallen asleep and from his horse, to the great amusement of the company. This tumble has fortunately no further result than to awaken him, whereupon a highly amusing dispute arises between him and the Manciple, who is naturally angry at the interruption. Nevertheless, through the intervention of the Host, this quarrel is settled to general satisfaction, whilst the Manciple pledges the Cook from his leathern wine-bottle. Meanwhile they have reached Harbledown (popularly called Bob up-and-down), the last village before Canterbury. Even at the present day the hollow road can be seen—the theatre of that cheerful scene which Chaucer describes, the part which was travelled over whilst the Manciple gave his excellent tale. There, on one of the hills, may be beheld to-day, as perhaps it was beheld then, the Hospital of St. Nicholas of Harbledown, highly honoured in the pilgrim-days of Canterbury, and

still wondrously picturesque, with its ivy and wild
wall-flowers—with its grey stones, clefts, and fis-
sures—to him who regards the old cloister from the
lonely quiet ravine which once formed the animated
road from London. As soon as, ascending from
this, the hill is reached, he sees beneath, extended
in the fruitful valley, the city of Canterbury; and
as it lies there in the evening sunshine, with its
numerous towers and churches, and its Cathedral—
the goal of the pilgrimage—the Priest, who now at
last speaks, may well compare it with the heavenly
Jerusalem, and greet it with serious speech. His
story, if such it may be called, is a treatise on
penance (in some manuscripts plainly called
' Tractatus de Pœnitentia '), and well suited for
the conclusion of a journey, gives occasion to the
holy man to remind the company symbolically of
the end of their human pilgrimage on earth. A
breath as of evening air moves around us, and the
fancy of the reader depicts the troop of pilgrims,
now in the early twilight, entering the town by
the Gothic arch of the West Gate—the only gate-
way which stands unchanged since the fourteenth
century in the London Road. Now they ride up
High Street, where already the evening lights
shine from the windows, and at last stop before
their inn, opposite Mercery Lane, that little street

in which they will assemble in the morning for
procession, and to which, although centuries have
passed away, the memory of the Canterbury Pilgrims still clings.

But it was not allotted to Chaucer to depict all
this. He was not to see his pilgrims in Canterbury,
nor accompany them back again to London; he
owes all the remainder to us, and his supper to the
brave host of the ' Tabard.'

He died in the seventy-second year of his life,
anno 1400, one year after the son of the Duke of
Gaunt, Shakspeare's Bolingbroke, Henry IV., ascended the throne. That was a year of triumph
for the grey poet, this last year of his life. Immediately after his accession the King granted a pension to him, and to his son Thomas an appointment
in the service of the Court. The last news we have
of Chaucer is, that he hired a house opposite the
royal palace, close under the walls of Westminster
Abbey, in the so-called Cloister garden, where to-
day stands Henry VII.'s chapel. Chaucer took
possession of this house on Christmas Day 1399,
but on the 25th of October, 1400, he died, and was
interred in Westminster Abbey, in that quiet part
which, under the name of the " Poets' Corner," has
become so world-renowned. He was the first poet
who was here laid to rest, the precursor of a long,

brilliant train who should follow him in the future.
Over his grave rises an altar with a Gothic roof—
a monument which was here erected to him by an
admirer in 1555. It has become black and rusty
in long time, and its inscription can scarcely be
deciphered.

The old inn in Southwark was also standing a
few years ago. The appearance of the neighbourhood has in every respect much changed during
five hundred years. Where formerly the pilgrims
assembled for their pilgrimage, is now the immense
station for the lines of the South-Eastern and South-
Western Railways, of which the one follows the
Old Kent Road, the way to Kent, and the other
runs towards the sea-coast of Hampshire. Still,
as formerly, the traffic goes over London Bridge
by the same streets; but these streets are become
railways, and how very impenetrable has the
traffic grown! The surging and roaring of the
human tide, the iron rattling of waggons, omnibuses, cabs, hansoms—all in a coloured, confused
whirl—the deafening noise, the spectacle which
bewilders the eye—the floating sea-colossi, the
ships beneath, the railway lines above — that
mighty black arch, extended across the street
diagonally before us, continually rattling with the
trains going to Charing Cross or coming thence—

the telegraph wires, which quiver in mid-air—
who could recognise beneath this flood of modern
London life the old quiet Southwark and the
streets of the Canterbury Pilgrims? And yet
here we are on the spot. On the left, as if sunk
down, but in truth only in a low position, in consequence of the neighbouring streets having been
raised, stands the old church, well known to us,
of St. Mary Overies, just as Chaucer saw it, and
in which his friend Gower lies buried. On the
right, in the direction of Southwark Bridge, not
far from Barclay and Perkins' famous brewery,
is the place where, in Chaucer's time, stood the
palace of the Bishop of Winchester, and in Shakspeare's time the Globe Theatre. New streets,
among them the handsome Southwark Street,
Borough, completed in 1865, animate everywhere
the old classic ground; and that part of the High
Street which led to Old London Bridge was some
thirty years ago demolished to make room between
the New London Bridge and the railway stations.
But the lower end of the High Street continued
long unchanged, and in it the inn of the ' Canterbury Tales,' the old ' Talbot,' as much of it at least
as remained after a fire in the year 1676. In the
year 1867 it was still to be seen in a court, which
was reached by going from the High Street through

a house, which was built after the fire, and which hid the court from the street. When you entered the court you had on the right hand the tavern, which dated from the seventeenth century, and even then already numbered its 200 years, and bore from an iron hook the sign, "The ' Talbot' inn, R. Gooch." Joined to it in the background, and forming a corner on the left, was that which still stood of the old 'Tabard,' the wooden house of the fourteenth century, with its pointed roof, its worm-eaten galleries, its staircase outside, its balconies and little green window-panes fixed in lead. Under one of the balconies was a sign, with " Allsopp's Pale Ale," and on one of the staircase-landings was another—" John Paice, car-man." Under the gallery, on the side, hung a board, on which the twenty - nine pilgrims were represented with the inscription, " The old ' Tabard' inn. This is the inn in which Geoffrey Chaucer and the 29 pilgrims lodged on their journey to Canterbury;" and near it hung another board, with the inscription, " Midland Railway Re-ceiving Office." What a contrast, the fourteenth and the nineteenth centuries !—the ' Canterbury Tales' and the railway! But till the last this court has remained true to its former destiny; " John Paice, carman," has taken care that it shall never be lacking in horses and packages of every kind, whilst " R. Gooch," as a fit successor of " mine Host," keeps ready a pewter pot, with a good drink in it for every thirsty man, as was done five hundred years ago.

But, when I consulted the newest edition of ' Murray's Handbook of Modern London—London as it is,' I found in the place where formerly stood its description, only the words, " 'Tabard' Inn, Southwark : the starting-place of Chaucer's Canterbury pilgrims. Pulled down."

SHAKSPEARE'S LONDON.

I.

ALTHOUGH London in the sixteenth century did
not number many more inhabitants than Cologne,
and not nearly so many as Hamburg now possesses,
it even then passed for one of the largest towns in
Christendom; and our German traveller Hentzner,
who was there in 1598, relates with genuine
astonishment that the circumference of this town
amounted to "*nearly* a whole mile." At that
time, as to-day, there was a City of London and a
City of Westminster; but the suburbs, whose
blocks of houses now swell the brick and mortar
sea of London, were then still green fields and
flowery meadows; and the City of Westminster
itself was not much more than a suburb of the
palace, the seat of the Court, and of the nobles of
England. Here was the then already old Abbey
and Cathedral of Westminster, the Houses of Parliament, and York Place, a handsome residence
built by Cardinal Wolsey, but, after his fall, forced
by Henry VIII. from his former favourite, and
afterwards, "with its rich stock of valuables, its
hangings of gold and silver cloth, its thousands of

G

pieces of fine Dutch linen, and its stores of silver,
and even of beautiful gold services, which covered
two large tables," taken by the monarch of the
high hand into his own use. Since that time this
residence has been, called "Whitehall;" and here,
in the splendour of England's most glorious days,
sat Elizabeth upon the throne, "by the grace of
God, Queen of England, France, and Ireland;
Defender of the Faith."

Where now the maze of dark courts and ill-
famed side streets of the Strand extends to the
banks of the Thames, there stood then the town-
houses of the bishops, the ambassadors, and the
great lords. Beautiful gardens surrounded them,
and against their walls plashed the water of the
then still *"silver"* Thames. Here were Bedford
House, Leicester House, and Essex House, now
vanished from the places where they stood, and
only leaving their old names to the streets, squares,
and districts of new London. Here was also
Durham House; and here, in a small study which
overlooked the Thames, sat Sir Walter Raleigh, a
hero in war, a discoverer of distant lands, a man
of letters, and a courtier. A circle of famous
names united itself around the throne of Elizabeth:
it was the youth and heroic time of England.
Philip of Spain, who from being a suitor for

Elizabeth's hand had become her enemy, had
threatened to annihilate England with a formidable fleet of ships, called the Armada. But " God
blew, and they were scattered in pieces." This
judgment of God was the commencement of
England's power on the sea. The progress of
her colonies began; and at home, consequent
upon freedom of faith, with growing prosperity,
awakened also the spiritual life of the nation.

In the firmament of philosophy, so long over-
clouded by the mist of scholasticism, a star of the
first magnitude was rising. Men had learned again
to speak with classic antiquity in its own language.
Poets found purer forms and grander subjects for
their songs, and the dramatic muse awoke. A
style, half chivalric and learned, half full of
artistic geniality, reigned in the Court of Queen
Elizabeth. " Queen Bess" has always been one
of the favourite figures of English history, of the
English people; and this she would certainly not
have been if, besides the talent to reign, she had
not possessed other qualities of appearance, of
mind, and of heart. The Elizabeth, who only too
often rises before us, is the queen who sentenced
Mary Stuart to death; and we have therefore accustomed ourselves to see in her the "old" Elizabeth of whom our traveller Hentzner, towards

the end of the fifteenth century, sketched certainly
a not very prepossessing picture, when he says she
had a wrinkled face, red wig, small eyes, a crooked
nose, thin lips, and black teeth, and yet was continually hearing from her courtiers flatteries on
her beauty. But we must also set before us the
young Elizabeth as she appears, for example,
in the beautiful portrait in the South Kensington Museum, with pleasant feminine features
and golden hair; the Elizabeth who studied
the Greek classics in one of the still inhabited apartments of Windsor Castle, who walked
alone on the terrace of this castle meditating;
the Elizabeth, in short, whom Shakspeare has
celebrated.

An Italian observer who saw her forty years
before the German—the Venetian Ambassador,
Giovanni Michele—describes her accordingly as a
lady equally worthy of remark in body and mind,
her face more agreeable than beautiful, her growth
slender, her figure well formed, with beautiful
eyes, and, above all, with a wonderful hand,
"which she liked to show." Why did she not
dispose of that hand? It is true that a strong
heart beat in her bosom ; but although free from
many weaknesses of her sex, it was not quite free
from the softer emotions which make that sex tender

and amiable. Once or twice at least, we know, Nature made her power felt even in this woman. But between her and Robert Dudley, Earl of Leicester, the shadow of Amy Robsart arose; and Robert Devereux, Earl of Essex, became a rebel and a sacrifice on the block. Once again, late, when Elizabeth had sat for twenty-three years on the throne, and was no longer a beautiful young princess but a mighty queen of mature age, the Duke of Anjou, a son of Catherine de Médicis, crossed the sea to ask her in marriage. He had wooed her for nearly nine years in a kind of continual mistrust, and now at length he desired the fulfilment of his hopes. The Queen received him most graciously, and the tilt-yard of Whitehall became the theatre of a knightly spectacle, for the description of which we are indebted to the old chronicle of Hollingshed. About 10,000 thalers, a good sum in Elizabeth's days, were spent in erecting a richly decorated banqueting-house. The Queen showed herself on a gallery, which the gallant lords of the Court immediately named the " Castle of perfect beauty." This castle was attacked by " Ardent Desire and her foster children," who sang the summons to surrender in a canon, of which the chronicler has preserved for us the following verse :—

" Yeeld, yeeld, O yeeld, you that this fort doo hold,
Which seated is as spotless Honor's feeld ;
Desire's great force no forces can withhold,
Then to Desire's desire, O yeeld, O yeeld ! "

After the song was ended, without the " beautiful vestal on the throne" making a sign of surrender, two cannons were fired off, one with sweet-scented powder, and the other with sweet-scented water, and afterwards a number of ornamented scaling ladders were applied, and the servants then cast flowers and all kinds of sweetmeats against the walls, with such devices as formed the suitable artillery of Desire.

But still poor Anjou missed the aim of his wooing, for political considerations intruded themselves, and the royal lioness of the house of Tudor remained henceforth a virgin on England's throne; her bridegroom the people, her last love her country.*

Where now in modern London a massive stone gate, black with the soot of centuries, divides the Strand from Fleet Street, there was then a turnpike of wood, newly painted, and hung with coloured cloth, called Temple Bar, after the neighbouring guild of lawyers of the Temple. Behind Temple

---

* *Vide* G. R. Emerson's ' London,' p. 50.

Bar, within its walls and remaining " bars" or doors, began the City, the true London of those days. Here with their City-Monarch chosen by themselves, the Lord Mayor, who had his Court and his Court-poet as well as the Queen on the other side of the Bar, lived all the good citizens of London. Some of the great nobles still continued to reside here, though others of them had already begun to emigrate westwards towards Fleet Street and the Strand. The first who left the City to settle themselves more commodiously in a more open neighbourhood were the bishops, to whom their ecclesiastical position assured that security, which for a long time was only to be found in the town by others. The nobility followed the clergy into the neighbourhood of the royal residence; yet in Shakspeare's time there was still many a nobleman's house right in the heart of the City, as for example, that of the Duke of Norfolk, in Duke Place, named after him, the Jews' quarter of London in aftertimes. The City, however, became more and more the abode of rich merchants, whose almost princely luxuriance kept pace with the growth of the colonies, of trade, and of the East India Company. Their houses, constructed of oak beams, with Gothic windows and gables, gave the streets, although they were narrow, a picturesque perspective. But very few

of these Elizabethan houses are left in the City of
London to give us an idea of the rich style of
architecture and the better taste of that time. The
great fire of 1666 destroyed them almost entirely.
But at that time they still stood in all their picturesque beauty, with their carved beam ends
and their fleurs-de-lis, and other flowers of oak-
wood over the door and at the windows. The
principal street of old London was then—as it is
still now for the City, though under quite altered
circumstances—Cheapside. Very different indeed
was " Chepe," the Golden Cheapside of Shakspeare's London, from the present street of this
name, with its houses black with dirt and age, its
bustle during business hours, and its death stillness
during the night. Then it was the great high road
from the tower to the Abbey and palace of Westminster, with the most beautiful shops on each side,
and inhabited by the richest burghers,—the theatre
of processions and pageants, and all the princely
pomp of those days. Here still stand the Guildhall and Bow·Church, from the gallery of which
kings and queens have looked down at great State
ceremonies; of which the tower lantern was lighted
every evening, and the bells always tolled the
curfew at nine o'clock—those same bells, to be
born within whose sound still makes the true

London "cockney." Here stood also the famous
Cheapside Cross, one of those numerous and handsome crosses erected by Edward I. to the memory
of his wife Eleanor, at each of the places where
the funeral procession halted on its way to Westminster, destroyed in 1643 by the Puritans, as
also was Charing Cross, which has, however, received the popular designation of Trafalgar Square.
Each house had, as likewise at that time in Germany, and still frequently in the Swiss towns,
its particular sign, after which it was called; for
there were then no house numbers. There were
signs of trades and guilds, and there were signs
which had reference to commerce and navigation
and remote countries. There were a Moor's Head
and a Greek's Head in their natural colours (or
at least, what were considered such), and there
were a Golden Ball and a Golden Cross. This
house was called the 'Black Bull,' and that the
'Red Lion.' At first, without relation to the position and trade of those who dwelt in the houses,
these signs not unfrequently served to show
what afterwards was the family name. So, for
example, we find a famous man, of whom we
have already spoken in this book, before he was
called Thomas à Becket designated as "Thomas of
the Snipe," after the sign of the house in which

he was born. Later we see house signs on the
addresses of letters, of which Carlyle among other
things has preserved so many for us in his book
on Cromwell ; for example: .

" To be delivered
  " To my worthy friend, Mr. Storie,
   " At the sign of 'The Dog,'
    " In the Royal Exchange,
     " London."

So the booksellers concluded their publications:
for example; " Printed for Thomas Underhill, and
to be had in his shop, at the sign of the Bible in
Wood Street."

Such a sign was a very weighty and massive
thing, hanging out over the shop-door, and there
swinging to and fro; and all these different signs
and figures and shields, with their bright colours
and strong gilding, were to be seen in the streets.
It must have been a very cheerful sight. The
river also had a different appearance. It was still
the broad stream of the Thames, well stocked
with fish, covered with boats and barges, and
graceful swans, as Fitzstephen described it in the
twelfth century. London Bridge was (until the
year 1750, in which Westminster Bridge was completed) the only bridge : it had houses on each
side, and a church stood in the middle. As

picturesque as the streets themselves was the crowd of men in them. There was not the iron noise of a thousand wheels in motion, but, as the old Chronicler Stow says, there was always a noise of convivial preparations. The cooks cried hot ribs of beef roasted, pies well baked, and other victuals. Much clattering was there of pewter pots, harp, pipe, and psaltery. The names of Pudding Lane, Cock Alley, and Pie Corner in modern London still remind us of the dainty morsels of a former time; and the two Wine Streets, one in the neighbourhood of Saffron Hill, now a dirty district between Holborn and Clerkenwell inhabited by beggars, thieves, and rabble of all kinds, preserve the tradition of the time when London was still called " the City of Gardens," when there were still beds of saffron, when the Catholic priest cultivated his vine, and the Protestant clergyman his gooseberry, while he comforted himself with the words " God might well have made a better berry, but he would not."

As little as in the houses did our monotony of brown and grey exist in the costumes of that time. All was then rich in colour and fancy, pleasant and interesting to the eye. There was more individuality and more liveliness in the world and in its garments. The age which knew how to enhance the lofty magnificence of the cathedrals, and to build the stately colonnades of the houses of the nobles and the comfortable corners of the houses of the citizens, had also a surprising inventiveness for costume. What an immense wealth of fancy was expended on shoes, hats, stockings, and cloaks! On the shoe, of which the points now turned upwards like a ram's horn, then spread out like an open fan; on the head-dress, which varied from the baretta to the hat with the steeple crown; on the cloak, which passed through every grade, from the wide Spanish mantle falling in rich folds to the short Norman spencer. Gay cavaliers in velvet, silk, and fine cloth, which glittered with gold and silver embroidery, paraded the streets; and the burghers had, like the nobility, their colour and their decoration; each guild, each trade, each profession had its arms and signs. Black was quite out of fashion; and in the midst of this continual display of lace and satin, of green, scarlet, pink, and sky-blue coats, of plum-coloured cloaks and yellow surtouts, a costume of dark stuff betokened the hypocrite, the slinker, the devotee, the Puritan.

To this London, then in so much enjoyment of life, so mighty in the feeling of national elevation, so sparkling with new riches, so noisy with the feasts

of the Court, the plays and pleasures of the
burghers, to this London came William Shakspeare in the year 1586 from his country home in
Warwickshire. He was three-and-twenty years of
age, and had left behind him a wife, who was
eight years older than himself, and three children.
Whether he fled from Stratford-on-Avon on account of poaching and the composition of a satirical
poem on the justice of the peace, Sir Thomas Lucy,
or whether he wandered away with the view of
seeking his fortune, of this we know as little as
whether his dramatic course began by holding
horses at the theatre-door or arranging the chairs
in the theatre. But behold there he is ; his genius
has led him at the right time to the right place.
The drama, which for centuries had been carried
on by the guilds and trades in the form of miracle-
plays, and mysteries in the streets and open market-places, was now taken out of their hands, and
in those of the poet and artist obtained admission
into the palace of the Queen and the halls of the
nobles. The desire to act and see actors became
general. Every great lord had his troop of players,
who called themselves his actors and servants, and
went about in the provinces when they found no
occupation in the capital. The first public theatre
in London, Blackfriars Theatre, was opened in

1576 : by the end of the century there were seventeen theatres in which there was daily acting.
Besides this the students at the Universities acted ;
the lawyers in the halls of their inns, even the
apprentices of London acted ; so that that became
true which the proverb said, and which was
afterwards placed as an inscription on the Globe
Theatre : " Totus mundus agit histrionem "—All
the world's a player.

Shakspeare joined the Blackfriars troop, which,
originally in the service of the Earl of Leicester,
was afterwards patronised by the Queen, and received the name of the " Queen's Players." This
title has been preserved, and is still held by the
actors of Drury Lane, who always call themselves " Her Majesty's servants." The young
member of the Blackfriars troop soon distinguished
himself: as early as 1559 he was made a sharer
in the theatre, which, as it was the first in
time, remained also first in rank. " Shakspeare's
dramatic entertainments became," as a contemporary author expresses himself, " the greatest support
of our chief theatre, if not of every one in London."
Before he had reached his thirtieth year " our
friendly Willy," the " honey-tongued Shakspeare,"
was a popular and famous man. " He is our
Plautus and our Seneca, the best man in England

for comedy and tragedy," says Francis Meres in
the year 1598.

But where must we look for him in this London,
which was already so large according to the notions
of that time? Now there were three places in the
London of those days where one might be sure
to meet, at least once in the course of an ordinary
day, every man who belonged to good society—
either St. Paul's Cathedral, the Tavern, or the
Theatre.

St. Paul's was then the great and fashionable
promenade of London; but it was much besides. What the Rag-fair of Houndsditch in
the morning, the Exchange at midday, Rotten
Row in the afternoon, and the Haymarket in the
late evening are in the London of the present
time, such during the whole day was St. Paul's in
the sixteenth century; the old metropolitan church
of London, not the square before the church, but
the church itself.

Altogether wonderful things went on in the
church. There were the theatres, the courts of
justice, the places of political combat, and the
lottery-houses of those days. The old drama, the
miracle play, before it went out into the streets,
had for centuries had its place in the church; and
even in the year 1592 we hear that, on the occa-

sion of a visit of Queen Elizabeth to Oxford, the
service in the University Chapel was no sooner
over than the chapel was changed into a theatre
for the amusements of the afternoon. About
the same time the academic authorities of the
same University forbade pipes in the churches
" on account of too great body of smoke." The
parish elections were almost universally carried on
in the churches, and frequently, especially in times
of contagious sicknesses, the assizes also were
held there. Men behaved in the most careless
manner in this metropolitan church of London,
which, destroyed in the great fire, stood on the
same spot where now rises St. Paul's Cathedral.
St. Paul's of the present London is a domed building, after the pattern of St. Peter's at Rome: St.
Paul's in Shakspeare's London was a Gothic
Cathedral, with a slender spire, which was half
destroyed by fire in the year 1561, with cloisters
and a Dance of the Dead on the outer walls. Within
were chapels and shrines, which glittered with
precious stones and gold; the painted glass of the
windows threw a many-coloured light on the
splendid silver service of the high altar, and on
the shrine of the holy Erkenwald, on which sparkled
a large sapphire, with which it was believed that
he healed diseases of the eyes. Whenever Queen

Elizabeth came with her noble retinue to attend
the service at St. Paul's she was almost invariably
accompanied by two white bears. But this was
not the worst. Ever since the time of the Reformation the nave of the Cathedral had become quite a
common passage for porters with beer-barrels,
bread-baskets, fish, meat, and fruit; laden mules,
horses, and other animals crossed incessantly
from one door to the other, strewing the marble
mosaic with straw, refuse, and dirt of all kinds.
Through the lofty aisles of the Cathedral resounded
the neighing of horses, and drunkards snored
on the benches in the choir. On the columns, in
the rich-sculptured decoration of the capitals, birds
built their nests, and it was a favourite amusement of the youth of the City to shoot them down
with a bow and arrow. Notices were affixed
to the pillars, and at the so-called "Si quis"
door thronged domestic servants who sought situ-
ations. Here the advocates of the neighbouring law-
courts of Dowgate and Paternoster Row had their
stands, at which they received their clients; and
even under Charles II. so much of this remained,
that a lawyer, as soon as he was called to practise,
went to St. Paul's to choose his particular stand.
In the side-walks the usurers had their place, and
the font was made use of as a counter for the

H

reckonings. The noise was very great; and while in one part of the Cathedral the organ was played and preaching held, in the other part was cursing, swearing, and cheating. It is true that Elizabeth had forbidden, by the punishment of the pillory (with which was not unfrequently joined the loss of the ears), driving, riding, shooting, and kite-flying in St. Paul's; but yet under Charles I., in the year 1630, Bishop Laud called down solemn imprecations on those who profaned that holy place, by recruiting soldiers there, holding profane law-sessions, and carrying burdens; and in Shak-spearian London more than ever was the nave of the Cathedral, " St. Paul's Walk," the fashion-able promenade, the place for novelties, the daily rendezvous of men of wit, and the gallant ladies of the town.

This middle part of the church was called in the jargon of those days the Inland Sea, or Duke Humphrey's Walk, after the solitary monument which stood in the nave, named after Duke Humphrey, although a simple knight, Sir John Beauchamp, rested therein. Why the Duke was called " his Lordship without flesh " is difficult to say, for during his life the good Duke loved no-thing better than a rich meal and cheerful guests. Yet at a later time he must have become famous

for the reverse, for " to dine with Duke Humphrey "
meant in the language of those days to have no
money with which to pay for a dinner. A diarist
of that time, Francis Osborn, gives us the following description :—" It was then," he says, " the
fashion for the best classes, for lords and courtiers,
and men of all professions, to meet at St. Paul's
about 11 in the morning, to walk in the middle
aisle till 12, and after dinner from 3 to 6, during
which periods some spoke of business and some of
news. Little happened in the world which arrived
not here sooner or later. At these hours, I used,
being a young man, to mix with the choicest company I could find." Here, to these curious assem-
blages of vices, fooleries, fashions, and fancies of
the London of that time often came Shakspeare.
Here he found the models for his plays and the
butts for his wit. Here he found Pistol and Bardolph, Sir Toby Belch, Sir Andrew Aguecheek
and Slender. " Here in St. Paul's I bought him,"
as Falstaff says of Bardolph.

But where was he himself, " the old fat
knight," this flower of the genius of pothouse
revelry? Nay, I think the place is not to be mistaken where the man stays whose saying is,
" Shall I not have mine ease in mine inn ? "
The taverns—' The Mermaid,' ' The Mitre,' 'The

Horn,' or 'The Boar's Head'—are not far ; and
in one of them we shall certainly find him, for,
according to the code of the men of fashion of that
time, " He must dine at one of the famous taverns."

But before we reach these places of merry company, full tankards, and sparkling wit, we have,
just on going out from St. Paul's, a sight worth
observing.   Here in the churchyard, round one of
those street-crosses in which old London was rich,
sits an assemblage of pious people in the open
air, and under the cross stands a man in black,
preaching.   It is a Puritan, who thunders against
the looseness of manners of his time, against its
pleasures, and, not least, against its theatres.   This
man too and his party will have their day to
cleanse the churches and close the theatres.

It is said that Shakspeare made the acquaintance
of Sir John Oldcastle (for so the original of our
admirable friend, Sir John Falstaff, was called) in a
tavern in Eastcheap, the 'Boar's Head.'   Perhaps
even Chaucer saw this 'Boar's Head,' for in the
time of Richard II. the house and the sign existed,
though perhaps not as that of an inn.   Among the
three taverns in the City, towards the end of the
fifteenth century, the 'Boar's Head' is not mentioned ; but it received a place of honour among
the forty taverns which were granted to the City

in the sixteenth century by Act of Parliament;
and in the statistics of the year 1633, which
number 211 taverns, it is designated an ancient
tavern. Its first authentic appearance is in
an agreement of lease in the year 1537, when
it was in the hands of a widow, Joanna Broke,
probably the mother of William Broke, who
was landlord of the 'Boar's Head' till 1588, and
whom Thomas Wright succeeded. The original
sign of the 'Boar's Head' Tavern, a boar's head
carved in wood, with the date 1566, and the name
of the landlord at that time, William Broke, was
the only thing that was saved when the inn
was burnt down in the fire of 1666, and in July
1868 it was sold in an auction for 26*l.* sterling.
The building, which after the catastrophe was
erected on the same spot with the same sign, had
a stone boar's head, with the initials J. T., and
the date 1668; and this is now preserved in
Guildhall. Another relic of this second inn exists,
which in the year 1834 was brought before the
British Society of Antiquaries—a figure of the
noble Sir John Falstaff, carved in oak, which, in
the costume of the sixteenth century, had supported
a beam ornament over one side of the door, while the
figure of Prince Henry supported that on the other.
With these memorials of the two Shakspearian

heroes the tavern very long enjoyed a great renown in the neighbourhood of the Billingsgate
Fish-market, bore the ' Boar's Head ' on its shield,
and underneath the modest inscription, " This is the
best inn in London ; " till, at the beginning of the
last century, its owner at that time, perhaps in re-
pentance for the sins of his predecessors, male and
female, bequeathed this abode of Mrs. Quickly to
the Church of Saint Michael, that a chaplain might
be supported upon its income. But the ' Boar ' never
really flourished well under Church government :
at the beginning of this century the old nest was
divided between a barber and a gunsmith, over
whose adjoining shops the ' Boar's Head,' carved in
stone, was to be seen until the year 1831. Then
the last inmates of the ' Boar's Head ' were dis-
possessed, the house was pulled down to make room
for the new London Bridge, and exactly on the
spot where old Jack caroused, and, when he could
not pay his debts, promised marriage to the hostess,
with an oath over his parcel-gilt goblet, stands now
the statue of a man, who in his time was not less
corpulent but much less witty, the mounted statue
of William IV. The parcel-gilt goblet is preserved
in the neighbouring Church of St. Michael, or at
least, the sexton says that a goblet, which he shows
for sixpence, is that goblet. The last landlord of the

' Boar's Head ' whom Shakspeare can have known,
" John Rhodoway, Vintner at the ' Bore's Head,'
† 1623," lies buried in the church, and the grave
of a drawer at the same tavern is shown in the
adjoining churchyard of St. Michael. The sexton
says it is the identical Francis, whom we know so
well in Shakspeare's ' Henry IV.'; but if it really
were, this drawer must have reached the patriarchal
age, remarkable in our present proportions, of some
120 years or more, for he only died in 1720. Besides,
the inscription which adorns his resting-place calls
him Bob Preston :—

> " Bacchus to give the toping world surprise,
> Produced one sober Son, and here he lies ;
> Tho' nurs'd among full hogsheads he defy'd
> The charm of wine, and every vice besides.
> O, reader, if to justice thou 'rt inclined,
> Keep honest Preston daily in thy mind,
> He drew good wine, took care to fill his pots,
> Had sundry virtues that outweighed his *fauts* (*sic*).
> You that on Bacchus have the like dependence,
> Pray copy Bob in measure and attendance."

The tavern which Shakspeare most frequented,
and where he held the longest and most famous
sittings with his friends, was the tavern of ' The
Mermaid.' It stood in Bread Street, a side street
from Cheapside, between the present Southwark
Bridge and London Bridge. A few steps from the

house in which England's greatest dramatist lingered so often and so willingly, stood the house in which, about the same time, England's greatest epic poet was born, the poet of ' Paradise Lost.' So near, according to time and place, moved these two geniuses, who were destined to shine not far from one another on the poetical horizon of England, Shakspeare and Milton. Milton's house had the sign of the ' Spread Eagle,' after the arms of his family, which the poet also bore, and which, surviving in a little blind alley in modern London, " Spread Eagle Court," indicates the spot where, before the fire of 1666, stood the house in which Milton was born. ' The Mermaid ' was also destroyed in the same fire; the place is, however, still shown, and a good series of traditions has been preserved. The name of the landlord was Dun. His guests assembled either for dinner, which was taken just after twelve, or for the evening glass about six, when the theatre was over. There were then, of course, no bills of fare; but yet some cookery books of that time remain. Perhaps it may interest lady readers to learn what Mr. Dun's kitchen could do for Shakspeare and his friends. Here are some of its delicacies : boiled tulip-stalks ; salted turkey, stewed in white wine and vinegar, and served with fennel sauce ; pickled goose, with pinks and ginger; clover-flower jelly, and omelets of mallow-stems with rosewater.

But we think that the fat man at the upper end of the table, who seems to say of himself, " You see I have more flesh than other men, and also more weakness"—we think that he holds with the " Roast Beef of Old England," and that he partook of more sack than rosewater. " I would not give up fat Jack Falstaff for half the great men of ancient chronicle," says Washington Irving. " What have the heroes of yore done for me, or men like me? They have conquered countries of which I do not enjoy an acre, or they have gained laurels of which I do not inherit a leaf, or they have furnished examples of hair-brained prowess, which I have neither the opportunity nor the inclination to follow. But old Jack Falstaff! kind Jack Falstaff! sweet Jack Falstaff! has enlarged the boundaries of human enjoyment, he has added vast regions of wit and good humour, in which the poorest man may revel; and has bequeathed a never failing inheritance of jolly laughter to make mankind merrier and better to the latest posterity."

Wherefore, health to the noble Sir John Falstaff, and health to the noble Sir John Oldcastle, who was the excellent original of this excellent character! There was, however, also a veritable Sir

John Falstaff, one of the bravest generals in the
French wars under the three Henries. He is
certainly not Shakspeare's Falstaff, but it is not
impossible that the remembrance of this soldier
combined with that of Oldcastle to produce him.
The historical Falstaff was a great benefactor of
Magdalen College, at Oxford, and among the property which he bequeathed to it was also, strange
to say, a ' Boar's Head,' not indeed the tavern of
Eastcheap, but of another inn of the same name in
Southwark, which was pulled down about the same
time and with the same object as the other Falstaff's
' Boar's Head' Tavern, in order to lay open the
approaches to new London Bridge.

Between eating and drinking there was vigorous
smoking, for since Sir Walter Raleigh brought the
first bag of tobacco with him from the West Indies,
smoking had become the fashion in the exclusive
circles of those days. Shakspeare's colleagues of
the Globe and Blackfriars Theatres — Lawrence
Fletcher, and John Taylor and Richard Burbage,
the original performers of Hamlet, Lear, and
Othello—smoked. Shakspeare himself does not
appear to have been inclined to the new habit,
since in none of his pieces does he mention it; but
Ben Jonson must have been a friend of the " snipe's
head," as a pipe was then called. In his comedies it

is often mentioned. Richard Burbage was the first
actor of his time. " No one can be called a gentleman who is unacquainted with Dick Burbage;
every country maiden can tell of him," says the
'Return from Parnassus,' a play of the year 1602.
Richard Burbage must also have been a very fine
man. Once when he had acted Richard the Third,
a pretty townswoman of London fell so much in
love with him, that she granted him a " rendezvous,"
under the signal-word " Richard the Third." The
poet of tragedy, Shakspeare, heard the agreement,
and resolved to undertake the adventure himself,
went, and really obtained admission by the signal
agreed upon. Later came Burbage. " Richard the
Third is at the door!" said he, speaking upwards.
" William the Conqueror was before Richard the
Third," said William Shakspeare, speaking down,
and carried the day.

Shakspeare was the most amiable and elegant
of companions; Ben Jonson was somewhat more
heavy and ponderous.

Ben Jonson, after Shakspeare the most famous
dramatist of his time, had led a very eventful life.
First he had studied, then he was a soldier, then
became an actor; he had then shot one of his
colleagues, and been sentenced to imprisonment
for life. But he was pardoned, and employed the

remainder of his existence in writing for the stage. A good fellow-feeling, only disturbed once or twice by passing petty jealousies, bound him to Shakspeare. Both were witty, both were clever and experienced in affairs of the world. Their talk enlivened the entertainments at the 'Mermaid,' and their wit and jokes were carried about freely in London. Some of them are preserved to us. One day, for instance, speaking of the motto of the Globe Theatre, " All the world is a player," Jonson asked, " If all the world's a stage, where are the spectators, the public ? " Shakspeare immediately answered, " Man is himself at the same time actor and spectator."

Shakspeare was the more genial, but Jonson the more learned of the two ; especially he was a good Latin scholar. Once, when Jonson had made his friend godfather to one of his children, Shakspeare sat at the table absorbed and melancholy. Ben Jonson sought to enliven him, and asked him why he was so sad. " Sad ? I ? On my word, Ben, I am not sad," said Shakspeare ; " I have only been reflecting a while what I shall give my godchild, and now I have it." " Pray, what is it then ? " inquired Jonson. " Well, Ben, I will give him a dozen good Latten spoons, and you shall translate them."

The subject of a verse which Shakspeare improvised in the tavern of the 'Mitre' is a canary wine-
glass, once belonging to that hostel. "Had Horace
or Anacreon," says the poet, "drank of this wine,
they had been as deathless as their verses."

O dear Jack Oldcastle! O stout Jack Oldcastle, who could sit among the players and drink
his glass of sack, and take his ease, and hear his
Will and his Ben!

But now two o'clock is striking from the Cathedral and we must conclude our sitting. We
must betake ourselves over the sea, as was said
in the language of that time; that is, take a boat
and be rowed to one of the theatres, which whether
on this or that side of the Thames, lie close
by the shore. For at the stroke of three in the
afternoon the representation begins.

II.

The beau and man of fashion who in Elizabeth's time takes his morning walk in St. Paul's, already knows the titles of the pieces which will to day be brought out in the theatres of London; for among other pious proclamations on the walls of this Cathedral church there are also play-bills. For the profane multitude, however, and the public in general, they are affixed to the posts which have been erected here and there in the streets for horses to be tied to. On them we perceive the seven play-bills of the seven principal theatres of London; the 'Rose,' the 'Swan,' the 'Red Ox,' and the 'Curtain,' probably named after a picture; and the 'Globe,' the 'Fortune,' and the 'Hope,' probably named after a figure which, placed on some particularly conspicuous place of these buildings, was used as its sign. The play-bills of that time contained only the names of the piece, its author, the troop, and its patron; but no list of the dramatis personæ. Unhappily we possess no original of such a bill, but the title-pages of the first edition of Shakspeare's

works may give us an idea of the style in which
they were drawn up.   Here is an example :

Her Majesty's servants will to-day produce
A very amusing and highly ingenious Comedy,

Entitled :

SIR JOHN FALSTAFF AND THE MERRY WIVES OF WINDSOR ;

Intermixed with wonderfully varied and pleasing witticisms
of Sir Hugh, a Welsh Knight, of Justice Shallow, and
his wise cousin Slender, together with the swaggerings of
old Pistol and

CORPORAL PIM,

by

William Shakspeare,

As it has been several times performed by the servants of the
most honourable Lord High Chamberlain, as well

before

Her Majesty as elsewhere.

Shakspeare's troop, the chief and most important of that time, had two theatres ; a winter
theatre called ' Blackfriars,' and a summer theatre
the ' Globe.' Blackfriars Theatre, the oldest in
London, and the first in which there was acting
of plays after 1576, stood in the neighbourhood
of the present Blackfriars Bridge, in the region
of that labyrinth of small lanes and dark courts
which now surround Printing-house Square.
Where now the four colossal steam-presses of

London work, and dark warehouse doors unceasingly vomit forth printed packages of newspapers, there formerly Shakspeare played the
ghost of Hamlet's father. The paper age has
followed the golden; Shakspeare's Theatre has
given place to the editing and printing houses of
the 'Times.' Blackfriars Theatre was a so-called
private theatre, that is, it was smaller than the
others, which, in opposition to it, were called public
theatres ; had a complete roof and seats in the
pits ; and the acting was before a select audience,
and by candlelight, while the daylight was arti-
ficially excluded. The Globe Theatre, on the other
hand, the summer theatre of the company, was a
public one ; it lay opposite on the other side of the
Thames in an oblique direction, and in order to
reach it, it was necessary to cross one of the
bridges or to hire a pair of sculls.

Carriages in London at that time were only rarely
seen. They came in with tobacco smoking, and
were ridiculed with it. "The first carriage," says
a satirist of that time, "was made by the devil in
China out of a crab's shell, and brought over to
England in a cloud of tobacco smoke." The first
carriage in London came from Holland, and was
given to the Queen as a present, in which she
drove from Whitehall to St. Paul's on the day of

the solemn thanksgiving service for the destruction of the Armada. Till the beginning of the seventeenth century four hackney coaches, which stood under the 'May Tree' in the Strand, answered the requirements of travelling London; but the "enterprise," which had gradually comprised the number of twenty, was soon decried as a public nuisance, and hackney coaches were in the year 1635 plainly forbidden by a royal proclamation, as they obstructed the passage and made the streets dangerous for His Majesty and the nobility. Henceforth hackney coaches were no more driven in the streets of London, but only from London into the country and *vice versâ;* and no one was to use them, except such persons as were in position to keep four strong horses in the stable for His Majesty's service, which, under heavy punishment, must be ready when required. The Republic showed itself more tolerant than the Monarchy towards the forbidden comfort; in an ordinance of the Lord Protector Cromwell, in the year 1654, 200 such carriages are allowed for the metropolis and six miles round, but not more, " as their continually increasing number threatens by blockading our streets to become insupportable." A century later there were 800; and in 1854 between 8000 and 9000 cabs, besides 3000 omnibuses.

I

The gentlemen of the Court and the cavaliers
of Shakspeare's time rode to the theatre, accompanied by their Irish stable-boys, who ran along
beside them, and by their French pages, who
followed them on horseback. But the majority of
the spectators came by water in small rowing-
boats. This was the favourite means of transport
from one part of the City to another. Those parts
of London which lie towards the parks and on the
hills were attached much later. The London of
that time, the City, lay almost entirely by the
water, and had fewer bridges than at present.
More than 40,000 men lived by their oars and
boats, and between 3000 and 4000 persons were
rowed every day to the theatres alone, which,
whether on this side of the river or that, lay close
to the bank.

But the Theatre had also its enemies. Already
we have seen that man beneath the cross at
St. Paul's, that clergyman, the worthy John Stock-
wood, who before his congregation of Puritans
declaims against this new misuse of time. " I say
nothing," cries he, " about various other sins, which
drag thousands along and at last drown them
in the stream of vanity. But look at the public
plays in London, and look at the crowd of men
that flock to them, and run after them. Consider

the gorgeous theatrical buildings, an enduring
monument of England's extravagance and foolish-
ness." Then after the preacher has depicted in
fiery words the horror of a theatrical exhibition, he
brings into connection with it the sickness which
raged almost every year, and closes with the assertion, "The cause of the plague is sin, and plays
are the cause of sin, therefore plays are the cause
of the plague."

The magistracy of London, Lord Mayor and
Aldermen, took up this argument. It was announced by this corporation, in a very learned
document, that to act during the plague spread the
contagion, and that when there was no plague it
produced the plague. Conformably with this it was
ordered that actors—with the exception of those
engaged in Her Majesty's service—should only
have permission to play when the town should be in
health; that is, when not more than fifty people
had died in the week for three consecutive weeks.
There was to be no acting at all on Sundays, and
not later on week days than so that each of the
spectators could be back at his dwelling before
sunset, or at least before it grew dark. This very
wise order of a highly praiseworthy magistracy
had no other effect than that the theatres were not
built in the City, but in its outskirts, mostly by the

I 2

water; and that Her Majesty and Her Majesty's
great lords took the poor persecuted actors into
their service, and covered them with their mantle
from the wisdom and prevision of the fathers of
the town. In this quality the actors of that time,
like other servants, wore the arms and colours of
their patrons; whoever laid hands on them had
to do with the lords of Her Majesty's household.
The members of Shakspeare's troop, and Shakspeare himself, as "Her Majesty's servants," wore
scarlet cloaks with velvet facings.

Queen Elizabeth was a great friend and pro-
tectress of the Play. She and her Court considered
it no sin, after they had their customary church-
going in the morning, to conclude the Sunday
with a comedy; and in their care for the pleasure
of the humbler classes they encouraged them to
follow their example. At that time Sunday was
not the day on which it was forbidden to the good
people of London, for their recreation after the
burden and toil of the week, to visit any kind of
public building but a church and a gin-palace.
Then Sunday was the best day for the theatres,
and people flocked into them to see Shakspeare
and to hear Shakspeare. The Queen certainly in
her own person never went to the theatre, but re-
presentations took place continually in her palaces

at Whitehall, Richmond, and Windsor; and some
of Shakspeare's pieces were first brought out before
Her Majesty. During one of these Court representa-
tions in the Banqueting-Room at Whitehall, when
Shakspeare played the rôle of Henry VI. in his
own drama, the idea occurred to the Queen to put
his presence of mind to the test. "I have often
been told," she said, "that he possesses a great
talent for improvisation, well, I will convince
myself of it." The Queen's box was immediately
over the stage, and was reached by a little staircase,
before which stood the two body-guards of Her
Majesty with great halberds, in the steel of which
glittered the arms of the Order of the Garter, and
the device "Honny soit qui mal y pense." At the
moment when Henry VI. in the midst of his nobles
came on to the scene which was to represent the
Parliament, the Queen let her glove fall down
over the front of the box just at Shakspeare's feet.
He, as soon as he saw it fall, stepped forward
without any hesitation, and breaking off his speech
in the middle, raised the glove, with the following
words, which he improvised in his character as
king :

> "And though now bent on this high embassy,
> Yet stoop we, to pick up our cousin's glove."

Then, after placing the glove on the halberd of

one of the body-guard, from which the Queen, smiling, took it, he went back again, and continued to play his part. A tolerably authentic anecdote also tells us that we have only to thank the wish of Her Majesty for the " Merry Wives of Windsor." She who, like all the world at that time, entertained a great admiration and friendship for Sir John Falstaff, was very curious to learn the behaviour of the fat knight in a love affair, and in the company of ladies, after always hitherto seeing him among men, either with his cup or in battle. Here was an exercise for Shakspeare's humour! It is said that he did not take more than a fortnight to produce the play. And so at the end of the year 1602, shortly before Elizabeth's death, the new comedy appeared, probably at Windsor Castle, in which the Queen then, by preference, resided, and after which, with delicate courtesy, the poet named his piece. An anecdote, which is certainly less authentic, adds that the Queen laughed so violently over the tricks of the Merry Wives and the misfortune of their knightly gallant, who is thrown into the Thames in a heap of dirty linen, that a cramp and cough came on, which proved fatal to her.

Alas! the poor Queen was not to die of laughter. Her end was sadder. For nights she sat on her

bed weeping, bedewing the silken pillows with
tears, and rending the air with cries over those
long departed—one among them poisoned and one
beheaded—till at last she died in her palace of
Richmond, lying on the ground, with the name of
Essex on her lips. . . . .

But the sun is still high, and our small vessel
floats on the waves of the Thames. There on the
right-hand shore is Bankside, the abode of pleasure
in Shakspeare's London, bright with the signs of
inns, and lively with music. There is the bear-
garden, and there are five out of the seven theatres
of London. There, where behind Southwark
Bridge in our London a gigantic host of chimneys
day and night pours forth black smoke which
darkens the atmosphere—where there is an inces-
sant roar of waggons, and a continuous smell of
hops and malt, and where on a soot-blackened
wall a board bears this inscription, "Barclay and
Perkin's Brewery"—on this same spot, three hundred years ago, and under the blue sky of Shakspeare's London, stood his theatre, which had for
its sign Hercules with the Globe, after which
it was called the Globe Theatre. It is still the
same unchanged Southwark, as we saw it two
hundred years earlier, in Chaucer's time, a rural
suburb with fields and gardens. Memories of

Shakspeare mingle with those of Chaucer; the old
' Tabard' in which the Canterbury Pilgrims formerly assembled has received a gay neighbour;
and as Shakspeare's genius in the ' Mermaid'
is connected with that of the future, so here in
Southwark, where his Theatre stands, it is connected
with that of the past, the worthy Father of
English Poetry; in this manner exhibiting, as it
were, backwards and forwards, the local material
connection between centuries. The Globe Theatre
is a hexagonal building of wood, almost like a
fort, with many windows around, which look like
loop-holes, with two small wooden houses on the
top, and a flagstaff. Now, as the clocks of London
strike a quarter to three, a fantastically dressed
man steps out of one of the little wooden houses
with a trumpet, to give the first signal. From all
the theatres in the neighbourhood sound the same
tones, which meet in the air, and urge to greater
speed the vessels with which the mirror of the
Thames is covered, and the riders who are coming
over the bridge. But before it is three o'clock the
trumpeter will blow twice more, and then with the
striking of the hour and the last flourish the
representation will begin, and a red silk flag will
appear on the flagstaff.

Meanwhile, boat is moored by boat to the bank,

the neighing and trampling of numerous horses are round about the theatre, and all press towards the entrance and paying-place; the young cavalier with sword and plumed hat, the solemn citizen, the modest and pretty townswoman, the learned man and the book-worm from Little Britain, the swashbuckler from his lurking-places in the Strand, the lawyer from the Temple, the country gentleman from his hall at home full of falcons and terriers, the runaway apprentice from the workshop, and the sailor, still smelling strongly of tar, from the sea; all these are Shakspeare's audience.

The prices of admission are very diverse. The cheapest places at that time as now are in the gallery; these cost about a penny. The great bulk of the public crowds together in the pit, which in the Globe, as in other public theatres, is called the "yard." The "yard" has no roof and no seats; here reigns unlimited freedom. Rain and sunshine come at will; and for twopence every British subject has here the privilege of seeing, pressing and being pressed, eating apples, cracking nuts, drinking beer, playing cards, and damning the performance. In this respect, if in no other, the groundlings were in great consideration; their applause determined the success of the piece. But, nevertheless, they were accounted neither respectable nor fit to judge critically, and the really educated frequenter of the theatre took good care not to be included among them. For about eighteen-pence or two shillings, he took his seat in one of the "rooms," as the boxes in Shakspeare's theatre were called. Sometimes he hired his "room" for the whole season, and kept the key in his own pocket.

It seems that the playhouses had also their especial power of attraction for the equivocal characters of that time ; in that respect the world has remained as it was, and little arrangements for suppers after the theatre were as much in fashion then as they are now. There was no lack of pickpockets, but the mode of their punishment was original ; if they were taken in the act, they were without further ceremony brought on to the stage and bound to a post, and there offered a worthy aim, as much for the derision as for the nutshells of the groundlings. Much more than in our own days was the stage then considered to be for the joint amusement of the public. Only the smallest part of it was appointed for the actors ; more than half of it served the gallants, the wits, and the men of profession and education, as a place for the display of their own persons, their white hands, or their silk cloaks. For a small gratuity, they had here their three-legged stools, or threw themselves at length on the rush-strewn floor. Rushes were at that time what carpet is now; the custom of covering the floor with them was general in the palace and in the house of the citizen, as we see by Holbein's English family pictures; and they were not wanting on the stage. Dekker, in his 'Gull's Horn Book,' gives very exact directions to the gallant how he is to behave on the stage, as these gentlemen not unfrequently amused themselves during the play by picking up one of these green plants from the ground, and with the point of it tickling the ear of his neighbour. The perfect gallant never appeared before the trumpet had been blown three times, then, as the above-named Decker describes, " presently advanced himself up to the throne of the stage, I mean not into the Lord's room (the stage-box), which is now but the stage's suburbs, but on the very rushes where the comedy is to dance; yea, and under the state of Cambyses himself must our feathered ostrich, like a piece of ordnance, be planted valiantly, because impudently beating down the mews and hisses of the opposed rascality."

The marks of approval and of disapproval were the same in Shakspeare's theatre as in our own. The first instance of calling for a favourite author was not indeed till a hundred years later, and hap-

pened to one who took upon himself to compare
Shakspeare with a " drunken savage;" namely Voltaire, at the first bringing out of his ' Merope ' in
1743. Lessing, who relates this event in his ' Ham-
burgische Dramaturgie' as something quite unusual, does not appear to have been much edified
by it. " When the representation was at an end,
the pit desired to see this wonderful man, and
called and yelled till Voltaire appeared, and let
them clap and gape to their heart's content." Since
then, all French dramatic poets have stood in this
pillory; but, adds the author of 'Emilia Galotti,'
" I would sooner have done away with such an evil
custom by my example, than by ten ' Meropes '
have given rise to it."

Now in Shakspeare's Theatre there was neither
this nor any critic ; immediate applause decided
all. It is true that the gentlemen of fashion who
sat on the stage, had named their note-books
" tables," in which they eagerly wrote during the
representation ; but they only wrote the witticisms
which most pleased them, in order to carry them
about afterwards at the Court and the tavern, or
to mingle them if opportunity allowed in their conversation. To have such a book at hand, and to
draw it forth at the beginning of the play, passed for
a sign of literary refinement and good taste. Be-

sides this, the gallant man of that time had his playing cards, his snuffbox and the silver spoon with which he took the snuff, his pipe, and his three kinds of tobacco, of which the genuine Trinidad was the most prized. To fill his pipe was the first thing a cavalier did after taking his three-legged stool on the stage; then he lighted it, handing round the burning match on the point of his sword, or begging one of his neighbour. Smoking was at that time a complete art : people learnt smoking as at the present day they learn dancing; they had the most varying manners of taking the smoke and blowing it out again, namely, the "whiff" and the "sniff," and the "euripus," and the stage was considered the best place to show what they had learned from their professors.

What in Shakspeare's time was a coarseness, not opposed to morality, took later the character of an immorality. Ladies at that time never went to the theatres, and much later, in the last part of the seventeenth century, only with masks. So Pepys, the diarist in the year 1663, saw a daughter of Cromwell, Countess Falconberg, at the theatre; but as soon as the house began to fill she put her mask on, and wore it through the performance. Neither had there hitherto been any actresses, the female characters were represented by boys or

young men ; and even under Charles II. it happened
one day, at the bringing out of one of Shakspeare's
pieces, that the director came to the monarch, who
was becoming indignant over the delay in beginning, with the excuse, "Sire, only a few minutes
longer, I pray ; the queen is not yet shaved!"

But when women not only appeared in the
places of the spectators, but even became customary on the stage, the seats of the gallants
excited a veritable opposition, although the morals
of that time were not particularly good, before
or behind the scenes.   At any rate, the presence of
gentlemen on the stage caused various disturbances,
and as early as the year 1664 an order was made
that no one who did not belong to the troop
should be seen in the dressing-room.   Later, means
were taken to procure a seat on the stage at a high
price, as, for example, half-a-guinea, in 1732, at
the opening of Covent Garden Theatre.   But the
evil continued, and became no better when efforts
were made to correct it in another way, namely,
by posting sentinels on the stage "to prevent the
disorders which the most unmanly race of young
men that ever were seen in any age frequently
raised," as says the 'Guardian' of April the 2nd,
1713.   The report of that time tells of one of these
soldiers who, at a certain part of the piece, was so

moved that he burst into tears, whereat the company were immensely delighted. Some laughed aloud, others applauded the poor fellow ; in short, such a noise was made that the representation was interrupted by it. But these guardians of order did not always restrict themselves to dumb tears of sympathy; sometimes their feeling drew them farther. One of them once shot an Othello, on the open stage, because he could not look on while that Moor murdered Desdemona. Another, in the midst of the tragedy of ' The Earl of Essex,' when Lady Nottingham denied having received a ring from her unhappy lover, rushed forward on the stage, seized the stage queen, frightened to death, by the neck, and cried, " She lies; she has the ring hidden in her bosom."

In Paris the war against gentlemen on the stage continued till past the middle of the eighteenth century. One evening, a certain actor named Beaubourg, who was distinguished for his great ugliness, was playing the part of Mithridates, and the famous Adrienne Lecouvreur had to say to him as Monime, " Ah, my lord, you alter your face ! " Then the gentlemen who sat on the stage began to laugh aloud, and to cry, " Let him do so. It won't hurt him." This manifestation, which took place in 1759, put an end to the disorder ; their

privilege was bought from the hitherto favoured
ones for a considerable sum; and at the same
time Garrick, the reviver of Shakspeare, purified
the English stage from an abuse which, under
different circumstances, had in Shakspeare's time
formed a necessary element of it.

Shakspeare's theatre was thus :—a stage 53 feet
broad and 27½ feet deep; a space of 12½ feet in
breadth round the rest of the building, for boxes,
galleries, cloak-room, and passages, so that the
inclosed "yard" measured something like 55 feet
by 40; the walls, of wood and whitewash, nearly
32 feet high—all full of people smoking, brawl-
ing, drinking, eating, lying, sitting, and standing;
and over them the roof of the sky, blue and sunny
to-day, to-morrow gloomy and full of rain.

The stage alone was protected from the changes
of the weather by a roof of straw, and the place
where the acting took place was divided by a
curtain of woven material from the place which
was occupied by the gallants and wits. It hung,
like every other curtain, by rings on a rod, and
was drawn apart in the middle towards each side.

Now it strikes three, and the third trumpet-
blast resounds from above. Immediately the curtain moves and parts. The Prologue advances,
usually in a long black velvet cloak, and with a

laurel branch twined round his forehead. Sometimes the poet prescribes a different costume, as,
for example, in ' Troilus and Cressida' :

> "Hither am I come,
> A Prologue armed."

or in ' Henry the Fourth,' where Prologue appears
as Rumour, painted all over with tongues. He
recites his poetical greeting to the audience, in
which he at the same time welcomes them and prepares them for the play, from a leaf which he holds
in his hand. As soon as he has ended and retired
the play begins. At the end of it Epilogue appears,
according to rule, one of the characters of the drama,
who invites the audience not to be niggardly in
their applause. " So, good night," says Puck, as
Epilogue in ' Midsummer Night's Dream,' " Give
me your hands if we be friends."

After the Epilogue came the " Jig," a medley of
talking, singing, and dancing, also of couplet and
ballet, full of allusions to the events and personalities of the day, brought out by the clown of the
company, and accompanied by music. The conclusion of the whole representation was made by
all the members of the troop appearing again,
kneeling down round the edge of the stage, and
saying a prayer for the Queen—a custom which is

K

maintained to the present day in England, where
no play, opera, or concert is left before the National
Anthem has been sung.

But how did Shakspeare's stage look during the
representation ?   Very primitive, readers may rely
upon that.   There was no decoration and no scenery
—there was nothing but a great board in the background, with the inscription " France," if the scene
lay in France, or " Venice," and " Verona," if the
poet wished to transport us to that country where
Othello murdered his wife out of jealousy, where
Romeo and Juliet loved, and died for love.   As
quickly as this board is changed, the scene of the
play changes also ; Puck himself cannot fly quicker.
Sometimes, in one act, we are in six different
corners and ends of the 'world, and all by means of
a board !   These, therefore, in Shakspeare's sense,
are, as Schiller says, the " boards which represent
the world."   The floor of the stage, as has been
already said, is strewn with rushes, the walls are
hung with tapestry, and a balcony and several
curtains are in the background.   The balcony is
for the sieges, when the citizens appear " on the
walls," or the soldiers " on the towers."   The
curtains, called " Traverses," are for making a
second room on the stage when it is required ;
or when, as in ' Hamlet,' a play occurs within a

play. They managed in all things as well as they could. In one piece a Mussulman hero is to be buried; the only thing the poet gives to help the imaginative powers of his audience is the notice, " Imagine the temple of Mohammed." In another piece a peasant invites his neighbour. In order to inform the spectators that the invitation has been accepted, and that they are both come into the cottage, the stage notice announces, " Here a dog barks," and the scenic effect is left to the actor who can bark best. Sometimes not even so much as this was done to acquaint the public with the where and how of the affair. In a comedy of Greene, for instance, a certain Jenkins challenges a shoemaker, who has struck him, to go with him " one or two miles" away, and then to fight with cudgels. The shoemaker at last consents, but wishes to fight as soon as possible. " Come, Sir, will you go with me outside the town?"

Whereupon Jenkins immediately replies—"Yes, Sir, come along."

In the next line they are already at the place and spot. "Now we are outside the town, what have you to say?"

No doubt the cudgelling begins here, for one or two steps upon the stage have borne the two heroes and also the public over one or two miles of

country. Still the theatre of Shakspeare was not
quite without arrangements for a more modest kind
of effect. There were, for instance, trap-doors, which
occupy the place of the German *Versenkungen.*
The witches' cauldron, in ' Macbeth,' went down
through such a trap-door. In another piece it says,
" The magicians strike on the ground with their
sticks, and a fine tree comes up from beneath."
There were also means of making figures float
above, but they were of coarser substance than the
invisible wires of our fairy-ballets. A piece of that
time says, " Venus exit; or, if it can be arranged,
let down a chain from above and draw her up."
In a stage inventory of the year 1598 are found
the following objects, which partly belonged to the
wardrobe, and partly compensated for the want of
decoration :—" Item : a rock, a prison, a jaws of
Hell, a Dido's grave. Item : eight spears, a staircase
for Phaeton for him to go up into heaven. Item :
two biscuits and the city of Rome. Item : a golden
fleece, two gibbets, one laurel-tree. Item : a wooden
sky, the head of old Mohammed. Item : the three
heads of Cerberus, a dragon in Faust, a lion, two
lion's heads, a great horse with its legs. Item : a
pair of red gloves, a papal mitre, three imperial
crowns, a block, for the beheading in ' Black John.'
Item : a cauldron for the Jews. Item : four coats

for Herod, a green cloak for Mariamne, a bodice for Eve, a costume for the ghost, and three hats for the Spanish dons."

Of Shakspeare's theatres, that in Blackfriars stood a long time, till it fell to pieces with age. But the Globe had only a short life. One evening in the year 1613, when Shakspeare's 'Henry VIII.' was being performed, a burning splinter fell on the stage, which was, exceptionally, covered with a straw mat. The flames caught, tore round the wooden building, and it was soon burnt to ashes.

This fire, which consumed one of Shakspeare's theatres in his lifetime, was symbolical of that other greater fire which fifty years after his death destroyed almost that whole City which we have pictured as Shakspeare's London. Of this London very little remains; only memory can point out the places which are associated with the story of Shakspeare's life. What the fire spared has been in the two following centuries thrown down, one piece after another, and cleared away. Of the palace at Whitehall, in which Shakspeare played comedy before Queen Elizabeth, only the smallest portion still stands, and that has been changed into a chapel. Of the houses in which he and his friends, his contemporaries, and his audience, dwelt, there is not a single one to be seen. The theatres in which

all his pieces were performed the first time have
had no better fate; but one building of Shakspeare's London still stands in its old glory—in
Shakspeare's days already more than six hundred
years old, it has since become about three hundred
years older—the Abbey of Westminster. The soot
and rust, the moss and the ivy of almost a thousand
years, cling to the outer walls—to the buttresses
and pointed arches of this honoured minster; and
in the sacred gloom that fills its arches, in the
solemn silence which always reigns in its choir and
side aisles, are the tombs of the Kings and Queens
of England. Here also in Poet's Corner, not far
from the grave of Chaucer, stands a monument of
white marble, which represents a man who wears
the picturesque costume of the time of Queen
Elizabeth—the broad lace collar, the richly-orna-
mented doublet, and the short knightly cloak.
He leans easily on his right arm, which rests
on a portion of a column, and in his left hand
he holds a scroll, which, half-unrolled, shows
the following verses:—

> " The cloud capp'd towers, the gorgeous palaces,
> The solemn temples, the great globe itself;
> Yea, all which it inherit, shall dissolve—"

These lines, whose echoes seem to die away
softly in the twilight which broods over the

graves, are Shakspeare's lines; and this monument, to which the bust of Milton looks, as if
it had on its lips the words, "What need'st thou
such weak witness of thy name?" is Shakspeare's
monument.

THE COFFEE-HOUSES AND CLUBS
OF LONDON.

THE COFFEE-HOUSES.

IT was, if I mistake not, Madame de Sévigné who said that "coffee and Racine would be forgotten together." This sentiment would do honour to the prophetic soul of that lady were it not opposed to this other observation, that he wrote his verses for the *champ mêlé*, "and not for the future."

Coffee and Racine came into the world about the same time; so much is true. Racine was born in the year 1639, and five years later Laroque introduced the first coffee at Marseilles. Its reception in France was not attended with enthusiasm. Soliman-Aga, Turkish Ambassador at the Court of Louis XIV., between whom and the Grand Seigneur was an *entente cordiale*, invited once, in the year 1669, the nobility of Paris to take coffee with him in his magnificent apartments. The French nobility arrived and were enchanted with his famous slippers, but made wry faces over his "black and bitter" drink. "Perhaps," says one of their witty compatriots, "the coffee would have tasted better if it had been cærulean blue, or at least pearl grey."

In spite of this not very encouraging experience, the Ambassador's servant, an Armenian, whom in French books I find called Pasqual, opened in 1670 the first coffee-house in Paris by the market of St. Germain. But the public found no greater delight in this new drink than the high nobility; and the next day he shut up his shop and departed for London.

We may satisfy ourselves with the belief that he succeeded here better than in Paris. Though coffee was still a novelty, he had not the dangerous responsibility of being the first to introduce it. Twenty years before his arrival, during the republic of Cromwell, a Jew, called Jacobs, had established a coffee-house at Oxford, and the 'Political Mercury' of 30th September, 1658, speaks of the Sultanes' Cophee-house in Sweeting's Lane. Between these two dates—either in 1652 or 1657, for the dates differ—another Oriental, of the same name with the Armenian, Pasqua Rosée, of Ragusa, established, in company with a London coachman, a third coffee-house in London, not far from the Exchange. This company, through the exertions of its head, attained considerable notoriety, and is the starting-point for all history connected with London coffee-houses.

Pasqua Rosée came to London, as the Armenian

to Paris, in the service of a nobleman, who allowed him to teach his countrymen the Oriental art of coffee-making. Somewhat later the head of the Sultan Amurath appears to have been a very common sign of coffee-houses, with this subscription :—

> "Morat ye great men did me call,
> Where eare I came I conquered all."

Our Ragusan, however, took his own head, of course, *in effigie.* That fortune and circumstances favoured him has already been declared, but he was not deficient in honest labour in extending this subject of his commerce. Even at that time journals were existent, and journals bore advertisements.* Meanwhile, from the probably moderate

---

* All the Journals of that time give advertisements. The 'London Gazette' had a particular rubric for "advertisements," which indeed, compared with our means of obtaining publicity, have a very childish appearance. A number of the 'Gazette,' for instance, that of the year 1689 —which I bought by auction in a second-hand shop in London—has eight notices, out of which three refer to stolen, and two to lost property. In the sixth a runaway son is intreated to return ; the seventh heralds "A History of the Coronation of James II." ; and the last is a species of educational treatise, with the title : "Earnest considerations on Time and Eternity, with Introductory Remarks about the manner in which the Jews celebrate the New Year." The price of insertion seems to us rather high

number of the subscribers to the papers of those days, and the intervals of at least half a week at which most of them were published, there was plenty of employment in the distribution of handbills—bills which were handed to the passenger along the streets—a practice still in use for certain communications of medical and scientific matter which the usually liberal advertisement sheets of English papers exclude, just as it was in the days of Hogarth. (Cf. ' A Harlot's Progress,' plate 5.)

One of these Pascal handbills has come down to posterity ; it bears the superscription ' The Virtue of the Coffee-drinking, first made and publicly sold in England by Pasqua Rosée.' These virtues are more than one at the present day could imagine, admitting all the excellent effects of a good cup of

---

and to have been reckoned, not by the number of lines, but the value of the subject. The ' Jockey Intelligencer ' of 1683 charged one shilling for a horse or coach, sixpence for a repetition. The ' Observator Reformed ' inserted eight lines for a shilling, but the ' Country Gentleman's Courant ' took a higher flight, seeing that the " advancement of trade was a thing to be encouraged," and charged twopence a line in consequence. Advertisements of books, as those quoted, appear very early. The first theatrical announcement of Lincoln's Inn Theatre is found in the ' English Post ' of 1701 ; and the first large page of advertisements in the style of the present journals, was in the ' General Advertiser ' of 1745.

coffee :—" It is a simple innocent thing," says he, " and makes the heart lightsome; it is good against sore eyes, and the better if you hold your head over it, and take in the steam that way. It is good for a cough. It is excellent to prevent and cure the dropsy, gout, and scurvy. It is a most excellent remedy against the king's evil, the spleen, hypochondriac winds, &c. It keeps the skin white and clean." As an especial advantage it is added, that one may drink coffee as hot as he will without its fetching the skin off the mouth or raising blisters on the tongue by reason of that heat.

The subscription of the document tells us that this drink is only made and sold in St. Michael's Alley, in Cornhill, by Pasqua Rosée, " under the sign of his own head."

Among many other things the bill contains a receipt for the making of coffee, in which it is said that the berry is first to be dried in an oven, then ground to powder, and then boiled with spring water. This primitive prescription, which, in fact, is very harmless compared to the fine meditation of Brillat-Savarin about the different methods of coffee-making, shows the present standing-point of the English. Far removed from that elevated, one might almost say ideal, conception of the famous physiologist of taste, the coffee of England is decidedly the very worst a man can drink; and this, combined with some other grounds of a climatic nature, may well be the reason that in the country in which it was first greeted, faith has not been kept with it, and people have generally returned to their natural beverage, tea.

At the time, however, to which we have referred, coffee was much in vogue, and the coffee-house became soon for the English—that is, Londoners— a place of hitherto unknown pleasure and new society.

There was, of course, that opposition which every innovation, it seems, whether of science, fashion, or gastronomy, must expect. The least one could say was, that, in spite of the assurance of Pasqua's handbills, it was easy to burn the tongue by drinking coffee too hot.

Satire and pamphlet arose against "a sort of liquor, called coffee," of which a specimen is saved for us in that valuable collection of Isaac D'Israeli's 'Curiosities of Literature,' ii. 322. In one of these writings—'A Cup of Coffee, or Coffee in all its colour'—of the year 1663, the anonymous author complains over the downfall of his genera- tion, whom he calls "English apes." He adjures the shades of their forefathers; and calls on Ben Jonson's manly ghost, the noble phantoms of Beau-

mont and Fletcher, who drank pure nectar, with
rich canary ennobled, while these coffee-men, these
"sons of nought," gave up the pure blood of the
grape for a filthy drink, "syrup of soot, essence of
old shoes."

Still farther in his anger went the author of
'A Petition of Women against Coffee,' 1674, who
makes his fair petitioners complain "that coffee
made the men as unfruitful as the deserts whence
that unhappy berry is said to be brought, and
that the offspring of our mighty ancestors would
dwindle into a succession of apes and pigmies."

Supposing this petition against coffee to be
fictitious, one in real earnest very soon followed.
On the 21st of December, 1657, a number of the
burghers appeared before the magistrate to complain of a certain Farr, who, as it appears, was a
barber before he became a coffee-man. This James
Farr, the founder of the now famous 'Rainbow,'
was accused of making and selling a drink, called
coffee, by the manufacture of which he offended
his neighbours with an evil smell,* and kept up a

---

* It is remarkable that the smell of coffee seems so
unpleasant to the true Briton. Each of the above-quoted
pamphlets calls it a "stink," and uses for the coffee-drinkers
the by no means elegant figure of "horses at a trough."

L

fire during the greatest part of the day and night, by which his chimney and house were set burning, to the great fear and danger of those who lived near him.

But these prejudices and persecutions, which affected not him alone, could not stop the rising popularity of the new institution.

Before the conclusion of the seventeenth century, the coffee-houses were one of the sights of London. As such they are noted in the ' Mémoires et Observations faites par un Voyageur en Angleterre' (Haag, 1698), one of those small but neatly got-up volumes with plates and illustrations, such as came in quantities from the Dutch press, in order, in the opinion of William III., to make propaganda on the Continent for the Protestant succession, and against the Jacobites. In this book, and in the above-mentioned year, we find under " Caffez " :—" These kinds of houses, whose number is very great in London, are exceedingly comfortable. You can hear there all the news before a good fire, can drink a cup of coffee or anything else, and transact your business with your friend, and all for a sou, supposing you feel disinclined to give more."

This price of entrance of a sou, or rather a penny, after which the coffee-houses in that time were soon called "Penny Universities," seems strange to us, but still exists in some of the London reading-rooms, where one, for this price or a higher, has the paper and a cup of coffee, and sometimes a cigar in addition, as, in Wylde's Coffee-House, Leicester Square, and Simpson's Cigar Divan, Strand. But this was not the only duty of the coffee-house frequenters. As soon as they entered they were informed by a large set of Regulations in verse, suspended against the wall, of what they might and might not do. John Timbs, in his compilation, 'Club Life of London,'* which we shall make use of in the course of our inquiries, has communicated to us one of these civil orders. We learn from it, first, that any one, of whatever position, was here welcome, there was no preference of seat (probably the Continental Congresses had set the example, *not* to

---

* John Timbs, F.S.A. 'Club Life of London, with Anecdotes of the Clubs, Coffee-houses, and Taverns of the Metropolis, during the 17th, 18th, and 19th centuries.' 2 vols. London, Bentley, 1866. A mere book of reference, sometimes sufficiently inexact, but, on the whole, a rich collection of almost inexhaustible material, for the best of which Timbs, though he has nowhere confessed it, is indebted to Peter Cunningham's excellent 'Handbook of London.' See the review in the 'Athenæum,' 3rd March, 1866. No. 2001, p. 294.

be followed). No one had to stand up when a
finer person came in after him; he who so far
forgot himself as to curse or quarrel must pay for
the first offence, twelvepence; for others a cup of
coffee for every guest present. One might be
merry and converse, but not in too loud a tone;
all talk of religion and politics was expressly
forbidden. Cards and dice were not allowed;
betting only to the extent of five shillings. The
last prescription was, that the guests should pay
their bills.

The veto on politics refers to an event in
Danby's Ministry, 1673–78. From the moment
coffee-houses became the fashion in London they
acquired a political significance. This was but
natural under the circumstances: when no Parliament had been called for years; when the magistrate
spoke no more after the opinions of the burghers;
when, with one word, the constitutional voices of the
estates were corrupted or reduced to silence, and
the voice of the new fourth estate, the Press, was
not yet sufficiently strong to be generally heard;
nothing remained but the coffee-houses, which, as
Macaulay says ('History of England,' chap. iii.),
were the "chief organs through which the public
opinion of the metropolis vented itself."

The rising of this new power in the State had

long been a cause of uneasiness to the Court, and
at the above-mentioned time an attempt was made
to close the coffee-houses of London.

Among the numerous tyrannical and unwise
political acts, which at last brought about the overthrow of the Stuarts, the proclamation " concerning the suppression of coffee-houses," December 20,
1675, is perhaps one of the most tyrannical and most
unwise. In the motives assigned for this decree
(communicated by D'Israeli, 'Royal Proclamations,' iii. 379) we are told, that it was made
because the multitude of coffee-houses lately set up
and kept within this kingdom, and the great resort
of idle and dissipated persons to them, have produced very evil and dangerous effects, whilst they
especially tended to spread rumours, and to tempt
tradespeople to neglect their business, and that this
idle waste of time and money was becoming an
injury to the Commonwealth. Hence it is ordered
for all coffee-house keepers that they should not pre-
sume on or after the 10th of January next, to keep
a public coffee-house, or to sell, or allow the con-
sumption therein, of coffee, chocolate, tea, or sherbet,
and that they would be answerable for so doing.

But it has, as we know, always been the fate
of these ministerial prohibitions to give to assemblies or meetings of this kind a character,

without which they would have probably continued
harmless, and thereby to bring about exactly what
it had been the desire to avoid. Kennet, a
very sensible man among the Crown lawyers of
that time, had given an unfavourable opinion
of the measure; he says that malcontents had
existed before they met with one another in coffee-
houses, and that the proclamation desired to sup-
press an evil which could not be suppressed. Let
us hear what Macaulay says : " Men of all parties
missed their usual places of resort so much that
there was an universal outcry. The Government
did not venture, in opposition to a feeling so strong
and general, to enforce a regulation of which the
legality might well be questioned."

The result was that the proclamation was withdrawn, and the coffee-houses were again opened,
under the following restrictions, that it should be
punishable alike for speakers and listeners to
spread false news and talk licentiously concerning
the State or Government.

Every one knows that these threats did not
prevent the fall of Danby and the exile of the
Stuarts, neither did they in the least delay them ;
and it would not be risking much to state that
those who by the royal decree were compelled to
be silent in the coffee-houses, greeted all the more

impetuously the Liberator and second Conqueror,
William of Orange, when he made his entry into
London on December 18th, 1688.

Since that day coffee-houses have been an institution, not only of London, but of British town life,
especially in the last century; and until the last
part of that century they held, in social and
political aspects, the position and importance, held
since then up to the present time by the clubs.
If we may listen to a voice which as late as 1708
cries out complainingly, " Who would have thought
London would have had near 3000 such nuisances,
and that coffee would have been (as now) so much
drunk by the best of quality and physicians ? "
(Hatton's 'New View of London'); we learn
from it that in the course of not more than
50 years 3000 coffee-houses had been established
in London, and that they were frequented by
all who had any pretension to rank, education,
or influence. Hence, D'Israeli is right when he
says that the history of the coffee-houses, before
the introduction of clubs, would be that of the
manners, morals, and politics of the people, and
from this point of view alone have we felt ourselves justified in inviting the reader to so close a
consideration of them.

Although every class of English society, and

every phase of English life, trade, science, literature, art, the theatre and fashion,—in fact, all those
peculiarities and eccentricities which one designates pre-eminently *English*, found their expression in coffee-houses, as they did later in clubs;
still the first and decisive characteristic with both
was politics. The noteworthy fact cannot escape
the observer, that journals began to exist thirty
years before the first coffee-house, and that they
had already attained a certain degree of civic
liberty when this was opened. Without journals,
one of the greatest charms of the coffee-house
and of the club would be lacking; and so little
could one think of one without the other, even
when they were in their early childhood, that the
satirist whom we have quoted above, mingles
together "syrup of soot" and "essence of old
shoes," as he euphoniously describes coffee, with
" diurnals and books of news :"

" Syrop of soot, or essence of old shoes,
   Dash't with diurnals and the books of news."

The first and original form of newspapers was
that of a little book of news, which appeared in
weekly editions, exactly like that to which the
refined Parisians returned towards the end of the
second empire. We seem to read a contemporary
report about Rochefort's 'Lanterne,' when we read

what Ben Jonson, a great opponent of the awakening public opinion, says of these news-books : that
there can be in Nature no greater malady, nor any
greater disgrace for the time, than this hunger of
the public for the pamphlets which are published
every Saturday.

The year 1622 may be noted as that of the birth
of the English newspaper press. The fearful war
in Germany, afterwards known as the Thirty
Years' War, had begun ; and the desire in England
to obtain news of it was all the greater as an
English princess, Elizabeth, daughter of James I.,
and wife of the unfortunate King of Bohemia, was
very nearly, at least at first, concerned in it. An
enterprising Irishman, Nathaniel Butter by name,
was the first who turned to advantage in the way
of trade this thirst for knowledge of the British
public, by publishing, after the model of 'The
Venetian Gazette,' 'Weekly Relations of News,'
which, after several successful attempts, he continued in regular succession as 'The Certain Newes
of this Present Week,' embellished with the arms
of the King of Bohemia. As far as the certainty
of its news went, he pretends to derive them at
one time from an eminent Jewish merchant in
Germany, at another from the lovely 'Mermaid'
wrecked on the coast of Greenwich.

M

Still for a whole year this paper was the only one that provided England with intelligence from the Continent; whoever would understand the importance at the time of the places and persons in Germany and the events of the war, is advised not to despise this 'Courant.'

But with the death of Gustavus Adolphus the public curiosity abated, and the business stagnated; so much so, that between the appearance of one 'Certain News' and another, time enough elapsed to fill the News-books with the whole of the Psalms of David, and half of the New Testament to boot, for want of other matter.*

English journalism received fresh food and an enduring form when the civil disturbances began under Charles I. On January 1st, 1642, there appeared at Oxford, where the King had taken up winter-quarters, the first number of the 'Mercurius Aulicus,' the Court and Royalist journal, which was in 1647, after the overthrow of this party, when the King sat in captivity at Hampton Court, followed by the 'Mercurius Pragmaticus.' The opposition journal, called the 'Mercurius Britannicus,' was established in August

---

* 'Early English Newspapers.' Cornhill Magazine, July 1868.

1643, and was edited by Marchmont Needham. This was the time of the 'Mercury,' under which name new journals of every shade of party on both sides sprang up, and were offered for sale in the streets by women, the so-called " Mercury women." The street itself was often the scene of the bitter strife of these ladies, who were not contented merely to sell their papers, but even took the field for the opinions expressed in them with such energy, that they, after belabouring each other with their fists, had recourse to snuff and ground pepper to throw into the eyes of their opponents, for the King or the Parliament.* But the editor of the Presbyterian journal, Marchmont Needham, was to meet his own evil destiny. A long time the idol of the London public, he fell out with those who had hitherto been his patrons, the dominant Presbyterian party, who suffered a free expression of opinion as little as did the Stuarts, and in his disgust went over to Charles I., for whom he wrote the already mentioned 'Mercurius Pragmaticus.' After the execution of Charles I. he fell into the hands of the Presbyterians, who threw him into the prison of Newgate and sentenced him to death, but the

---

* 'Literature of the People.' Athenæum, January 1870, p. 11.

Presbyterians themselves were overthrown just
soon enough to save his neck. Cromwell granted
him his life, and made him editor of the 'Mercurius
Politicus,' which became the journal of the Protectorate. Hitherto the members of the "ecclesia
militans" of the Press had fared by no means well;
with gaol, pillory, mutilation of the body, cutting
off the nose, chopping off the hand, if not even
with worse inflictions, they had been persecuted
unmercifully. The first, if only passing, gleam
of a better time was now to appear. Here Cromwell comes in as the eminent modern character
which he, though long unappreciated, really is.
Under his Protectorate the journals knew what it
was to enjoy the luxury of freedom, says the latest
historian of the English Press.* In vain had
Milton begged of the Presbyterians the liberty of
the Press. Cromwell secured it. The true image
of this great man, one of the greatest history
knew, is only in our time fully revealed; yet blind
party spite has not been able so much to blacken
it, but that here and there amid misrepresenta-
tions of opponents the truth breaks forth. The
elder D'Israeli, known to be a staunch Royalist,

---

* James Grant. 'The Newspaper Press, its origin,' &c.
(2 vols. London: Tinsley Brothers. 1872.)

and fully participating in the cavalier-like horror of Cromwell, is compelled to admit in his treatise upon censors, that under the Protectorate this office was abolished, but was reintroduced immediately on the restoration of Charles II.

The censor of this reign, Roger l'Estrange, was also at the same time its journalist *par excellence*. The amalgamation of the two offices was, at all events as things stood, the most convenient plan. For still the prosecution of the Press continued; the evil doers were evil-intreated in their bodies, their liberty, and honour; they were sentenced to transportation and hard labour like hardened criminals. Roger l'Estrange, who, as a true adherent of the Stuarts, had suffered so much and so valiantly in their cause, that he had excited even Cromwell's admiration, reflected how he could soften the troubles of his comrades of the Press, and suggested as a milder form of punishment all kinds of marks of infamy, which the culprits should wear; as, for example, instead of a hat-band a rope; or one blue stocking and another red; or a blue cap, with a red " T " or " S " upon it, to signify treason or sedition.

We hear nothing about his success with these humane contrivances; but he soon had himself to experience the teaching of the 'Two Souls Theory,' whilst within his breast the censor continually strove with the editor. In reward for his services rendered to the dynasty, the monopoly of a newspaper was awarded to him, which, under the name of ' The Public Intelligencer,' flourished in the first year of the Restoration. His spies went to all parts of the country—spies were then what we in the present day designate by the somewhat less doubtful name of " Special Correspondents." They frequented St. Paul's Walk, which a few years later was destroyed by the great fire, and sought for news in the taverns and in the coffee-houses, then just springing up. Even some " respectable persons" made him occasional communications, with the condition that he should keep their names secret, for which he granted them, as a fee, the free postage of their newspapers. Still, while the ' Mercury' women sold his journal in the streets and obtained subscribers in the houses, he continually trembled lest they should at the same time carry about contraband wares; and to protect them from temptations to such criminal conduct he gave them, besides forty shillings and some free copies, yearly something still greater—dinner at Hornsey, " with coach there and back." The year of the plague, 1665, found him fearlessly at his post; but in this year, when the Court emigrated to Oxford on

account of the fearful sickness, his well-merited privilege was taken from him, and the official paper,
the ' Oxford Gazette,' was established, which still
exists under the title of the ' London Gazette.'
He, the true servant of the Stuarts, experienced
the proverbial ingratitude of that family; and
as Stafford previously, when it was imparted to
him that Charles I. had signed his death-warrant,
cried out, " Nolite confidere in princibus," so now,
wrote Roger l'Estrange, " I have been promoted to
beggary, shame, in short, the worst that can befall
a man's honour; but God's will be done, and his
Majesty's."

Once again, towards the end of the reign of
Charles II., the much-tried journalist brought out
a weekly paper, in the curious form of question and
answer, the ' Observator.' But with regard to the
measure which deprived him, the most official of
officials, of his privilege, it might well be said, " If
they do these things in the green tree, what shall
be done in the dry?" In fact, now began an era of
the most complete desolation, unprofitableness, and
sterility for journalism. Still at the moment when
the Press, this public conscience, was sentenced to
silence, the coffee-house in a manner took its place,
and made itself known for the first time in its
full importance for political life. " Thither," says

Macaulay (i. 383), " crowded the people of London, as the old people of Athens to the market-place, to ask continually if there was any new thing."

But the activity of the coffee-houses extended over more than London : the material of conversation, which was there collected, was fixed in manuscript in so-called news-letters by persons who made this work a special profession, and these written newspapers, which were sent weekly into the provinces, informed their inhabitants of all which was *not* to be found in the printed ones.

So things continued during the reign of James II. till the. expulsion of the Stuarts. The day after his abdication appeared immediately three new newspapers; under William III., the almost crushed newspaper-press rose again quickly, and in the year 1694 the censorship was abolished. Manifold, in the following century, were the battles of the English Press, till, with complete freedom, it reached the height which we see it occupy at the present day. We cannot accompany it on this long and glorious way; it was sufficient for our object to point out the peculiar connection between the coffee-house and the newspaper—to show how they grew together, and in the earliest stages of their development supplemented and often supported one another up to the happy days when the classic 'Tatler' appeared, and the short face of 'Mr. Spectator' was seen. Then in the first flowery time of English periodical literature, with its stars, Addison and Steele, London coffee-house life stood in its zenith, and having arrived at this point, we may return thence to our special subject.

Each party, even each shade of a party, had its particular coffee-house, in which its members met. There were Whig and Tory coffee-houses, coffee-houses for High Churchmen, for Latitudinarians, for Papists (for England's religious belief was, and is now, notoriously in part influenced by its political); there were coffee-houses in which the Scotch debated for or against the Union with England, and coffee-houses in which the Jacobites hobnobbed over the "black gentleman," by which they understood the mole on whose hill King William's horse had stumbled and broken the neck of its rider.

In Daniel Defoe's 'Journey through England,' 1714, invaluable as a history of the culture of his time, there is a passage in which the famous author of 'Robinson Crusoe' depicts fashionable life in London at the beginning of the eighteenth century, which will, therefore, serve as an illustration of the above general remark. "Our life," he says, "is

thus : we rise at 9, and those who attend levees are
employed thus till 11, or go, as in Holland, to the
tea-tables; at 12 the *beau-monde* is assembled in
various coffee or chocolate houses, of which the best
are so near one another, that we can see the society
of all in less than an hour. We are carried to these
places in a kind of chair or litter, at the very reasonable cost of a guinea a week, or a shilling an hour.
The bearers act also as messengers, as the gondo-
liers of Venice. Different parties have their different houses, where a stranger, indeed, would be
well received; but a Whig would as soon go to the
'Cocoa Tree,' or 'Ozinda's,' as a Tory to St. James's.
The Scotch usually go to the 'British,' and a number of all sorts to the 'Smyrna.'" There are other
small coffee-houses, says the tourist, in the neighbourhood of Pall Mall,—then as famous for coffee-
houses as now for clubs,—and the most frequented
were the 'Young Man's' by officers, the 'Old
Man's' by stockjobbers, and 'Little Man's' by
indifferent gamblers.

The 'Old,' 'Young,' and 'Little Man,' were three
establishments by the Thames, not far from Charing
Cross and Whitehall. The 'Old Man,' or the
'Royal Coffee-house,' was the oldest of the three,
and had been established under Charles II. by
Alexander Man, after whom later it was named.

The 'Young Man' arose in the reign of William III., but the former always held the precedence; and we possess a description of it by Ned Ward, one of the most adventurous and notorious characters of that time, a mischievous pamphleteer, many times punished by pillory for slanderous libels, and at last, when he would have no more to do with the work of an author, landlord of a punch-shop in Holborn, in which capacity he died in 1731. But all that lessens the worth of his writings, in whatever disfavour they may have been held among his contemporaries, is nothing to us; and the readers of Lord Macaulay's 'History' will, no doubt, re-member the 'London Spy,' a kind of talkative description of London, of the remarkable details of which the great historian has not disdained occa-sionally to avail himself. Ned Ward's writings are exceedingly rare; and the writer of these lines is only indebted to a fortunate chance for his 'Secret History of Clubs'* with the significant motto, " Poeta qui pavide cantat, rarissime placet ;" a book, shabbily bound, badly printed, and full of the coarsest vulgarity, but for the subject which we

---

* 'The Secret History of Clubs: with their Origin, and the Characters of the most noted Members thereof.' London. Printed and sold by the Booksellers. 1709.

have under consideration a source of the richest information. Scorned by booksellers, either ignored or deservedly and severely censured by authors (as, for example, in Pope's satirical poem, ' The Dunciad'), entirely excluded from and tabooed by good society, Ned Ward was just the man to re- mark that which is apt to escape the member of a fraternity, and only strikes the eye of one who stands without its circle, especially when malice sharpens his sight, namely, the peculiar, the characteristic, the ridiculous. This, in fact, makes up the sum of his book, of which the epistle dedicatory is not addressed, like that of most other works of his time, to some great Lord, but " to that Luciferous and Sublime Lunatic, the Emperor of the Moon, Gover- nor of the Tides, Corrector of Female Constitutions, Cornuted Metropolitan of all revolving Cities, and principal Director of those Churches most subject to mutation."

Only the irregularities of coffee-house and inn life of that time are here treated of, partially under highly indecorous and feigned names, in a kind of prosaic history of their origin, with which is united a flow of poetry, both full of in- vectives and abuse which are scarcely half compre- hensible to us. Nevertheless, after the deduction of all of that of which we speak, there is a remainder which, if we do not mind the tone, is very instructive, and will add more than one feature to the picture which we are now about to sketch; only we must not forget that we here have to do with a man who can never feel at ease in good society.

According to Ned Ward's description in the 'London Spy,' the 'Old Man' must have been the finest coffee-house of London. " We now ascended a pair of stairs which brought us into an old-fashioned room, where a gaudy crowd of odoriferous *Tom-Essences* were walking backwards and forwards with their hats in their hands, not daring to convert them to their intended use, lest it should put the foretops of their wigs into some disorder. We squeezed through till we got to the end of the room, where at a small table we sat down, and observed that it was as great a rarity to hear anybody call for a dish of *Politician's Porridge*, or any other liquor, as it is to hear a beau call for a pipe of tobacco; their whole exercise being to charge and discharge their nostrils, and keep the curls of their periwigs in their proper order. The clashing of their snush-box lids in opening and shutting made more noise than their tongues. Bows and cringes of the newest mode were here exchanged twixt friend and friend with wonderful exactness.

They made a humming like so many hornets in a country chimney, not with their talking, but with their whispering over their new *Minuets* and *Bories*, with their hands in their pockets, if only freed from their snush-box."*

That which appears to have most troubled the 'London Spy' was that here he could not smoke at his ease. When he called for a tinder-box and a pipe, certainly they brought him what he wished, but as unwillingly " as if they would much rather have been rid of our company; for their tables were so very neat, and shined with rubbing like the upper leathers of an alderman's shoes, and as brown as the top of a country housewife's cupboard. The floor was as clean swept as a Sir Courtly's dining-room, which made us look round to see if there were no orders hung up to impose the forfeiture of so much mop-money on any person that should spit out of the chimney-corner."

We see Ned Ward has here fallen into society from which the sooner he removes himself the better. The gentlemen of fashion of that time took snuff, but they abhorred smoking, hence in the coffee-houses which they frequented there was no

---

* By Bories are probably meant *Bourrées*, a kind of Spanish-French dance. *Vide* Czerwinski, ' On Dancing,' p. 90.

smoking. Here, as Macaulay says, and our 'Spy' corroborates, the atmosphere was like that of a perfumer's shop; and if any booby unacquainted with the ways of the house desired a pipe, the ironical remarks of the whole assembly, and the short replies of the waiter, soon showed him he had better betake himself somewhere else. This was quite the case of Ned Ward, who concludes his account with the remark that his conduct at the 'Old Man's' drew the surprised faces of the Sir Foplings into as many peevish wrinkles as those of the beaux at the Bow Street Coffee-house, near Covent Garden, when the gentleman in masquerade came in among them with his oyster-barrel muff and turnip buttons to ridicule their fopperies.

Nevertheless, in most of the coffee-houses smoking formed the chief means of entertainment. Among numerous other testimony to this we have also that of the 'Spectator,' who, under the date of July 6th, 1714 (No. 568), writes:—"I was yesterday in a coffee-house, not far from the Royal Exchange, when I observed three persons in close conference over a pipe of tobacco; upon which, having filled one for my own use, I lighted it at the little wax candle that stood before them; and after having thrown in two or three whiffs amongst them, sat down, and made one of the company. I need not tell my reader that lighting a man's pipe at the same candle is looked upon amongst brother smokers as an overture to conversation and friendship."

The 'Spectator,' as also its precursor, the 'Tatler,' and its successor, the 'Guardian,' those world-famed moral periodicals, which, comprising some of the most interesting years at the beginning of the last century (1709–14), and written by the most witty men of the time, present a picture of society as it then existed, drawn with incomparable delicacy and most charming humour, naturally contain also invaluable material for our subject. For their authors were men of the world, who moved exclusively in high society; Addison, husband of a countess, and for a time Secretary of State; Sir Richard Steele, a Member of Parliament; Jonathan Swift, Dean of St. Patrick; and many others who belonged to the most distinguished wits of the time.* They were all friends to conviviality, " bon vivants " to a certain degree;

---

* Addison's Contributions to the 'Spectator' and 'Tatler' are given in German in Adolph Stern's 'Popular Library of Literature of the 18th Century,' with a Preface by H. Hettner, Berlin, 1866. In the same collection may be found ' Swift's Diary to Stella.'

and of Dick Steele it is only too well known that
he loved the entertainment of the coffee-houses, and
the red wine of the taverns, far more than was
advantageous to his domestic peace or his moderate
income. But so much the greater will be the
confidence with which we trust ourselves to the
guidance of such hands; and so much the more
faithful will be the picture, composed of those
many strokes and touches of reality with which
they understood how to enliven the classic elegance
of their writings.

In that often quoted passage of the 'Tatler,' in
which its editors allot to the different coffee-houses
the different subjects which would offer themselves
for consideration in the course of their undertaking
(so that a stated topic might always be expected
with certainty at a stated coffee-house), politics fall
to the lot of St. James's Coffee-house.

As staunch Whigs, Addison and Steele naturally
chose this coffee-house, the headquarters of the
Whigs in St. James's Street, not ten steps from
the palace of the same name, in which, from Queen
Anne to George IV., the monarchs of Great Britain
resided. Here, until the latter part of the last
century, the party was represented by its most
eminent members; from here, as long as he
was a Whig, Jonathan Swift (under Addison's

N

address) communicated with Stella; and here,
sixty years later, before the great change took
place in him, the youthful Burke was to be
seen. By that time the coffee-house had changed
entirely into a restaurant—the usual way with
coffee-houses before their total disappearance—
upon the establishment of clubs. St. James's
Coffee-house was closed in the year 1806, and on
the spot where it formerly stood stands now a
row of stately buildings looking towards Pall
Mall.

The 'Spectator,' and indeed the pen of Addison,
gives a description of the principal political coffee-
houses, at the time when coffee-house life had
reached its highest degree of refinement. It
appears that in March 1712, the report had spread
in London that Louis XIV. was dead. "As I
foresaw," says the 'Spectator,' "that this would
produce a new face of things in Europe, and many
curious speculations in our British coffee-houses,
I was very desirous to learn the thought of our
most eminent politicians on that occasion. Since
every district in the city has its coffee-house, and
every coffee-house has some particular statesman
belonging to it, who is the mouth of the street
where he lives, this is the surest means of ascer-
taining the opinion of the town."

In order to reach as nearly as possible the
fountain-head of all news, the 'Spectator' begins
his wanderings at St. James's Coffee-house. "Here
I found the whole outward room in a buzz of
politics. The speculations were but very indifferent
towards the door, but grew finer as you advanced
to the upper end of the room; and were so very
much improved by a knot of theorists who sat in
the inner room within the steam of the coffee-pot,
that I there heard the whole Spanish monarchy
disposed of, and all the line of Bourbon provided
for in less than a quarter of an hour."

In a coffee-house in St. Giles's, now, as is known,
one of the most ill-famed, as it was then one of the
most aristocratic quarters of the town, and since
the Revocation of the Edict of Nantes inhabited
principally by celebrated French refugees, the
'Spectator' found a table of French gentlemen,
who sat in judgment upon the life and death of the
"Grand Monarque;" and in the ' Little Man,' already noticed, the sanctuarium of sharpers or false-
players (Addison must have meant this, although
he calls it ' Jenny Man's '), he saw an *alerte* young
fellow cocking his three-cornered hat, on a friend of
his, who entered at the same time as the 'Spectator,'
addressing him in the following manner, " Well,
Jack, the old prig is dead at last. Sharp's the

word.   Now or never, boy.   Up to the walls of
Paris directly."

Between Charing Cross and Covent Garden
there was no great difference in the aspect of
politics, and in one of the Temple coffee-houses,
he heard the circumstance discussed from a judicial
point of view.   But in the inner part of the City
the case was otherwise.   Here he went to a coffee-
house in Fish Street.   The chief politician of that
neighbourhood, when he heard the news, after
first filling his pipe with tobacco and then rumi-
nating for a while, said : " If the King of France
is certainly dead, we shall have plenty of mackerel
this season ; our fishery will not be disturbed
by privateers as it has been for these ten years
past."

In the little coffee-house of a neighbouring alley
he afterwards overheard the conversation of a
theological Ultra and Non-juror, with a lace-dealer
—probably a Huguenot from Spitalfields, and in
that case a staunch Protestant.   " The matter in
debate was whether the late French King was
most like Augustus Cæsar or Nero.   The contro-
versy was carried on with great heat on both sides ;
and as I was under some apprehension they would
appeal to me, I laid down my penny at the bar,
and made the best of my way to Cheapside."

In this and the neighbouring streets of the City, through which at the present day during business hours the stream of commerce flows, whilst afterwards they lie almost deserted, there lived at that time all the great merchants, whose residences now stand in quite a different region of the metropolis, far from their houses of business. Here, therefore, at that time there was a greater number of coffee-houses than in any other part of London, and it was not easy for the ' Spectator ' to find the right one among the numerous signs which appeared to invite him from all sides. The politicians of these coffee-houses are men of business, and the motives which influence them for or against, are commercial. Owing to the difficulty with which at that time news spread, that which we now call " a rumour on 'Change " could not take effect so generally or so quickly. According to the before-mentioned assertion of the ' Spectator,' eight days elapsed before it was known in London whether the King of France was dead or not; and when at last the contradiction of the report arrived, this weighty political intelligence was still very far distant from the hands of those whom it most interested. Upon his entrance into the coffee-room, the first thing the ' Spectator ' observed was a man who expressed himself as much distressed at the death of the King; but on further explanation, it appeared that his sorrow had its ground, not nearly so much in the loss of the monarch, as in the circumstance that three days previously he had sold, instead of having bought, when, in case the news were confirmed, paper must inevitably rise. "Upon which a haberdasher, who was the oracle of the coffee-house, and had his circle of admirers about him, called several to witness that he had declared his opinion above a week before that the French King was certainly dead, to which he added, that considering the late advices we had received from France, it was impossible that it could be otherwise." While he was still occupied in summing up his reasons, and dictating to his hearers with great authority, the door opened, and there entered a gentleman from Garraway's Coffee-house, who related, that several letters had just come from France with the news that the King had gone to the hunt on the same morning on which the post was despatched; whereupon the haberdasher took his hat from the wooden peg and returned to his shop in great consternation, while the stock-jobber—although we do not know it positively—must probably have rubbed his hands with pleasure.

Here the 'Spectator' breaks off: it has, as he

says, amused him not a little, to hear in what different ways men judge of one and the same piece of information according to their different interests; and he shows us, I hope, in a very plausible manner, that in this respect matters are not far different now from what they were then, when political tidings, which concerned questions of existence, found their way to the public, while they quietly wandered from one coffee-house of the Capital to another.

If we consider the defective quality of all means of correspondence, which we now possess in such great completeness, we shall understand the weight and importance of coffee-houses in the whole political life of the nation.

Another feature, not less interesting or decisive for the development of another side of public life, is presented by the literary coffee-houses, which introduced that which the clubs completed, and which on many grounds has hitherto failed with us in Germany—that is, the formation of a literary class, and the solidarity of literary interests.

The oldest and most honourable of the coffee-houses "sacred to polite letters," says Macaulay, was ' Will's ' (named after its owner William Urwin) at the corner of Bow Street and Russell Street, Covent Garden, in a neighbourhood, which is still adorned by the principal theatres in London, but was at that time particularly fashionable. Macaulay's description of 'Will's' Coffee-house has been very often quoted : it is in its way as classic as the classic spot itself. " Then the talk was about poetical justice, and the unities of time and place. There was a faction for Perrault and the moderns, a faction for Boileau and the ancients. One group debated whether ' Paradise Lost' ought not to have been in rhyme. To another, an envious poetaster demonstrated that ' Venice Preserved' ought to have been hooted from the stage. Under no roof was a greater variety of figures to be seen. Earls in stars and garters, clergymen in cassocks and bands, pert Templars, sheepish lads from the Universities, translators and index-makers in ragged coats of frieze. The great press was to get near the chair where John Dryden sat. In winter that chair was always in the warmest nook by the fire; in summer it stood in the balcony. To bow to him, and to hear his opinion of Racine's last tragedy, or of Bossu's treatise on epic poetry, was thought a privilege. A pinch from his snuff-box was an honour sufficient to turn the head of a young enthusiast."

This last highly significant point the great historian derived from the ' London Spy,' who

probably made but a very sorry figure among the
aristocrats of literature in ' Will's ' Coffee-house (he
calls it the Wit's Coffee-house), but, nevertheless,
once entered it. It is described in the ' London
Spy' in the following terms: " Accordingly up-
stairs we went, and found much company but little
talk. We shuffled through this moving crowd of
philosophical mutes to the other end of the room,
where three or four wits of the upper class were
rendezvoused at a table, and were disturbing the
ashes of the old poets by perverting their sense.
At another table were seated a parcel of young,
raw, second-rate beaux and wits, who were con-
ceited if they had but the honour to dip a finger
and thumb into Mr. Dryden's snuff-box."

It is true that Dryden was the great household
god at ' Will's ' ; the fame of each, that of the poet
and that of the coffee-house, was about the same age,
and must pass together through the history of literature. Samuel Pepys, the diarist of the Restoration
and first years of the reign of Charles II., saw him.
" Dryden, the poet, whom I knew at Cambridge,
and all the wits of the city, and Harris, the player,
and Mr. Hoole of our college, sit here in the great
coffee-house, in which I had never been before," he
says, when he went one evening (Feb. 3, 1663) to
Covent Garden to fetch his wife, probably from

the play, which this married couple much loved. Society at that time had not become accustomed to late hours, for they were on the point of breaking up as Pepys entered. Still it must have very much pleased the worthy gentleman, for he considered it a very spiritual and pleasant entertainment, and talked of coming again. But he appears not to have carried out his resolution; for in his diary, kept with minute exactness, in which he remarks upon every play that he saw, every man with whom he spoke, every book which he read, this is the sole notice of ' Will's ' Coffee-house.

When, about a hundred years later (it must have been in the fiftieth year of the last century), another Samuel, not less famous in English literature, Doctor Johnson, the great lexicographer, then still an obscure man, came to collect materials for the ' Life of Dryden,' there were only two old people living who could remember the glory of ' Will's'—Mr. Swinney, successively director of Drury Lane and Haymarket (died 1754), and Colley Cibber, comedian and dramatic poet (died 1757). What he learned from both may be reduced to two lines. Cibber could only say that he remembered Dryden as a decent old gentleman, and umpire of the critical contests at ' Will's.' Swinney's information is still narrower, and re-

lates only to Dryden's particular chair, which in
summer was named his summer-chair, and his
winter-chair in winter.*

This chair, which since the death of Dryden in
1700 had stood vacant, was again occupied in
1709 by a person of renown, no less than Isaac
Bickerstaff, Esq., an old man, a philosopher, a
humourist, an astrologer, and a censor. It is
known that these were the manifold capacities
under which Jonathan Swift held up the weather
and almanack maker, Partridge, to the ridicule of
his contemporaries; and we learn from the 'Tatler,'
in the preface, that the wit of the rector of Laracor
had called forth an inclination in the City for all
that appeared under that disguise. Steele afterwards made use of the figure of this unfortunate
man, famed throughout all Europe, to place him
before the public as the editor of the new periodical,
the ' Tatler,' and to the advantage of his authority,
he attributes later (in the dedication of the fourth
volume) the sudden success which his works
acquired in the world.

In the first number of the ' Tatler ' (which in
the collections of the last century appeared as

* 'Boswell's Life of Johnson.' Routledge edition (London,
1863), iii. 45.

often under the title of 'The Lucubrations of Isaak Bickerstaff, Esq.') is said, "All accounts of gallantry, pleasure, and entertainment, shall be under the article of White's Chocolate-house; Poetry under that of 'Will's' Coffee-house; Learning, under the title of Grecian; foreign and domestic news you will have from St. James's Coffee-house; and what else I shall on any other subject offer shall be dated from my own apartment."

We may consider that only a feeling of reverence, of courtesy, perhaps, induced the editors of the 'Tatler' to misrepresent the seat of Poetry as being at 'Will's;' that was at one time the case, but the special glory of this coffee-house, after lasting for forty years, passed away with Dryden. For although Addison is sufficiently courteous to the shade of this poet, to say, in that number of the 'Spectator' in which he registers the political opinions of the different coffee-houses upon the death of Louis XIV:—"On my going into 'Will's' I found their discourse was gone off from the death of the French King to that of Monsieur Boileau, Racine, Corneille, and several other poets, whom they regretted on this occasion as persons who would have obliged the world with very noble elegies on the death of so great a prince,

and so eminent a patron of learning." In spite
of this graceful homage at the graves of the re-
nowned, Steele was probably more sincere when
he acknowledged, in the first number of the
' Tatler ': " This place is very much altered since
Mr. Dryden frequented it: where you used to
see songs, epigrams, and satyrs, in the hands of
every man you met, you have now only a pack of
cards; and instead of the cavils about the turn of
the expression, the elegance of the style, and the
like, the learned now dispute only about the truth
of the game." And in No. 16 : " We used to sit
here in old times in judgment over a game of chess,
but the entertainment is now in quite another
direction." The truth is not that the coffee-house
was untrue to its company, but that the company
was untrue to the coffee-house.

When the continuation of the ' Tatler ' had
dropped the guise of ' Censor of Great Britain '—
which had become burdensome to him, as every
one who had borne it knew—henceforth to pay
his respects in the character of Mr. Spectator,
Button's Coffee-house had stepped into the place
of ' Will's.' The new generation of wits assembled
here around a new centre—Addison. When he
returned from his post in Dublin, after the overthrow of the Whig and Marlborough adminis-

tration, Daniel Button, a servant of the Countess of Warwick, whom Addison afterwards married, had opened the new coffee-house in the same street as, and exactly opposite to the old one, and Addison became its great patron. This became Addison's coffee-house, as that had been Dryden's. Here the poet celebrated the triumph of his 'Cato;' but hither he also came after his marriage with the Countess of Warwick, to forget in the midst of his good friends of yore that he had married discord in noble life, and that the noble Countess had given him, as Lady Howard previously gave Dryden, " the heraldry of the hand, not of the heart." Often he sat here till late into the night, longer than Dryden formerly sat in his coffee-house; the bottle of red wine stood on the table, and we may imagine what advice brave Steele, honest Dick, gave to her and him, his old friend, who was unhappy—although he had a Countess for his wife, the Palace of Holland House for his residence, and no debts—far more unhappy than he, the author of the 'Christian Hero,' who wrote his wife the tenderest letters from the debtor's prison. Pope also used to come to Button's Coffee-house, till one day he was soundly beaten with a birch stick by Ambrose Philips, the pastoral poet, on account of an unfavourable

criticism upon some of his idylls. And hither,
lastly, came Swift, " the mad doctor," as they called
him. One evening when Addison and the rest of
the company were here, there also appeared a man
in great boots, evidently just come in from the
country. Swift looked at him long, at last ap-
proached him, and without farther introduction
inquired, " Excuse me, Sir, have you ever seen
such good weather in this world ?" When the man
addressed had wondered a little at the peculiarity
of Swift's manner, and of his question, he made
answer : " Yes, Sir, thank God, I have seen many
good days." "That is more than I can say,"
returned Swift; " I cannot remember any weather
which was neither too hot, too cold, too wet, or
too dry; but God Almighty manages to arrange
it so that it all comes to the same thing at the end
of the year."

Button's Coffee-house is only occasionally mentioned in the ' Spectator;' the ' Guardian ' (the
third and last of the periodicals edited jointly by
Addison and Steele) first placed before this place
of assembly for wits that letter-box in the form of
a lion's head with open jaws, which appears to
have made no small sensation in the London of
that time. The head was an imitation of that of
the Doge's palace at Venice, through which all the

secret information of that Republic passed. It opened its wide mouth ready to take in and devour any letters or treatises destined for the ' Guardian.' This lion's head, designed by Hogarth, described by Steele as an excellent work, and in July 1713 set up at the western side of the coffee-house, is the sole thing that remains of Button's. When the periodical ceased with the number for October 1st, 1713, the lion's head, after passing through many hands, came at last into the possession of the Duke of Bedford, at whose country seat at Woburn it is preserved. But the coffee-house was pulled down in the year 1865. I myself remember to have seen it. Often have I come into this neighbourhood, standing between the two houses, in the comparatively quiet street, to think of the departed times and men. On the right was Covent Garden, whose two piazzas—once highly fashion-able, the great and the little piazza, built after the designs of Inigo Jones, surrounded by red brick houses with balconies—have long ago been changed into the famous vegetable market ; on the left was Drury Lane, the old street and the theatre blackened by smoke and soot, if not by age. In a little side street, Maiden Lane, in the time of Queen Anne inhabited by the finest milliners, there lived in the house of " the white peruke," Voltaire (1728–30), when he was writing his 'Lettres de Londres sur les Anglais;' and before me, over the arches of the Adelphi, rose the terrace on which the 'New Exchange' Bazaar exhibited its tempting treasures in gloves, ribbons, and choice of fine essences, to the fair world in hoop-petticoat and peruke. 'Will's' Coffeehouse alone survives, but it is now inhabited by a respectable butcher.

> "Sic transit gloria mundi."

Our subject is still far from being exhausted; how could one think of completeness, when the title of the coffee-houses in London would fill more leaves than we have here designed to employ for their history? To describe the particular phenomena of a certain characteristic time, the focus of public life, with some of the persons who have left the impress of their mind upon the time, this was rather the task which we set before us, not a nomenclature. We wished to prove, by some examples, how very early we may discern in England, even on this ground, the appearance of a regular strife against arbitrariness, a wise use of victory, and a constant tendency towards association of interests. We had then in Germany scarcely any national life; and in our towns

o

had certainly nothing which at that time we could have set beside the coffee-houses of London and of Paris, as we know them from Rameau's ' Neffen,' to adduce one example instead of many —these meeting places for the originating of political plans and for intellectual intercourse, whose rays and beams extend in all directions— these places of learning with select conversation and refined society, in which science and life met together.

And yet, as we have said, the political and literary coffee-houses constitute but a small part of the number of those in which every position and every calling found its representative. For it is this principle of general interest, under which the different forms of the same appearance assume, far above an anecdotal, a truly historical aspect; and it is this principle which points impressively to that so called practical side of the English, which at all times and everywhere has so fortunately preserved them from pedantry. Has it at all injured the immortality of Sir Isaac Newton, that, after the sittings of the Royal Society, of which, as we know, he was President, he betook himself to the Grecian, there to spend the evening in the society of his two secretaries, Dr. Halley and Keil, and other professors from Oxford, perhaps at the same table with Mr. Spectator, whose face, as he informs us in No. I., is very well known in this coffee-house; whilst at another table "there are inquiries about Antiquity, and the heroic deeds of Homer's 'Iliad'?" ('Tatler,' No. 6.) As theologians, the Doctors of Divinity also had their coffee-house, Child's, in St. Paul's Churchyard, close to the chief Cathedral of London. Prelates have always been liberal patrons of landlords, from that Walter Mapes, who composed the noble drinking-song, 'Mihi est propositum in tabernâ mori' (translated by Bürger, 'Ich will einst bei Ja und Nein, vor dem Zapfen sterben') to Lawrence Sterne, "the sentimental travelling Yorick," who once gave out the text, "It is better to go into the house of mourning than the house of feasting," and began his sermon with the words "I dispute that." A certain coffee-house in Cheapside, called the 'Chapter,' was famed for the so-called "Three-penny Curates," clerical day-labourers who were hired for two pence and a cup of coffee to hold service anywhere within the boundary. Doctors of Medicine were at Garraway's; lawyers in the neighbourhood of the three great inns—Lincoln's Inn, Gray's Inn, but especially near the Temple, in Fleet Street. The coffee-house of the painters (old Slaughter's) was in St. Martin's Lane, in the vicinity of the present National Gallery; and that of the booksellers (the Chapter Coffee-house) was naturally in Paternoster Row, the home of the English book-trade; that narrow, gloomy street under the shadow of St. Paul's, in which, whilst all around the mighty roar of London is like the raging of an unseen sea, no waggon drives, no noise is heard, so that nothing disturbs the reflection of the "Fathers of the Row," or the solemn stillness of the immense shops, in which, house by house and wall by wall, are stored packets of books behind dusty windows, as high up even as the sooty roofs. The Chapter Coffee-house still stood, forsaken by its old spirit, empty and uninhabited, in the year 1848, when Mrs. Gaskell visited it. It had the appearance of a dwelling-house two hundred years old, such as one sometimes sees in old country towns; small, low rooms, with heavy beams across the ceilings; walls wainscoated breast-high, and shallow, broad, and dark stairs. This was the coffee-house in which a hundred years ago all the booksellers and publishers met, and to which the literary hack, the critic, and even the wit, used to go to seek ideas or employment. But that, however the honourable company may have changed, their views on certain literary matters remain the same, we may learn from the following passage in the first number of the 'Connoisseur' (a periodical of the year 1754), which says, "When the booksellers speak of a good book, they neither intend to praise the style or the sense, but only its rapid and wide sale. That book is the best which sells the best."

Of the coffee-houses of that period, those of the merchants in the neighbourhood of the Exchange and Change Alley, in name, design, and locality, existed the longest; some even remain to the present time. Garraway's was first closed on August 11th, 1866. "Delicacy of feeling is no article in City life," says the 'Illustrated London News,' in the farewell words which it devotes to the venerable establishment. Ground is sold at a considerable sum in these days of love of building. Garraway's was one of the oldest coffee-houses in London; its first possessor, Thomas Garraway, "Tobacco-dealer and coffee-man." Twice, in the great fires of 1666 and 1748, the house was burnt down, and twice it was rebuilt. From the time of its establishment in the seventeenth century, it was a place for auctions; at first of wine, then of tea, at last of mahogany and logwood. During the year of the South Sea scheme, the waves of speculation and of swindling rose nowhere higher than here. In a poem on this subject, Swift says that Change

Alley is a gulf deep as hell, in which thousands
are wrecked, and Garraway's is the rock on which
the wild race of wreckers lie in ambush to plunder
those who are cast ashore. The great auction-room
was on the first floor; here public sales took place
"by the candle," that is, at the beginning the
auctioneer lighted a little piece of wax candle,
usually an inch in length, and then decided in
favour of him who, when the light went out, had
made the highest bid. Twenty or thirty sales on
an average were undertaken here every day. The
refreshment-rooms were on the ground-floor, and
the great meeting-place from ten in the morning till
nine in the evening was the bar; the sandwiches
(a kind of overlaid bread and butter) of Garraway's
were famous. Until the last the walls of the
locality were covered with auction placards; a sign
of the change of possession to which this house
itself was at last obliged to succumb.

Jonathan's Coffee-house has, up to the present,
escaped a similar fate : it was a place for stock-
jobbers as early as the time of "Mr. Spectator,"
who in that assemblage was often taken for a Jew;
and Lloyd's, of world-wide renown, as far as ships
sail, and wares go under insurance across the sea,
is at present greater and more flourishing than it
has ever previously been, although, as far as age

is concerned, it may vie with the oldest houses of
this kind. Lloyd's Coffee-house is one of the oldest
in London; we find the name mentioned in the
'Tatler' and in the 'Spectator' as early as the
year 1700. Nevertheless, it is in fact only this
name which it has preserved; for it was trans-
ferred from the original building to the Exchange
as early as the year 1774; and there in the north-
western corner, after the Exchange had been
burnt down in 1838, and erected anew in 1841, the
coffee-house still remains. A noble flight of steps
leads from the great quadrangle of the Royal Exchange up to the handsome vestibule, where stands
a statue of Prince Albert in remembrance of the
laying of the foundation-stone; and a marble tablet,
let into the wall, the so-called "Times Testimonial,"
relates the history of that great and widely rami-
fying fraud which threatened the existence of
the banks of all European commercial towns,
but which was happily exposed in time by the
'Times.' As the proprietors refused every compensation in money, the grateful City erected this
monument to the great journal, and established
over and above (*œre perennius*) two 'Times'
pensions. Lloyd's is the great centre of the organisation of the City, and of all its interests, which,
scattered over wide and stormy seas, reach the

most distant shores.   Its illimitable cords—one might call them the nervous system of the world, which encompasses it and agitates its smallest point—here mingle in one room, which is no larger than any other apartment in which coffee is drunk and cigars are smoked.   It is very difficult to give an idea of it.

Every one who is in this room has, by the last intelligence, the position of the globe before his eyes, trade and politics, wind and weather : he hears the roaring of the storm which rages in the Indian Ocean, and he sees the iceberg which endangers the Liverpool Packet on the coast of Canada.   An instrument, the so-called anemometer, is here put up, with very fine machinery, which shows every change of every wind which blows, its direction and power, as well as the quantity of falling rain. Two great folios bound in leather, on high stands, on the right and left of the entrance, contain, one, the intelligence of all the ships which have gone into any haven in the world ; the other, the accidents at sea.   After a storm great crowds throng around the two books, whose contents are published in print every evening as ' Lloyd's List.' Here may be seen the faces and costumes of every zone.   Hither come captains to conclude in their room, the Captain's Room, contracts for new journeys; hither also shipowners and underwriters, in the underwriters' room, to do the business of insurance. Here the body of a ship is weighed as one weighs a handful of corn; the names, the numbers, the tonnage, the crew, the losses and profits of each separate vessel in the British merchant service, are here precisely known. No English merchantman may leave an English port without having been previously declared seaworthy, and then entered in 'Lloyd's Register;' * every ship carries her certificate, and the amount of insurance is determined accordingly. The third room at Lloyd's is the Merchants' Room, a reading-room, with a supply of newspapers, of which one can hardly form an approximate idea. The great expenses of this establishment are defrayed partly by the returns of ' Lloyd's Lists,' subscriptions, and insurances, partly by the contributions of the members, about 2000. For although Lloyd's still has the name of a coffeehouse, it is in reality a modern club, with ballot and entrance-fee of new members, and regular subscriptions from the old. Lloyd's has had this

---

* This Register, ' Lloyd's Register of British and Foreign Shipping,' is kept at No. 2, White Lion Court, Cornhill, and was established in the year 1834.

character since it came into The Exchange in 1774, the year which denoted the period when the old coffee-houses of London began to change into the modern clubs.

II.

THE CLUBS.

IT is difficult to say when this process of change was completed; such periods cannot be precisely determined: this much is certain, that there are no more coffee-houses in London, and the name, where it is found, designates something quite different. A coffee-house in London of the present day is an eating-house of the third rank; in hotels of the second rank the " coffee-room " signifies the dining-room; and in an hotel of the first rank the room for breakfast and supper. The coffee-room serves also for strangers in the hotel, when they only have beds, the place of sitting-room, in which they assemble, sometimes in slippers, to read the newspapers, to write their letters, or to take their afternoon nap on a sofa or in a chair. In the large hotels the so-called coffee-room is a most elegant saloon, furnished with English comfort and French elegance, where one moves about upon carpets, and every word that is said is only a whisper; but in middle-class hotels it is really a reminiscence of the old coffee-houses, a heritage of the tavern, which the destruction of the coffee-house has bequeathed to the club. The number of taverns, too, in London is considered to be on the decrease. "Under this consecrated word," says an author in 'London Society' (March 1866), "we understand the regular old-fashioned and dark-tabled room, with its green or red curtains, in which our grandfathers and great grandfathers, and their great grandfathers before them, ate their suppers, drank their port wine and punch, smoked their.pipes, and talked of politics and literature."

There are now few of these venerable houses in London, but some still exist in Drury Lane and in the neighbourhood of the Temple; and who, with a predilection for old London, will not once have visited one of them, 'The Cock,' or 'The Cheshire Cheese,' or 'The Mitre,' to look out from the richly-browned coffee-room on to the quiet court of the Temple, with a row of trees in the middle, on which the dreamy afternoon sun shines, while memory, so to speak, encircles the ceiling with a garland of leaves from the 'Tatler' and 'Spectator?'

"Sir," said Dr. Johnson, to his 'Eckermann' Boswell, "there is no other place in the world, where the more noise you make, the more welcome you are."

The Doctor was the great patron, the "vates sacer" of taverns, although he also contributed his portion to the cultivation of club life, as it is now understood.

The word club, or Klub, is as much German as English; the Anglo-Saxon root *clypian,* or *clypan,* English, cleave; German, *kleiben;* hence *Kluppe, Klubb,* Club, something split up, and at the same time holding closely together, the signification, in our derived use, of an exclusive company and its locality. Sanders' 'Dictionary of the German language,' pp. 944 and 946.

The Club is a union which rests upon division; that is, of charges and expenses, and its central point, naturally, the covered table. " Our modern celebrated clubs," says No. 9 of the 'Spectator,' "are founded upon eating and drinking, which are points wherein most men agree, and in which the learned and the illiterate, the dull and the airy, the philosopher and the buffoon, all of them bear a part."

Clubs of this kind we have had also in Germany, and still have at the present day; and historical names, as the Jacobin Club and the Clubbists of Mentz, to which may be added the different Clubs of Frankfort at the time of the assembly of the States of the German Empire,

show that the idea was brought forward also on
other, higher grounds, in periods of political movement. Still England is the land in which the
club had its special development, and is the sole
home of the modern club, which we find nowhere
else as a popular element in public life.

Certainly those small nightly assemblies, usually
known under the name of clubs, were formed and
subsisted close to the coffee-houses, and at the time
of their greatest prosperity; still their acknowledged object was only that first and most natural
bond between sociable animals—eating. Intellectual food was sought in the coffee-houses, material
food in the taverns and clubs. The tavern was
the place in which the club was held. As still
in many parts of Germany people join for a
Martinmas goose, so they did then in London for
various things, only regularly and continuously.
" Reasons are as plentiful as blackberries," and the
good Londoners of that time made use of every
occasion for worthy doing, statesmen, plain citizens, men of letters, " *histriones, balatrones, et hoc
genus omne ;*" at last each street had its particular
clubs, the so-called Street Clubs. This was from
the beginning the mark which distinguished the
club from the coffee-house, and which has remained as the foundation of the modern club

system; only members had admission, who were received according to rules, and paid their portion. Perhaps it is this continuity in the development of a social institution, which thereby becomes historical, that most attracts the inquirer, as it presents to the reader the most instructive part, perhaps, of our theme.

We find the word " Club " used with its present meaning even before the Civil war; for instance, in a poem of Sir William Davenant, " The Long Vacation in London," in which the poet depicts how in the time of the Long Vacation the streets of London are desolate, because all betake themselves to the country :—

> " Our mules are come! dissolve the club!
> The world till term is ' rub, O rub! ' "

There is no doubt that this poem was written by the former General Intendant of Royal Plays under Charles II., whilst Davenant was still Poet Laureate to Charles I., for in it mention is made of the Globe Theatre, which was pulled down in 1647, and of the Bull Theatre, which, at the time of the Restoration, stood so neglected that Davenant says, in his 'Playhouse to be Let' (1663), "it has no other inhabitants than spiders." *

---

* Payne Collier. 'History of English Dramatic Poetry,' iii. 302, 328.

During the Republic, and under the Protectorate, there existed a club, by no means unimportant in the history of that time, the Rota Club, a social union founded by Harrington, the author of 'Oceana,' for the object of political discussion, to which, among others, belonged Milton's pupil and friend, Cyriac Skinner. The meetings took place in the 'Turk's Head,' a coffeehouse in New Palace Yard, in the vicinity of Westminster Hall. They sat at a round table, the table of old knighthood and of modern equality, with a passage through, so that they might have their coffee warm, without interruption of the debates. The resolutions were decided by ballot, by means of a balloting-box; and Harrington says of this box, that there was no false play in it, " a box in which there is no cogging." Discussions were publicly held here upon questions of political organisation, in a feeling but little friendly to Cromwell's Government, so that there was frequent temptation to close the sittings by military power. But Cromwell contented himself with watching over these philosophic coteries without persecuting them.*

---

* Guizot's 'Histoire de la Révolution d'Angleterre,' iv. 104, 105. D'Israeli's 'Amenities of Literature,' p. 699.

By a similar union the " Green Ribbon
Club" was formed under Charles II., which
held its sitting under the house-sign of King
Henry VIII., opposite the Temple, and among
whose members during the last year of the Protectorate was Andrew Marvel the poet, and
Milton's assistant.

But those clubs of whose history we are
more exactly informed began in the time of
Queen Anne, a time of greater intellectual freedom, and of more social activity. The oldest
and most considerable of them was the Kit-
Kat Club, which, as the 'Spectator' says, owes
its origin to a mutton-pie. This means that
the club met at first in the house of a pastry-
cook, by name Christopher Katt, or according
to others, Christopher, the sign of whose house
showed one of those incomprehensible, but thoroughly English combinations, the 'Cat and
Fiddle,' so that " Kit " (abbreviation of Christopher) and " Kat " could be explained in one
way or the other. At any rate, the mutton-
pie appears to have been the great medium
through which the members of this club in
the time of good Queen Anne came together
in a brotherly manner. The Kit-Kat consisted
of forty members, noblemen, men of position,

P

rank and influence, authors of distinction ; all
the forty no less sincere lovers of pie than
devoted friends of the House of Hanover, and
zealous supporters of the Protestant succession in
Parliament and in the Press. Six dukes (among
them the great Marlborough, German Prince of
Mindelheim) and five counts—the celebrities of
the Whigs of King William's time ; Sunderland,
Halifax, and Somers, and the leading minister
of the coming era, Sir Robert Walpole, sat, ate,
and drank here amicably with the two fashionable comedy writers, Vanbrugh and Congreve,
with Addison and Steele, those Dioscuri whose
names were never wanting in the social lists of
that time ; together with a whole troop of other
witty celebrities, among whom Sir Samuel Garth,
afterwards physician to the King, did not hold
the lowest position. One evening he came into
the club with a list of fifteen patients, whom
he had yet to visit. " Deuce take them," he
cried, when Steele maliciously reminded him
of it, "nine of them are so ill that no physician can help them, and six so well that no
physician can hurt them! " Also Sir Godfrey
Kneller, born at Lübeck, the Court painter to
two monarchs, and the immortaliser of countless
beauties, who without him would probably have

been forgotten,* was of the party; and he painted the portraits of the whole club in a series of pictures, the so-called Kit-Kat portraits, which were to be seen, the property of one person, at the two exhibitions of Manchester (1857), and of Kensington (1862), certainly well worth seeing, as the first celebrities of an historically-distinguished time, and painted by the first painter of that time; who was so little gallant withal, and so avaricious, that he only sketched the faces of the great ladies who came to his studio, and afterwards added the figure and hands of his maidservant. Perhaps this was to their advantage, for it is known how Kneller's portraits of ladies are distinguished by their wonderful arms and hands. On the other side, when he was blamed on account of his hasty and careless work, he cried out, "Bah! it will not be believed that the picture is mine; no one will believe that the same man painted this picture and the Chinese at Windsor!" To the curiosities of the club belong also the so-called "toasting-glasses," a number of glasses on each

---

* . . . . "For two ages having snatch'd from fate
Whate'er was beauteous or whate'er was great."
Pope's *Epitaph on Sir Godfrey Kneller*, in
Westminster Abbey.

of which was inscribed a verse or toast on one
of the reigning beauties of the time. Among
these were four daughters of the Duke of Marlborough, who was fortunate in this respect; and
a niece of Sir Isaac Newton. The custom of
drinking toasts was then new, and each glass was
named after the lady, in whose honour the first
toast from it had been drunk, the Duchess or
Countess so and so. The glass "Lady Mary
Churchill" (named after the youngest of Marlborough's beautiful daughters) had an inscription,
on the whole complimentary to the lady, but com-
plaining that her eyes take away the liberty which
she was sent to bestow :

"Fairest and latest of the beauteous race!
    Blest with your parent's wit and her first blooming face,
Born with our liberties in William's reign,
    Your eyes alone that liberty restrain."

The composer of this elegant poem on glass was
Lord Halifax; and the secretary of the club was
the great publisher of that time, Jacob Tonson, the
immortal Bocai (anagram on Jacob) in the satire
of Ned Ward, who had more than one ground for
being angry with the excellent publisher. This
man Bocai was at the best no better than God
appears to have always made publishers; even

Dryden himself was obliged to write of him a very malicious epigram, with the postscript, "Tell the cur that he who has written these three lines can write more," to make him pay up an agreed *honorarium* (Dryden, 'Poetical Works:' description of old Jacob Tonson). Nevertheless, perhaps Ned Ward is a little too hard in his judgment upon him, when he calls him the "Chief Merchant to the Muses;" and asserts of him that he had compelled one of his unlucky authors to give up poetry and to establish a pastry-shop, in which he, Bocai, once a week presided as chairman of the new pudding establishment. Hither he had summoned all his authors; and as he found that pies to poets were as agreeable food as once ambrosia was to the gods, he paid for the fruits of their inspiration with pasties, with the double advantage that his *protégé*, the pastry-cook, took as waste paper what he could not sell in his profession. In this manner Bocai did a better business with his bookselling than his authors with their wit; and although among noblemen he always looked like a bookseller, he conducted himself, *vice versâ*, when he came among booksellers, like a nobleman.

More indulgently by far does our Biedermann pronounce upon the Beef-steak Club—this new

" Rump Parliament," as he calls it—whose members have the double advantage, in his eyes, of being neither booksellers nor authors. " Like true Britons," says he, "and to show their contempt for Kit-Kat pies, they gave a rump-steak the preference, wisely considering that the word beef was of a manly character, and sounded better than ' pie ' or Kit-Kat, in the title of an English club; " and that a gridiron, which has had the honour to be made the badge of a saint's martyrdom, was a nobler symbol of Christian integrity than two or three stars or garters. Although this club, like the former, was founded to bring together a number of friends on stated days to the pleasures of the table, and not with any political object, yet very naturally in this country, where party differences give their impress even to society, and, as a more recent writer (D'Israeli) remarks, " public life is perhaps the only foundation of true friendship," it took a political, and indeed Tory colouring; and for a long while the clergy and beef-steak remained the truest supporters of the opposition, while the ruling party, in return, recruited in their highest places from the Kit-Kat. The president of these beef-eaters, who, according to Ned Ward, so bravely represented the heart of the nation, wore a golden gridiron on a green silk-ribbon round his neck, and was, in the words of our authority (mark the year, 1709!)—"as proud of his new fangle as a German mountebank of a Prince's medal!"

The beef-steak and the club are two such national institutions, that alone and united they will never be allowed to die out from English life. There have been at different times, as there are still, different Beef-steak Clubs; but that Beef-steak Club which, under the name of 'the Sublime Society of Beef-steaks,' was the most famous of all, ceased to exist in April 1869, after it had attained the glorious age of 134 years. Founded by a scene-painter, Mr. Lambert, the Gropius of his time (1735), in the painting-room of a theatre, this sublime company, true to its original foundation, assembled invariably, as long as it continued, on the "boards which signify the world," first in Covent Garden Theatre, then, when this house was burnt down, in the Lyceum Theatre; where till the last, on every Saturday afternoon, at five o'clock, from November to June, a beef-steak dinner was served behind the scenes in a room which, according to the description of Mr. Cunningham, "was a little Escurial; the doors, the panelling, and the ceiling of good old English oak, adorned with the

bars of the gridiron as thickly as the Chapel of
Henry VII. with the portcullis of its founder."
The scenery, customs, and signs of a lodge hung
round the nightly sittings of the steaks, and what
the trowel is to the freemason, such the gridiron
was to them. The damask table-cloth, the drinking-
glasses, and the silver service, had woven, cut, and
engraved upon them the sign of the gridiron.
Through the iron bars of a great gridiron the
cook could be seen at his work, and the original
gridiron (that emblem which was saved from
the fire at two great theatres) had its place of
honour on the ceiling. The record book of this
club included the first names of the British aristocracy. Here Counts and Dukes might be seen
helping the cook; also members of the Cabinet
and magistrates of the good City; and here, in
the bloom of his youth and of his rising fame,
Brougham might be seen, with bottles packed
under his arm, which he brought out of the cellar.
The number of steaks was limited to twenty-four,
but was exceeded at one time, namely, when the
Prince of Wales, afterwards George IV., wished
to be received. This memorable occurrence took
place in the year 1785, and the ' Annual Register ' considered it sufficiently important to
devote to it the following paragraph:—" On

Saturday evening, 14th May, the Prince of Wales
was made a member of the Beef-steak Club. As
there was no vacancy, it was determined to make
him an honorary member : when the Prince refused
this, they agreed to increase the number from
twenty-four to twenty-five ; thereupon H.R.H. was
unanimously elected."

Beef-steaks with onions, and port wine, formed
the *menu*, and the first toast was, " Success to the
ten acres ;" by which was meant the ten acres of
land on which Covent Garden stood, in the parish
of St. Martin. On the 7th of April, 1869, the whole
of their splendour came to the hammer; furniture,
service of silver, portraits, and all remaining property of the ' Sublime Society of Steaks' went,
one after the other ; and the chief feature of the
auction, the old gridiron, the palladium of the
Society, was knocked down to the great restaurant-
keepers, Spiers and Pond, for 5*l.* 15*s.*

Corresponding with the numerous peculiarities
and eccentricities of the English national character,
a crowd of all kinds of wonderful, and to a Continental understanding sometimes quite incomprehensible societies, accompanies club life from its
very commencement. Volumes might be written
upon the remarkable ideas which were in this
manner incorporated, till they disappeared, perhaps

to make place for those still more remarkable.
Ned Ward, the earliest chronicler of the clubs,
has brought together a really beautiful sum of
what the Germans call "blooming nonsense," or
"*höhern Blödsinns*," to speak in the most modern
language. He tells of the club of the Split-
farthings, of the False Heroes, of the Mountebanks,
of the Bird-fanciers, of the Atheists, of the Beggars,
of the Thieves; he tells of the club of the Nose-
less Ones; and he tells, besides, of one or two
other clubs, whose name and description cannot
well be told in respectable society.

There was also a club of nightly disturbers of
rest, the so-called Mohawks, a *réunion* of young
people, belonging, for the most part, to the best
position, whose club-pleasures began by their
getting drunk, and ended by their rushing into
the streets, breaking windows, beating the night-
watch, attacking harmless wanderers, and pack-
ing old women in casks, to roll them down Snow
or Ludgate Hill. This nuisance became at last
so great, and the fear of venturing in the streets
after dark so general, that a Royal Proclamation
was issued on the 18th of March, 1712, which, however, only partially allayed the irregularity; for
this noble club did not expire till the end of the
reign of George I. Another club, the so-called

Hell-fire Club, consisting of the scions of the first
nobility of the country, and celebrated by its
blasphemies and wild excesses, was suppressed by
a decree of the Upper House. The president of
this club was the young Duke of Wharton, son of
the Minister under Queen Anne, and its spirit is
reflected in the following conversation between
two old club-companions, Lord Sandwich and
the famous Wilkes. When Lord Sandwich—so
says Horace Walpole—asked Wilkes whether he
thought he should die by the rope or by a certain
disease, he replied, "That depends upon whether
I adopt your Grace's mistress, or your Grace's
principles."

The "Je ne sçais quoi" Club (in the 'Star
and Garter,' Pall Mall) was a little less baneful,
although the name of the Duke of Orleans, afterwards Philip Egalité, which is among the members, appears to show that virtue and propriety
were not its device.

But is ugliness a necessary quality for men of
freedom? It almost seems so. Honoré Gabriel
Riquetti, Count Mirabeau, upon his visit to England, was unanimously chosen an honorary member of the Club of Ugly Faces, whilst earlier the
same distinction had been conferred upon Jack
Wilkes, the great revolutionist of England. This

club owed its origin to an insurpassably ugly man, by name Hatchet, with a nose of such immense extent, that one day a butcher boy cried out that it had knocked his tray of meat from off his shoulder, while Hatchet's head was still, at least, a foot distant from the tray. The natural antithesis to the Ugly Club was the Handsome Club, which consisted exclusively of men who had studied at Cambridge, and who, before joining the club, painted dimples upon their cheeks, if they were not blessed with them by nature. This club established the golden rule, which Brummel, the king of dandies, afterwards adopted, that the necktie made the man ; and one of them spoke the whole truth when he one day stated that to undress at night was a foretaste of heaven, but that, nevertheless, a man must suffer to be irresistible. Truly, one walks not under laurels with impunity !

The Club of the Unhappy Ones received no members who had not been already once, at least, made bankrupt, or else had in some way come into collision with the law ; and the Lying Club ordained, by one of the paragraphs of its statutes, that the president should wear a blue cap, with a red feather, and these signs of worth were to be given up with the chair to him who, in the course of the evening, told a greater and more unblushing lie than it had been possible for the president to do. Between nine and eleven o'clock no true word was to be spoken, under severe punishment, unless introduced by the sentence, " With your permission, Sir Harry ;" for Sir Harry Gulliver, the Münchhausen of England, was the patron of this select society. There was also another Club of Kings, the King Club, consisting of uncrowned heads, who had not the dignity but the family name of King; and an Adam Club, consisting of members who shared their surname with the husband of Eve, and on that account also assembled in Adam's Coffee-house, in Paul's Alley. From a contrary point of view to the Club of the First Man, rose the Club of the Last Man, which, from the beginning to the end, was so constituted, that it always consisted of a fixed number of members, which, under no condition, was ever to be increased. A bottle of port wine stood sealed in the room where the club assembled; and when out of all only one member remained, the last man was to sit in this room, unseal this bottle, and drink to the memory of the dead. Still it is said that this statute was never fulfilled to the letter ; when the number had melted away to two, these two met in the room, emptied the bottle, and declared the club to be closed. ('Athenæum,' No. 2001.)

It would be possible to prolong considerably the list of these eccentric clubs; but it is now time to approach that man, who has secured for himself the title of the "most clubable man," and who indeed, as he has left behind the traces of his singularity in English literature and in English life generally, has also imprinted them on English clubs. There can be no doubt that we mean Samuel Johnson, the Doctor, as he is still always called by preference.

The peculiarity of this man consisted in this, that he was far more important in his personality than in his works, and that he worked far more enduringly through what he said than through what he wrote. Obstinate in his political, narrow in his religious, and quite old-fashioned in his æsthetic views, he still is, and will probably long be, the most popular character of English literature, dealt with by the historians of both parties with equal affection, and standing nearer to the heart than any other English classic.

No one who does not know England can without difficulty form an idea of the charm which the name of this man always exerts over every Englishman. From the school which the boy attends, he takes this with him among his earliest impressions to Cambridge or Oxford, where he probably will

not fail to visit the room in which Johnson read
the classics as a student; or the coffee-house, where,
nearly fifty years later, after the University had
made him a Doctor "honoris causâ," he delivered
his opinion on Macpherson's 'Ossian.' The image
of Johnson will accompany the traveller who seeks
out the distant Hebrides; and although the destruction of old buildings, and the erection of new,
has done so much to alter the shores of the
Thames and the interior of the City, yet from the
old courts which lie on each side of Fleet Street,
the figure of the Doctor, as their " genius loci,"
rises to meet the spirit of him who travels down
them. His figure, inclining to corpulence, his
clumsy gait, his puffy face, his three-cornered hat,
his brown coat, and his cane, are before the eyes of
thousands, who perhaps have never seen one of his
books, except the 'Dictionary of the English Language' and his 'Lives of the English Poets;' and
many who find his tragedy, 'Irene,' tedious, and
his Abyssinian romance, 'Rasselas,' unenjoyable,
are delighted with the sayings which he brought
out at table; with the beautiful and sublime meditations which a morning walk through the park
excited in him; with the information which he
gave his fellow-travellers in a post-chaise; or with
the happy remarks which he made in the evening

in the comfortable rest of a country inn. The
smallest circumstances of his life—which was not
very exciting, but very rich in examples of virtue,
human love, and strength of character—people are
never tired of quoting or feeling proud of, thanks
to the valuable ' Biography of Johnson,' by Boswell, that book which is in every English house
where are Shakspeare and the Bible.

When Johnson wrote he was stiff, pedantic, and
strove after a grandeur which very often led to
a pompous, prolix, and un-English diction ; when
he spoke he was just as simple, short, condensed,
natural, and thoroughly English; he hit the nail
on the head. He was no poet, but a philosopher,
a teacher of men ; and although the humble position of his youth and the melancholy of his later
years, joined with a very great pride, held him far
from those who are usually called " society," he
was, nevertheless, a master of society in its higher
and highest sense. Never were there words
deeper and more full of significance exchanged, or
more comprehensive opinions expressed, than in
the small circles in which Johnson was reverenced.
A treasure of worldly wisdom lies in the con-
versations, richly furnished with anecdotes and
happily-chosen quotations from the poets, which
beautified the modest symposia at which Johnson

presided, whether in the house of his bookseller Osborn, or in the villa of his friend Mrs. Thrale, or in his own club.

Johnson's Club, first the club *par excellence,* afterwards called the Literary Club, continues to the present day under the name of Johnson's Club. In its existence of more than a hundred years it has changed its quarters and its name several times, but its substance, so to speak, has remained the same. When Johnson founded this Club in 1764 it included only his nearest friends, together not more than nine, who every Monday assembled in a tavern for a supper. Here was to be seen, close to the honourable dictator of English language and literature, a young man, in every respect the opposite of this massive person—who was accustomed to rule over all—a timid man of thirty years, little powerful in word, overlooked by everybody, and surpassed by many of the company, who were far less important than himself; for the most part silent, and when he spoke, confused, indistinct, unimportant, and wanting in striking expression, but full of life and loveliness when he wrote; a keen observer, a mild critic of the human heart, and approaching to sublime in his picturing of the whole home-charm of English landscape—Oliver Goldsmith, the singer of the ' Deserted Village,' and the

Q

author of the 'Vicar of Wakefield,' of immortal
memory. He was deficient in the gift of conversation to such a degree that he was often absurd
when he spoke. Hence he was, in all good-nature,
made the butt for the wit of his friends, and
especially of Garrick. To revenge himself for
this, Goldsmith wrote his famous poem, 'The
Retaliation,' in which he dedicates epitaphs to his
companions, and says of Garrick, hinting at his
small figure—

"Describe him who can,
An abridgment of all that was pleasant in man."

" Sir," said Dr. Johnson, " no man was such a
fool when he had no pen in his hand." But he
loved him very much; and in the Latin epitaph
which he devoted to the monument of his departed
friend in Westminster Abbey, says, that there was
almost no kind of literature which he did not
touch; and none, which he touched, that he did
not adorn (qui nullum fere scribendi genus non
tetigit, nullum, quod tetigit, non ornavit); and
that the love of his companions, the confidence of his friends, and the veneration of his
readers (sodalium amor, amicorum fides, lectorum
veneratio) have honoured his memory by this
monument.

There was also a gentleman with spectacles on

his nose, a trumpet to his ear, and a snuff-box
in his hand—Sir Joshua Reynolds, Kneller's successor, and first President of the Royal Academy
of Arts; who has adorned the walls of the lordly
castles and baronial halls of England with all
that was or became excellent, noble, and famous,
during two generations, for it is well known that
of the portraits which he has left behind, those
of children are the most remarkable.   Another of
the nine was Burke, upon whose fiery eloquence
perhaps the only restraint imposed was the
superiority of Johnson.   " I am contented to toll
the bell for him," said Burke.   There was also
here a young man about twenty, of noble and
imposing exterior, recently returned from Italy;
and always inwardly busied with a thought,
a picture; how at Rome, when sitting among
the ruins of the Capitol, he had heard barefooted
monks sing vespers in the Temple of Jupiter.
Three-and-twenty years passed away before, one
night in June, between eleven and twelve o'clock,
in a summer residence by the Lake of Geneva, he
wrote the last line of the last page of the work,
whose first idea had been called up before him
that evening in Rome.   The name of this work,
one of the greatest in historical literature, is ' The
History of the Decline and Fall of the Roman

Empire;' and the name of the author, then still
young and unrenowned, his coming greatness only
foreseen by a small band of select minds, was
Edward Gibbon. Admission to this Club was
forbidden to many famous men. "To be chosen
a member of this Club is no less honour than to
be the representative of Westminster or Surrey,"
said one of the bishops of that time, who was
fortunate enough to share this honour. It was not
easily bestowed on David Garrick, the Director of
Drury Lane. Although he was a pupil of Johnson
—one, indeed, of the three whom, in the years
of his calamity, the poor pedagogue had to teach,
the only one who, faithfully sharing this calamity
with his master, accompanied him to London and
afterwards brought out his 'Irene' on the stage—
yet Johnson was averse to the reception of the
modern Roscius, whose brow was crowned with the
laurels of all England, and who, not only a great,
but also a rich man, walked upon Persian carpet
and dined off silver plates. "Sir," said Johnson,
"I love my little David heartily, more than all, or
many of his flatterers do; but surely in such a
a society as ours one should not sit elbowed by
players, pimps, and mimes."

At last, however, Johnson yielded to the argument of the rest of his friends, and probably of his

own heart. Garrick became a member, and was
until his death not the least ornament of a club
which, including by degrees all the celebrities of the
day, became a power in literary and artistic matters,
upon whose verdict depended the fate of a new
book or of a new piece. At Garrick's death, in
1779, the club, which then numbered over thirty
members, first took the name of the 'Literary,'
and five years later, Johnson dined for the last
time in the cordial friendly union. " He looked
ill," Boswell remarks of the day (it was June 22nd,
1784), " but he put on a brave appearance, not to
disturb the company. He was very pleased with
the friendly speeches which all made him, and
endeavoured to be as entertaining as his condition
allowed."

On December 13th of the same year he died.
Weeping in the doorway stood Frances Burney,
the authoress of ' Evelina,' whose youthful fame
had filled the soul of the old man with an
almost fatherly joy ; and his hand grew cold in
that of a young friend from the club, the mild,
enthusiastic Bennet Langton, who, in his eighteenth
year, delighted with Johnson's writings, came to
London to become acquainted with him, and since
then had not ceased in a modest manner to admire
him. Eight days later Johnson found his well-

earned place in the Abbey, where rest England's great dead, almost the last of a generation of authors who perhaps are more important in the history of the culture of their nation than for that of its literature.

Among the members of the Literary Club are the great men of England of every province, of literature, of art, of science, of politics, and of the church. It is noteworthy that the great historians belonged to it almost without exception. Among them were two, who in their works have devoted a page of kind remembrance to the club: Lord Macaulay, who was never wanting at its dinners during the Parliamentary season; and Earl Stanhope (Lord Mahon), who was among the guests, when in 1864 the society celebrated its centenary, and the club received the name of Johnson's Club, in honour of its founder.

Besides this club, which has lasted, there was a number of similar unions, which had their day, and then disappeared. They could scarcely be called clubs in the new and complete sense, for they only depended on occasional meetings; still the desire for social union was in this way satisfied. For the predominant inclinations of that time—we mean the last part of the past century—were drinking and playing. The noble heads of society faithfully divided their leisure between these two passions, if they could not be united, and their regular places of assembly were ostensibly dedicated to the latter. The first real clubs were playing-clubs. Some of these proceeded from the old coffee-houses, after the Augustan age was over, when " that little circle of listeners," of which the ' Spectator ' has spoken, grouped itself round the chair of a prominent politician or critic. After the taste for this " elegant " entertainment had generally given way to another more substantial taste, the room was altered. From that time the dice-box rattled and gold pieces rolled; and instead of the door, as formerly, standing open to any one who paid for his admission, now only members had entrance. Such changes the ' Cocoa Tree ' underwent, a Tory coffee-house in the time of Queen Anne, and in the time of the Pretender, 1740, a Jacobite coffee-house; a play-club in 1780, where in later years Lord Byron might be seen. Thus, only still earlier, White's Chocolate-house became a play-club, and, only much later, in our own century, a regular club, which still, in remembrance of its former purpose, carries the arms designed for it by Horace Walpole, a dice-box with the device, " Cogit amor nummi," and in which to the present day a book is kept open for the entry of bets.

Betting and hazard attained their summit in that unnaturally excited period which reached fever-heat in East Indian speculation, owing to riches of returning Nabobs, witnessed the general outbreak at the occurrence of the French Revolution, and at last, in the subsequent war, found the steel and iron cure, of which the world was so much in need. One hundred guineas were betted at White's as to whether a certain member of the club, who was a widower, would take a second wife sooner than another member, who was likewise a widower. Heavy sums were depending upon whether a certain minister would be in office at a certain time; and whether a young lady of rank who was just married, would have a child sooner than the Countess N. N., who had already been married four or five months. A man fell down before the door of White's, and was carried into the house. Large bets were immediately made as to whether he was dead or not; and when some one suggested bleeding him, those who had betted on his being dead protested against such a proceeding, because it would lessen their chances. "One of the young folks at White's," writes Walpole, "has committed one murder, and has an intention of proceeding with another. He bet 1500*l.* that a man could live twelve hours under water ; hired some desperate fellow, sank him in a boat, and neither man nor boat have appeared again. He is now preparing another man and another boat for the same experiment."

Lord Mountford betted that Nash, who was eighty-three years of age, would outlive Cibber, who was eighty-four. The lord would have won his bet, for Cibber died (1757) four years earlier than Nash (1761). But both outlived the lord. He had lost stupendous sums at White's, and had set his last hope on a place under Government. When this hope failed, he invited his friends to a dinner at White's. It was New Year's Eve, and they played afterwards till far into New Year's morning. They drank " a Happy New Year," and the lord went home. Thence he sent for an advocate and three witnesses, made his will, asked the lawyers whether the will would stand good if the testator shot himself; and after this question had been answered in the affirmative, said, " Please wait a moment, while I go into the other room," went into the other room, and shot himself. In the ' Cocoa Tree ' 180,000*l.* sterling were won and lost in a single night. Two brothers, the sons of Lord Foley, had played away so much here, that they had to pay 18,000*l.* sterling yearly as interest on their debt. Admiral Harvey, afterwards so famous as one of the heroes of Trafalgar, in his youth, when a midshipman, lost his whole property—worth 100,000*l.*—at one stake to an Irish gambler by profession, by name O'Byrne, and won it again when he hazarded on a second throw an estate just inherited from his brother. The evil grew, whilst, as always in cases of moral corruption, it spread quickly from higher circles downwards. E. O. tables (" Even and Odds," a kind of roulette) stood in almost every ale-house ; at a Parliamentary discussion (1782) it was said by a Member, that in the two parishes of Westminster alone there were 296 of these, and another Member added, that in the whole of London there were no fewer than 500. Servants and apprentices were led astray by number-cards which were thrown into the kitchens and cellars ; and, even on Sundays, gambling-halls of the lowest kind were open all over London.

Some of the fashionable gambling clubs have continued till the beginning of our century, among them the universally known Almack's, in which Pitt and Wilberforce played at hazard ; for neither high Toryism nor humanity shielded from the

general passion, nor did the opposition make any
difference in that. Among the most frequent
guests at Almack's might be counted Pitt's genial
opponent, Fox. In the debate on the 6th February, 1772, upon the "Thirty-nine Articles," he
had made a rather heavy speech, and Walpole said
that this was not to be wondered at under the
circumstances. He had played at hazard at
Almack's from Tuesday evening the 4th till five
o'clock on the 5th; an hour earlier he had won
back 12,000*l.* which he had lost, and by dinner-
time, at five, he stopped with a loss of 11,000*l.*
On Tuesday he spoke in the above-mentioned
debate; went to dine at half-past twelve o'clock at
night; from thence to White's, where he drank
till seven on the following morning; thence to
Almack's, where he won 6000*l.*; and between
three and four in the afternoon went to New-
market, a famous place for horse-racing for wagers.
His brother Stephen lost, two evenings later,
11,000*l.*, and Charles another 10,000*l.* on the
13th; so that in three nights the three brothers,
of whom the eldest was not twenty-five, had lost
32,000*l.*

Lord Robert Spencer and General Fitzpatrick
held a faro bank at Brookes's, which in a short
time brought in 100,000*l.* sterling to the former,

whereupon he retired from business. The great
banker, George Harley Drummond, did the same,
when in one night he played away his property
to Beau Brummel. One of the most famous
gaming clubs, Watier's, was closed in 1819 ; when
the ornament of this and of all other clubs, Beau
Brummel, having a long time wandered in exile,
and been a trouble to the Consulate of Caen, at
last had made the vain attempt to win back the
favour of his Royal friend, "the first gentleman," by a packet of snuff, the famous Prince
Regent mixture. Although sums to the amount
of 30,000*l.* or 40,000*l.* sterling were occasionally
lost here in "Quitte or Double," Watier's was still
the great house for whist. "The same pack was
never used twice. At the end of a game the
cards were cast on the floor, so that, at the conclusion of the entertainment with dawn, the players
sat, to use the Beau's own words, ' knee-deep in
cards.' " *

It is very clear that men of a contemplative
quality of mind, and with an inclination towards
the quieter enjoyments of life, must have experienced a deficiency in social intercourse. The older

---

* ' Personal Reminiscences of Beau Brummel,' in ' Chambers's Journal,' April 21, 1856.

D'Israeli says of the year 1790 ('Curiosities of Literature') that the company at the coffee-houses has always, as long as he can remember, been on the decrease, that at that time there were as good as no proper clubs, especially were there no literary clubs, and those that were political were very narrow and exclusive. The friends of literature, the younger D'Israeli adds, in the biography of his father, had therefore taken to meeting in the booksellers' shops: the Whigs at Debrett's, the Tories at Hatchard's.

One of the few clubs which, developed from the old coffee-houses, did not devote itself exclusively to dice-boxes and card-tables, was 'Tom's,' an old neighbour of 'Will's' and 'Button's,' in Russell Street. Here, without doubt, at the end of the century, some of the most distinguished people of every branch of public life met some of the most clever; still this club also was closed in 1814, and the house in which first the coffee-house and then the club had flourished for nearly a century, was shortly after pulled down. For in the meanwhile another spirit had awakened, a new fashion had come up, the West End had arisen in all its glory; and the erection of those palaces had been begun, in which the modern club united the pleasantness and profit of a refined and influential society with

that solid luxury and highest comfort which corre-
spond with the richest city in the richest country
in the world, and which at the present day form
the true and justifiable pride of London life.

The club has become such a deeply-rooted and
national institution of thoroughly British spirit
and character, that it cannot be considered merely
as a factor of society in general, but also of all
those interests which unite or divide men, and it
may well be said, it has influenced the whole
civilised life of England of the present day more
than any other arrangement of a social nature.
The numerous clubs of London and England form
so many centres through which politics, science,
and literature, these definite forces in the cultivation of a people, continue to exist in lasting connection with each other, and with different circles
of society, and which, while they favour the group-
ing according to interests of position and calling,
at the same time protect them from isolation. It
is the principle of the Corporations of the Middle
Ages improved and employed in the spirit of the
present time, the genuine German essence of
fellowship under its most modern aspect. Circumstances have occurred which have been especially favourable to the development of club-life in
London.

As the English Sunday, in conjunction with the regular uniformity and quietness of the English evenings, has conduced to much more reading in England than among ourselves, so also a certain peculiar one-sidedness of English life has encouraged the club as its complement. The London man of business is in reality confined to the City by day, and to his house in the evening. Those manifold shades, which lend so great a charm to German, and to Continental life generally, are wanting in English, and especially in London life. They have there but an imperfect idea of those numerous pleasures "out of doors" which are known in our great towns. Going to the theatre, as such, has long ceased to be fashionable in London; the season for operas and concerts is short. Not as among ourselves do the Foyers offer to their *habitués* a place of meeting every evening. On account of these we have not hitherto had the need for clubs; but at present, however, we are beginning to feel, as in Berlin, for example, that some of the necessary conditions of its existence have arisen; a strong national feeling, a united national interest, a large and rich capital, and an earnest Parliamentary meeting. Also on other grounds, literary and artistic, the current is becoming stronger which draws com-

munity of interests to a fellowship, which more
or less approaches the nature of a club. But in
spite of our having the name, and making the
substance of the arrangements similar, it may well
be doubted whether the German Berlin Club will
ever attain to the general importance of the
English London Club, because the sphere of ours
can only be a narrower one.

In England, where hitherto there had been no
third stage besides business and the family, home
and publicity, the club came in as a mediating
element. It stands between the two, and embraces
somewhat of each; it combines the ease of social
intercourse, as it reigned in the coffee-houses of old
London, with the more solid enjoyments of the
good time of taverns. It supplies the place of the
Continental inn, the Restaurant, the Boulevard,
the Foyer, and the Conditorei; it is to the Londoner all this, and even something more. The
association of interests, of position, and calling, was
the first, and the association of material interests
followed. To be a member of a club, means that
a man has the right to regard one of the handsomest buildings in one of the best parts of the
town as his house, and servants in plush breeches
as his servants; to read the newspaper in a saloon
with gilded ceiling and thick carpet, and the

Magazine or Review in a library, with carved
oak book-cases; to dine off silver and Wedgwood
in a room, through the half-open window of which
the summer wind blows in from the Park; to smoke
after dinner his Cavendish or Havanna, drink punch,
and sleep, if he likes, in a comfortable smoking-
room, in whose antique fireplace in winter a good
fire burns. It means that he may go from his
house into a circle of society he has selected for
himself, to enjoy all those comforts and enjoyments
which can only be found in the houses of the rich
and refined; and all this at a price, the moderation
of which might almost excite more astonishment
than that which is raised by what is given in return,
through its detailed completeness. It was, if I remember aright, the Duke of Wellington who was
one day charged fifteenpence, instead of a shilling,
for a dinner at his club. The Duke declined to
pay the arbitrary overcharge, and did not rest till
it was struck off. "It is not on account of the
threepence," he said, "but on account of the disci-
pline of the club." This is preserved with the
utmost rigour. Nothing is more regular, nothing
more orderly, than the inner life of the club. No
loud word is heard, all goes on in an exemplary
manner. Every servant has his post, everything
its place, and a noiseless, quiet, gentlemanly tone,

R

free, however, from constraint, prevails everywhere.   Club-life has quite changed the manners
of English society, compared with the condition
of things which prevailed forty or fifty years ago.
Then, and indeed almost as long as the " first
gentleman " gave the tone, was the time of wild
carousals. ": As drunk as a lord," was a proverbial
saying, which, far from casting a shadow on the
character of one of the "upper ten thousand,"
made him appear rather as one of their particularly
manly and virtuous representatives.   When they
assembled, it was to become drunk ; and when they
broke up, many a noble lord and many an
honourable Member of Parliament might be seen
staggering uncertainly across the street, compas-
sionately led by the arm by a good companion,
not to speak of anything worse.   To-day a drunken
man in a club would only excite contempt.   Those
refined enjoyments have again come to be valued
which have given something truly urbane to English life, English manners, and English literature,
without taking from them a happy, excessively
attractive feature of reality.

But the alteration which the clubs brought about
in the constitution of British society is scarcely
greater than that which they introduced in the
architecture of the streets of London.   Formerly,

and even until the time when the clubs led the
way with a new example, the specific English
style, monotonous, gloomy, and dull outside, however much comfort there might be inside, was
the only kind to be seen in London. The clubs
were about the first to imitate the Continental
pattern, and to adorn the neighbourhood of Pall
Mall, St. James's, and Westminster with buildings, whose classical models stood in Venice and
Florence. What a number of splendid frontages!
What stately façades, executed in beautiful red or
grey marble, in the noblest spirit of architecture!
Polished columns support the magnificently carved
friezes; a sunbeam from Corinth or Athens in the
midst of the fog of London, and a vision of the
Parthenon, above the thousand-wheeled traffic of
the modern metropolis.

Although in general effect still unsurpassed,
the broad, large, and imposing quadrant which
Regent Street describes, has long ceased to be the
architectural wonder of London. Everywhere the
narrow and dark streets are giving way, and
new handsome buildings, in the Tudor and Re-
naissance style, are springing up in their place:
Parliamentary and Government buildings, in the
style of Westminster Abbey, Gothic churches,
handsome schools, asylums, benevolent institu-

tions, banks, and hotels. London is changing slowly, but more and more, year by year, from a brick and mortar town to a town of stone and marble.

The noble and characteristic treatment of club-buildings, which gave the impulse to this great change, vies in all its parts with the luxurious and comfortable arrangement of the interior. No wonder that with the temptations club-life offers there is scarcely a Londoner of any pretension who is not a member of a club. Not altogether with injustice modern satirists have seen in club-life a new hindrance to marriage, and have said that the club is an institution for the " encouragement of bachelordom," an abode of earthly bliss, in which women alone will not believe. Fortunately, however, domestic comfort is not the sole object for which man marries; for certainly comfort, such as the club offers, cannot be offered to the richest man by his own house. There he may also have servants in plush breeches, but he has the trouble of ruling them and the expense of paying them; here he is master, without any burden or responsibility. He can come when he will, and go when he will. His staying away causes no confusion. The small troubles of domestic life do not await him here. He is always met with the same politeness. When,

after a tiring day's work, he leaves his dark office
in the City, or his musty court in the Temple, for
his club, he is at once in a world where all breathes
rest and comfort; cool and shady in summer, bril-
liantly lighted and thoroughly warmed in winter.
Here he is always sure of finding some of his friends,
recreation, and an excellent dinner. Small tables,
with snow-white linen, covered with sparkling
crystal and polished silver and steel, stand ready
everywhere for the guests. On a mahogany desk,
in the middle, lies the "carte du jour" and little
forms near by, for the members to fill up according
to their taste: notes in the margin announce how
many minutes the preparation of each dish requires.
One knows exactly how long a time he has at
disposal, and the interval can be employed in
going to the dressing-room, where everything that
can rejoice the heart of man is ready: scented
Windsor soap, as much water as he likes, clean
linen and Turkish towels in abundance, and those
deep, handsome basins, in which it is a delight to
bathe one's face and hands. " Another and a better
man," you now descend to the reading-room, look
over one of the evening papers, which are everywhere fixed up on high stands, seek out a friend
with whom to share dinner, arrange with another for
a cigar or rubber in the evening, and betake yourself

to the dining-room, after the little page, in blue
jacket with silver buttons, has announced, " The
soup is on the table, Sir." For three shillings and
sixpence you can have a dinner, as well served and
as luxurious as in the household of a Duke : soup,
fish, roast meat, bread, cheese, and beer, *ad libitum*,
or a bottle of red wine, Burgundy or Bordeaux.
Such entertainment and service, with a dress-coat
and white cravat behind each chair, can only be
attained through the excellent economy of the clubs.
Certainly the entrance-money amounts only to
between 20*l.* and 30*l.* sterling, and the yearly
subscription from 5*l.* to 10*l.* sterling ; but with the
number of members up to 1200, a club, with an
income of from 5000*l.* to 15,000*l.* sterling, can keep
a good cook, a good cellar, and a staff of good servants.   At the head of the club stands a Committee
of management, elected according to statute; there
are also a secretary, a librarian, a manager, a
steward, a door-keeper, a butler, an under-butler, a
chamberlain, a clerk of the kitchen, a head-cook as
chef de cuisine, several under-cooks, kitchen-maids,
house-maids, waiters, pages, and attendants. This
is indeed the household of a prince, and who knows
whether many a prince in Germany is half as well
served as the member of a club in London.   Here
the invaluable advantages of co-operation or of con-

federation appear in two aspects: in the first place, every member of a club, for the expense of a few pounds yearly, has comforts which the greatest riches would scarcely be able to obtain for him elsewhere in such completeness; and in the second place, forty or fifty persons suffice to satisfy the needs of 1000 or 1200 members, each of whom would need five or six persons, if he wished to have in his own house all that he has in the club.

To belong to one of the great London clubs passes for a sign of respectability, and in many cases does even the service of a recommendation : hence no member omits to note his club upon his visiting card after his residence, and sometimes (especially by unmarried gentlemen, who perhaps do not live in particular elegance) this is the only address given. The club is all in all to its member : there he can receive his visits and his letters; he has at his disposal a drawing-room or reception-room, a writing-room, a writing-table, note-paper and envelopes with the club stamp, a card-room, a billiard-room, a bath-room, and in some of the political, especially the Tory Clubs, even a sleeping-room for the convenience of the country gentlemen, who, at the times of elections, are frequently summoned from their country seats to London.

Of the two Tory Clubs, one, the Conservative,

in St. James's Street, stands on old Tory ground,
where the shadow of Swift still indicates the place
of the old ' Thatched House ' Tavern—in which he,
at one time after his change in politics, dined, conferred, and conspired with the Tory magnates—an
imposing building, with Corinthian columns and
pilasters on the upper story, in the ornamental
frieze of which appear the crown and the oak-leaf,
with Roman-Doric columns in the lower story,
from which projects the massive portico. An
immense bay-window to the morning-room unites
as in a picture the architectural beauties of Pall
Mall, St. James's Street, and Old Palace Gate.
Here, set in a modern frame, is a piece of history
for every Englishman. On this spot of earth,
which his glance overlooks, the destinies of
England, for good and for bad, during the last
200 years have been acted out. The era of the
Stuarts and the era of the Georges have here left
their traces. Here stood, or still stand, the houses
in which lived their polished men, orators and
authors, and their celebrated women ; and here
are the streets in which they walked.

A dignified stillness, a dreamy pensiveness,
rests on the club-land of London ; all around the
flowers and lawns give their perfume, the lakes in
the Parks glitter, the trees in the squares rustle

and whisper; and the venerable pile of Westminster
Abbey amidst a mass of green, and the new tower
of the Houses of Parliament, whose bright gilded
point rises high above all the towers in London,
bound the horizon.

The Carlton Club is recognised as the headquarters and centre of the Conservative party in
England. In the political world Carlton and Tory
are two words of about the same meaning. Of all
the club-houses which adorn Pall Mall this is,
without doubt, the handsomest, on account of
its delightful fulness of form, its marble balus-
trades, polished columns of red granite, and ex-
pensively executed decorations, a work which
strikes one as picturesque in a high degree—a
copy of Sansovino's Library of St. Mark, trans-
ferred from the neighbourhood of the Piazza and
blue Lagunas of Venice to the moist sky of
London—an image of opulence, which is capable
of anything. The great landed estates of England, the unexampled riches of its princely
domains, and the influences, grown extensive
together with their estates, of its widely-rami-
fying families, look out upon the passers-by out of
the deep windows, and the Doric and Ionic columns
of this palace. The inside does not fall short of
the outside. The rooms, among which is the

coffee-room, 92 feet long, 37 feet broad, and 21 feet 6 inches high, show the most refined splendour. Here assemble Members of both Houses, men, almost without exception, of the highest social position—the little kings, who have divided the territory of England amongst themselves, and have left nothing for others but moving estates, steam, paper, ships, and the sea; the born representatives of the Conservative interests, from that old-fashioned country gentleman, whose ancestors, a hundred years ago, drank their red wine to the King " over the water," and called the now reigning dynasty " a pack of Hanoverian rats," to that most modern shade of party, whose politics have a colouring of feudal romance in D'Israeli's ' Young England.' The Conservative is younger (1840) than the Carlton Club (1832), and, in a manner, an offshoot from it for those Tories who could not obtain admission to the other. It numbers 1200 members.* The founder of the Carlton Club is " the iron Duke" of Wellington, and the number of its members, with the exception of Peers and M.P.'s (Members of Parliament), amounts at present to 950. Although these, as has been said, belong

---

* These and the following statements of numbers are according to ' Whitaker's Almanack ' for 1871.

to the richest class in England, the entrance-money
to the club amounts only to 20*l.* sterling, the yearly
subscription only to 10*l.* 10*s.* sterling—the former
being no more, and the latter less, in fact, than in the
majority of other clubs, whose supporters are not
possessors of the estates of this world.   But it only
needs the opportunity to show of how much these
" gentlemen of England " are capable.   When the
overthrow of a Whig Ministry is concerned, it may
be observed that the driving-wheels of this political
laboratory are of gold.   When it becomes important
to obtain new votes or to secure old ones, and when
at an election whole villages and market-places
must be taken to the poll in handsome carriages
and whole counties must be made drunk, then in
this club, in one evening, between forty and fifty
thousand pounds sterling are put down ; and in one
of the last crises, which threatened the reigning
Government, there must have been at its disposal
a sum not less than half a million.

A real Whig will never have much to praise in
a real Tory, and it is obvious that his club-house
will please him but little.   " The Carlton is a
showy building," says the Whig, " with its
pompously-coloured pillars and overloaded orna-
mentation, like a man with rings on all his fingers,
thick gold chain, and heavy seal, or worse still,

like an over-dressed woman; its height does not
accord with its length, nor its splendour with its
proportions, and altogether it does not accord with
the climate of London, in which its red granite will
pretty soon be spoiled by the weather." This last
assertion has, indeed, not been confirmed, for the
brightness of the columns has not in the least
diminished since 1832; it is, however, quite
true that the Reform Club, the head club of the
Whigs, built in a very grave style, appears almost
without ornament next to its showy neighbour.
Founded in the year 1834, it counts 1400 members.
The two clubs stand side by side in Pall Mall, only
divided by a narrow way which leads to Carlton
Gardens, and present scarcely a greater contrast
in their politics than in their architecture. The
club-house of the Whigs gives the impression of
thorough simplicity, of complete harmony, and a
certain subdued grandeur : it looks like a Roman
republican close to a luxurious Venetian noble ; and
it has in its exterior nothing which excites the
mind, nothing for the fancy, but only something
strong, which rather reminds us of the duties of life
than of its enjoyment. The style of this building
is the pure Itálian of the sixteenth century, in
which, as Kugler says, that more poetical inspiration, that more lively fancy of the fifteenth

century, appears lessened ; and, in fact, the model
of the Farnese Palace in Rome, begun by San-
gallo and completed by Michael Angelo, was in
the mind of the London architect, Barry, who
borrowed from it his deep-set windows, with
columns at the side.

There is no question that of the two clubs of the
great political parties that of the Whigs is the
truer to the English national character, which,
from its development, but little loves ostentation.
By contrast with the simplicity of this club-house
as seen from the street, he who enters is the more
delighted with the truly princely luxury which
reigns within. A large hall, of the whole height
of the building, receives him, and an ascent of a
few steps leads him to the saloon, which is surrounded by an artistically-designed colonnade, the
rich Scagliola marble pillars of which rest on bases
of dark red porphyry. The colonnade supports a
gallery, from which Corinthian columns gracefully
rise, and above all is arched a glimmering dome of
glass. The walls are of coloured marble, in which,
behind the colonnade, are introduced life-sized
portraits of the most celebrated Reformers, and
over the gallery are fresco paintings, representing
Poetry, Music, Painting, and Sculpture. The floor-
ing is of mosaic, and the whole presents an aspect

of almost overpowering splendour. As in an Italian
palace, a staircase leads from the hall to the upper
gallery, upon which the various apartments of the
building open—the dining-rooms, the card and
billiard-rooms, the reception-rooms, &c. Perhaps
the most attractive of all is the library, an imposing
room, a whole story high, full of quietness, comfort,
and books. Beautiful pillars support the arches
of the roof, rich hangings conceal the doors, thick
carpets cover the floor, rows of valuable books
adorn the walls, soft seats invite to reflection, and
through a great window may be seen and breathed
in all its freshness a glimpse of the green and the
smell of the mignonette from Carlton Gardens.
Such a room and such a library might well excite
the quiet envy of a man who loves books. Perhaps
there is no more beautiful room for study in the
world. A wonderfully pleasant air which fills the
breast with comfort, and a mixture of light and
shadow beneficial to the eyes and to the spirit, are
here always. The dark grey of the marble walls,
thrown up by a narrow but sufficient decoration of
gold ornament, appears suited to that repose of the
mind which is so necessary to him who would
meditate ; and the scarlet of the damask curtains,
morocco seats, and leathern bordering of the book-
cases, brings into the temperature of the room just

a breath of that warm tone which communicates itself imperceptibly to the temperature of the soul. A collection of 10,000 volumes is contained in the cases, handsomely bound, carefully chosen and arranged in order, according to the system of Panizzi, the great reformer of the British Museum ; and besides the part which includes polite literature and travels, this must be the most comprehensive political library in the whole kingdom.

But the true wonder of the Reform Club is its kitchen. For even a man of liberal principles can love the pleasures of the table, as it is known that shortly before the decease of Lord Palmerston (old Pam), a member of the diplomacy had said to his Austrian colleague, in compensation for all which he had censured in the old Whig, " Mais on dîne fort bien chez lui." Now, the Reform Club was fortunate enough to secure the service of such an artist as Soyer, of immortal fame in the annals of gastrosophy.

Several of his most successful discoveries have had their origin in the dinners which this club has given to eminent guests ; for it was on such occasions the ambition of this extraordinary man to adorn the table not only with good, but also with new and even sometimes witty dishes, and among his greatest successes were the " vol au vent à la

Clontarf," in honour of O'Connell, and the "ice
à l'Ibrahim Pacha," in honour of the Pacha of
Egypt, 1846. The atelier in which this master
worked—in other words, the kitchen of the Reform Club—would be one of the things best worth
seeing in London, only people do not succeed
in seeing it. Still there was one lady, the Vis-
countess of Mallville, so favoured as to enter this
sanctuarium, the secrets of which are described by
her in the following manner, in the 'Courrier de
l'Europe':—

"The kitchen is spacious as a ball-room, and
white as a young bride. All-powerful steam,
the noise of which salutes your ear as you enter,
here performs a variety of offices: it diffuses an
uniform heat to large rows of dishes, warms the
metal plates upon which are disposed the dishes
that have been called for; it turns the spits, draws
the water, carries up the coal, and moves the
plate below, like an intelligent and indefatigable
servant. Stay awhile before this octagonal appa-
ratus which occupies the centre of the place.
Around you the water boils and the stewpans
bubble, and a little farther on is a movable fur-
nace, before which pieces of meat are converted
into savoury *rôtis;* here are sauces and gravies,
stews, broths, soups, &c. In the distance are

dutch-ovens, marble mortars, lighted stoves, iced
plates of metal for fish, and various compart-
ments for vegetables, fruits, roots, and spices.
After this inadequate though prodigious nomenclature, the reader may perhaps picture to himself
a state of general confusion. If so, he is mistaken,
for in fact you see very little or scarcely anything
of all the objects above described. The order of
their arrangement is so perfect, their distribution
as a whole and in their relative bearing to one
another so intelligently considered, that you re-
quire the aid of a guide to direct you in exploring
them, and a good deal of time to classify in your
mind all your discoveries."

The remaining clubs of Pall Mall and of the
neighbouring Squares, whose speciality is for the
most part indicated by their names, are: the Army
and Navy Club, with 2250 members; the Garden
Club, founded in 1813, with 357; the United Service, founded in 1815, with 1550; the Oxford
and Cambridge Club, founded in 1830, with 1170;
the Union Club, composed of merchants, lawyers,
members of Parliament, and gentlemen in general, in Trafalgar Square, founded in 1822, with
1000; the Travellers' Club, founded in 1819, with
725 members, among whose number, according
to rule, no one can be accepted "who has not

s

travelled out of the British Isles a distance of at least 500 (English) miles, in a direct line from London."

The club of literature and art is the Athenæum, founded in the year 1824 by a number of notabilities, among whom were Walter Scott and Thomas Moore. The present club-house, built in 1829, and opened in 1830, in the Grecian style, and with a frieze supported by pillars, upon which appear in beautiful imitation the Athenian youths and splendid horses of the Pan-Athenaic procession from the roof of the Parthenon, is one of the most noteworthy buildings in Pall Mall, and partly covers the memorable ground where, until the year 1826, stood Carlton House, the Palace of the Prince Regent. Wisdom and virtue, the fame of the author, painter, and sculptor won in honourable work, and preserved immaculately, here followed upon the heels of those errors of the heart, that life without seriousness or sacredness, that indifference to public opinion, which will always be avenged when the name of George IV. is uttered. A colossal figure of Minerva over the Roman-Doric entrance-door has taken the office of the watchman, which formerly, in the days of blood of the Regency, was held by " Big Ben," the colossal door-keeper of the Prince ; and where formerly the companion of his feasts met, there in the high hall, under the columns of Lysicrates, better men have assembled and with better objects. Chaste statues adorn the room, and an excellent library, adapted to the especial character of the club, is also here. The club numbers 1200 members; and it is certainly not too much to say that all celebrities of the present time are included in this number, and that nowhere else as here have spiritual and temporal peers, bishops, noblemen, and those belonging to every position, patrons of literature and art, mingled with their real representatives in free intercourse. The Athenæum was for a long while the central point of the circle of authors in London. Here it was always customary formerly to introduce foreigners of distinction ; and to obtain admission became more and more an aim of ambition to Englishmen. Perhaps too much so for its original tendencies ; for, if we may believe the paper, which we may well call the paper of this club, because it originated in its midst, and among the English critical journals occupies the rank which is held in English society by the literary club, the name and picture of which it bears—we mean the 'Athenæum'—it has in later times somewhat lessened its significance, through the preponderance of that foreign element. "A prominent

ecclesiastic," says that Journal, "whose name had
been on the list of candidates for two or three
years, asked the Secretary when he might hope
for a chance of election. The answer was, 'What
a pity you are not a bishop! the thing would be
done at once.'"

With extraordinary boldness the 'Athenæum'
maintains the opinion that, even among bishops
of the Church and judges of the high Courts of
England, there are some very tedious, unenjoyable,
and unclubable people; and that these, united
with the rich merchant-element of London, have
contributed, for the greatest part, to change the
nature of a club, which had been originally founded
for members of learned positions, artists, authors,
and men of congenial dispositions; and which,
although the brotherhood of intellect is still sufficiently numerously represented, and the cream of
the Athenæum still exists, has, nevertheless, ceased
to be what it was at first.

This may have been the reason for which, in
the year 1864, a new Athenæum Club, the 'Junior
Athenæum,' was founded, which was so fortunate
as to find a shelter in the splendid house of the
Amsterdam millionaire, Van der Hope, in Picca-
dilly, and which at the present time numbers
600 members. Altogether it appears as though

each greater club must have its "Junior;" for instance, there is the 'Junior United Service,' since 1827, with 2000 members; the 'Junior Carlton,' opposite its venerable ancestor, since 1864, also with 2000; and the 'Junior Garrick Club,' since 1867, though with only 350 members.

Before this 'Junior,' however, the old and original Garrick Club—from 1831, with 650 members—still maintains precedence. This club, first formed for the members and friends of the art in which the man whose name it has received shone so highly, but afterwards a favourite rendezvous for authors and artists in general, has kept sacred the old ground, upon which in the time of "little David" rank, wealth, society, and fashion moved—the neighbourhood of Covent Garden.

In this club, till a few years ago, might be seen daily a man with grey hair, although his figure was still powerful, and his countenance showed no marks beyond those of matured judgment, refined mind, and benevolence. Daily from the bright environs of the West End he came here to tread this spot of earth, which he loved and knew as did no other in London, and to call up his prototypes from the greatest English humourists, he, the greatest of England's new humourists—Thackeray. He had to perform a pilgrimage through a great length of time from those small and smoky rooms, "where the best company usually gathered together after the theatre, to play piquet and to amuse themselves, where one saw blue and green ribbon with stars, and not merely English newspapers with foreign news, but also moral treatises," as Defoe says. Far was the way from those taverns where the president of the time was expected to bring his own wine, if we may believe Swift, to the high halls and dining-rooms glittering with silver, of the different clubs to which the author of 'Vanity Fair' belonged. Of all these clubs the Garrick was his favourite place of sojourn. Here, surrounded by the last remembrances of Queen Anne and the four Georges, was his world. "The two great national theatres on one side, a church-yard full of mouldy but undying celebrities on the other; a fringe of houses studded in every part with anecdote and history; an arcade often more gloomy and deserted than a cathedral aisle; a rich cluster of brown, old taverns—one of them filled with the counterfeit presentments of many actors long since silent, who scowl or smile once more from the canvas upon the grandsons of their dead admirers; a something in the air which breathes of old books, old pictures, old painters, and old authors; a place beyond all other places one would choose in which to hear the chimes at midnight, a crystal palace—the representative of the present—which peeps in timidly from a corner upon many things of the past; a withered bank that has been sucked dry by a felonious clerk, a squat building with a hundred columns, and chapel-looking fronts, which always stands knee-deep in baskets, flowers, and scattered vegetables; a common centre into which Nature showers her choicest gifts, and where the kindly fruits of the earth often nearly choke the narrow thoroughfares; a population that never seems to sleep, and that does all in its power to prevent others sleeping; a place where the very latest suppers and the earliest breakfasts jostle each other on the footways"—such is Covent Garden, with some of its surrounding features, as Thackeray often saw it, and for the last time on 22nd December, 1863.

That brown tavern, "filled with the counterfeit presentments of many actors long since silent;" among them the portrait of Perdita Robinson, who played so sweet and sad a *rôle* in the romance of the Prince of Wales,—the old building of the Garrick Club is no more, and a new one stands a few hundred steps farther westward. A few months after Thackeray went for ever to the companions of his fame and of his immortality, the old house was destroyed, pulled down, and cleared away, "and the place thereof will know it no more."

But among the great shadows which the historian, the novelist, and the lover of the past meets with there, is now also that of Thackeray.

THE JEWS IN ENGLAND.

I.

THE history of the emancipation of the Jews is
pre-eminently, and in an universal sense the history of the triumphant progressive development of
modern thought and freedom. With the word
which burst open the gates of the streets of the
Jews, was loosened the last fetter of the Middle
Ages which yet oppressed that thought; and it fell
to the ground in the same moment in which those
freed from the Ghettos began to mix, as citizens
and comrades, with their former persecutors.

The relation of the Christian to the Jew in
another than a religious point of view is of value
as the barometer of political civilisation. The
setting free of the one goes hand in hand with
the setting free of the other—from prejudices!

"Prejudices are the kings of the multitude,"
says Voltaire. The same man, so haughty and bold
towards kings wearing a crown, bows before that
of the populace, whilst he, in his 'Literature of the
History of Philosophy,' declares: "The Jews are
but an ignorant and barbarous people, which for
a long time has joined the foulest greed to the most

frightful superstition, and most unconquerable hate against all who endure and enrich them. But," he adds, " *Il ne faut pourtant pas les brûler.*"

Especially excellent and noble appears this sentiment in the mind of the great philosopher who had illumined his age, given the lie to religion and prejudice, but unfortunately never pardoned this one circumstance in the Jews, that they, in money transactions, had once or twice outwitted him ; as did Abraham Hirsch, in Berlin, who had received a bad bill of exchange from Voltaire for good stones, and to whom subsequently Voltaire had to pay both stones and bills to extricate himself from his embarrassing situation. " *Il ne faut pourtant pas les brûler.*" How tolerant of Monsieur Voltaire, after such experience ! and how just was Lessing when, in his famous epigram, he says Voltaire was the greater rogue !

Like almost all questions of State, Germany has decided this more by means of preparatory mental labour in the quiet chambers of its philosophers and poets than on the constitutionally conducted Parliamentary battle-field, to which, indeed, two things were wanting, namely, Constitution and Parliament. When these came the thing was ripe, for Lessing's ' Nathan der Weise ' was worth as much for the Jews in Germany as an entire victorious Parliamentary campaign. Conformably to German habit the case was carried through, bearing weight internally, and its marks first became externally evident when the enlightened spirit of the age pronounced its verdict. In one word, the question in Germany has been one of civilisation— in England one of politics. The phases of this movement mark themselves more sharply in England, because here, very early indeed in a bygone century, raised from the province of mere philanthropic and philosophic speculation and debate, it was made a subject of constitutional inquiry, which we see run through all the stages to a final triumph.

The story of the emancipation of the Jews in England, therefore, offers to the observation a clear distinct prospect, in which we may perceive more than in any other land the beginning, the middle, and the end.

II.

For a long period the Jews in England have
found themselves possessed of full civil and political rights. Seven Jews sit in Parliament, and
twice, in the course of a few years, have Jews
been invested with the highest of municipal
honours—the Lord Mayoralty of London. But it
was not so with them always.

·. Barbarities, such as in our own age we have seen
practised towards them in the less civilised lands
of the East, did the Jews once endure in England.
It appears that already, in the eighth century,
they were settled there. William the Conqueror
carried over a larger number of them out of Normandy ; under him and his successor, and the first
Kings of the House of Plantagenet, they flourished
in the new land. There, as almost at that time
everywhere, they were the guardians of knowledge,
the doctors and physicians, the honoured friends
of Kings, *dilectus et familiaris noster.* They had
their own protected quarter in London, and one
of the most famous colleges of Oxford was their
property. On the day when Richard the Lion-

hearted ascended the throne in 1189, the leaf was turned. When, after his coronation, a deputation from the whole body of the Jews of England did homage to him, and desired to bring rich and gracious gifts, they were turned away upon the instance of the Archbishop of Canterbury. None should receive presents from Jews, neither should Jews tread the court of the Castle. The roughness of the common people, who had never loved them, was thus sanctioned and unfettered by a holy mouth. Unwillingly had they seen the small community increase and grow—progressing towards wealth and power. They had become their debtors in money, and found it inconvenient to repay them; therefore they laid upon them taxes which they could not afford, and accused them as usurers when they took high interest, in order to meet the requirements.

We can form a fair representation of this for ourselves when we reflect on what has happened under our own eyes in Roumania. That which an English paper ('Saturday Review,' March 1872) has said of it suits well enough, if we carry back its date, England in the thirteenth century. " There must have been something especially sweet for the barbarous mind, first to take the money of a man, and when he demanded it back,

to buffet, strike, and half kill him, on high religious grounds." It is the old story, which has
been repeated unhappily too often, and everywhere
where there have been Jews.

The mischievous fire spread itself from the Court
of the King at Westminster over the whole of
England. The Monarchy was the accomplice of
the Prelacy, and the people a blind tool in their
hands, for the greed of the one and for the fanatical
zeal of the other. The old fearful tale of the blood
of Christ, which the Jews were supposed to use on
the night of Easter, was again brought forward;
those to whom, in the five Books of Moses, the use
even of the blood of brutes was forbidden—those
to whom barbarity was a horror, and murder a
nonentity. The persecutions of the Jews began.
Hunted and massacred with inhuman insensibility
by their foes and adversaries, who in those times
were usually their debtors and hoped to become
their inheritors, on one occasion, when no other
hope of safety or honour remained, a multitude of
them, to the number of 500 men, women, and children, buried themselves, with their Rabbin at their
head, on that notorious night of fire and murder at
York, beneath the smoking ruins of the Castle—a
deed of heroism well worthy of the spirit of the
Maccabees.

From that time, through nearly a hundred years, the Jews in England were fated to buy their existence day by day with gold; and at last, when the cup of fury was filled, did the angry God of Israel pour it out upon those who had gone astray of his people, even to the coasts of the sea.

Under Edward I., in 1290, the Jews were banished from England. A cause has been assigned for this cruel measure, which drove thousands upon thousands away from their own endeared soil—from their modest homesteads and the graves of their dead—that the Jews had been guilty of false coining. Recent inquiries have, however, brought to light a different result.* The Jews would not have been given up for such a trifling price. On the contrary, great endeavours were made to draw them over to Christianity. The last of those endeavours was pregnant with fatality for them. A Dominican monk, by name Robert de Redding, a skilful orator and able Hebraist, was intrusted with the office, but instead of converting them to Christianity, he was himself converted to Judaism. The Dominican monks, horrified at the disgrace which they believed inflicted on their Order,

---

* Grätz, ' Geschichte der Juden,' and Adler, ' Jews in England.' Longmans. London, 1870.

T

besieged the Queen-Mother Eleanor, and she, through her son Edward I., carried into execution the decree of banishment. Hume, who when he wrote his 'History of England' could not have known the particular ground of the banishment of the Jews from England, yet, from a just instinct of the truth, lays no especial stress on the "Imputation of false coining," but turns the whole guilt upon the King, whom a perverted feature of hero-worship in the present day has undertaken to extol as the greatest of the Plantagenets. Hume calls things by their right names when he says that "Edward, influenced by his zealotism and his avarice, was resolved to purge the kingdom from the hated race, and to take their property as the reward of his deed." The heart shudders to read how 16,000 poor Jews quitted the Island kingdom—how the boatmen, even on the Thames, maltreated them—how the inhabitants of the five ports took from them, as travelling money, that which the rapacity of the King had yet left to them—how thereon the shipowners refused to admit them on board, and how by hundreds they perished in sight of the open sea: "A crime," says Hume, "for which severe punishment was destined to the King, who had resolved to be the sole plunderer in his possessions. So were the Jews robbed of their fortunes and cast out of the kingdom. But," continues he, " since it is impossible for a kingdom to exist without money-lenders, and no one will lend money without compensation, so was usury, as it was then called, from that time protected even by the English."

So ends the first stage of the History of the Jews in England.

But only a few traces are left of their first residence here. In the old town of Bury St. Edmund's in Suffolk, well known from its remains of old Roman buildings, the noble wall of a stone synagogue is preserved, which in the present day has been converted into a police-station, but by the people is still called "Moses' Hall," and the "Jews' Synagogue." In the same way, the Jews' quarter, in which at that time they dwelt in the City of London, and had their places of worship, is called even to the present time Old Jewry.

For almost four hundred years—from 1290 to about 1650—there were no Jews seen in England; and only now and then do they appear in English poetry, in what guise we may well imagine.

Always when Jews are brought on the stage is painted their fierce hate towards Christians, their thirst for Christian blood is the gloomy theme of the song. In the earliest English ballads, which are preserved in Percy's 'Reliques,' is one entitled 'The Jew's Daughter,' belonging to the second half of the thirteenth century. The Jews, before they left England, must have heard the "Mord und Nachtklang"—music recalling night and murder—of this popular song, which Herder, who has translated it in his 'Stimmen der Völker,' calls a terrible tale, the tradition of which once cost very many Jews their land and life. It rests upon a narrative of the monkish historian, Matthew Paris (†1259), according to which, in the year 1256, a Christian child in Lincoln was crucified by them. The boy Hugo is running about playing at ball, when the Jew's daughter entices him towards her with an apple :—

> "And scho has taine out a little pen knife,'
> And low down by her gair (dress),
> Scho has twined the zong thing and his life
> A word he nevir spak mair."

Laughing, she rolls him into a leaden coffin, and throws him into a well fifty fathoms deep. The grief of the mother when she misses her son is touchingly painted :—

> "Quhan bells wer rung, and mass was sung,
> And every lady went hame :
> Than ilka lady had her zong sonne,
> Bot Lady Helen had nane."

At last, when she comes to the well, and cries for

her "bonny Sir Hew," her "pretty Sir Hew," she
hears a voice answer out of the depth :—

> "Gae hame, gae hame, my mither deir,
> Fetch me my winding sheet."

Evidently from this tradition was inspired, about
a hundred years later, when for a long time not a
Jew had been found in England, the tale of
the 'Prioress,' in Chaucer's 'Canterbury Tales,'
only that here miracle is introduced, which lends
the bloody deed a legendary background. This
very glimmer of piety which surrounded the
legends hostile to the Jews was all the more cal-
culated to stir up the fanatical hatred towards
these poor persecuted ones. The boy in the ballad
is merely playing at ball ; but Chaucer introduces
him, though so young, as a paragon of piety, who,
as he goes through the Jewish town to school,
sings his song aloud, ' *O Alma Mater Redemptoris.*'
The Jews resolve thereon to murder him, and he
becomes a sacrifice for his faith. They bury him
in a heap of manure ; there his mother finds him.
There, with throat almost cut in half, he still sings
his song, ' *O Alma Redemptoris Mater.*' The pro-
vost naturally has the Jews led to the most dis-
graceful death amidst the pain of torture :—

> "Therefore with wilde hors he did hem drawe,
> And after that he heng hem by the lawe."

The boy, on the other hand—the young martyr—
is by the abbot and monks solemnly laid to lasting
rest in a marble tomb; and, that in the register of
the sins of the Jews nought may be omitted, the
poet, in conclusion, recapitulates that other history
of murder which, for almost a century and a half,
had lived in the remembrance and in the mouth of
the people :—

> " O yonge Hew of Lincoln, slain also
> With cursed Jewes, as is notable
> For it nis but a litel while ago."

From this, however barbarous yet extremely naïve
representation, we see the Jews presently brought
by the first dramatists into a somewhat higher
sphere. Here, at least, is a man who has an aim.
Although barbarity is still his principal quality,
yet is it a means for him by which to gain something else. He is no longer the vampire sucking
Christian blood solely for his own enjoyment. Two
motives actuate him—Avarice and Revenge. And
these, if indeed bad and blamable, are, at all
events, the characteristics of a human being.

   In the famous tragedy of the ' Rich Jew of
Malta,' by Christopher Marlowe (1563–93), one of
Shakspeare's predecessors, we find these chaotically
combined, but amidst the wild mass of monstrosities
which we are accustomed to find in Marlowe, they

are yet always recognisable. His ' rich Jew ' poisons the wells (also one of the darling occupations of the Jews of the Middle Ages), cuts the throat of the sick during sleep, sets fire to the monasteries, blows the whole of the fortress of Malta into the air, and, with unslaked lime, prepares a grave for the Governor, into which he is himself finally precipitated, there miserably to be reduced to ashes. Corpses must have been lying about on the stage by dozens, the result of the rage of Barabbas, Marlowe's Jew ; and there is, indeed, no kind of death which he has not employed in order to obtain his victims.

But there is here an intelligible, human foundation for these outbursts of rage, even though there was no need of illustrating it by such a wholesale massacre. Because he will not become a Christian, his property and wealth are taken away, his house is changed into a nunnery, and at last he loses also his daughter Abigail, dear to him as Iphigenia to Agamemnon. She is converted—after her two Christian lovers have murdered one another through the artifice of her father—to Christianity, and becomes a nun.*

It is evident that we have nearly the same two motives here, viz., love of gold and love of his

---

* Bodenstedt, ' Shakspeare's Zeitgenossen,' iii. 319, &c.

daughter, that Shakspeare has adopted in his Shylock. But how entirely different is Shakspeare's from Marlowe's Jew. It is not to be understood that Shakspeare loved the Jews any more than his dramatic predecessor; but he was the greater poet. He felt that an object of moral detestation, not softened by any addition, be it ever so slight, of sympathy, as here, of compassion, could never be a subject for the stage. It is therefore on æsthetical, as well as on the highest moral grounds, that, at the very beginning, he lays so much stress upon making us understand the Jew Shylock as a *man*, in order afterwards to make us clearly see his *inhumanity*. " If you prick us, do we not bleed ? if you tickle us, do we not laugh ? if you poison us, do we not die ? and if you wrong us, shall we not revenge ? The villany *you teach me* I will execute." Thoroughly to appreciate what Shakspeare has done for his Jew, we must compare the two sources from which he has taken his story—the novel of Gianetto and Anselmo, from the ' Pecorone ' of Giovanni Fiorentino,* and the ballad ' Gernutus, the Jew of Venice, from Percy's ' Reliques.'

* Given by Delius in English, in the Introduction to ' The Merchant of Venice.'

The novel as well as the ballad give, feature for feature, the minutest details upon which Shakspeare, whilst he enriches them with the wealth of his poetical power, has constructed this portion of his wonderful drama. The friendship of Antonio and Bassanio; Portia's saving interposition; even the fond fooling with the ring is to be found in the novel, whilst the ballad (to be sung according to the tune ' Black and Yellow ') contains the very picture of the scene of judgment, especially Shylock's behaviour towards his debtors. But that which is wanting in both the one and the other is the Jew's daughter Jessica. She is the poet's own work. Through this character a fresh significance is given to all that has gone before, so far as concerns the Jew. We see in him first, and before all, not the Jew, not the usurer, not the dog-like, cruel man, but the father, the deeply-moved father ; the father injured in his most holy feelings, who is robbed of his daughter—the only thing besides his gold that he loved—and robbed, indeed, by the object most hateful to him—a Christian.

> " I have a daughter ;
> Would any of the stock of Barrabas
> Had been her husband, rather than a Christian."

So great, indeed, is the strength of his affection for his daughter, that while a ray of it falls on that

other low love of gold, even this appears less hateful
in our eyes, insomuch that where both stand forward together, we are induced to excuse the one
with the other, and deepest compassion, which even
outlives the horror of the scene of judgment, seizes
us when we see that he has lost both,—his daughter
and his gold. The one is of no value for him
without the other. "The curse never fell upon
our nation till now," he cries, when he hears of
his Jessica's seduction; "I never felt it till now.
I would my daughter were dead at my foot, and
the jewels in her ear! Would she were hearsed
at my foot, and the ducats in her coffin!"

Far from finding in these words, as Kreyssig,
an example of denial in the usurer of the great
national virtue of his race, the strong, devoted
family feeling—that feeling here speaks to us in
its wildest accents of despair. The fearful desolation of death yawns about him on all sides, with
but the one point of light attaching him to life—
the desire of revenge. This, however, becomes
the tragic cause of depriving him of the last thing
he can call his own—his fortune. Now bursts the
piercing cry from his lips, "Nay, take my life and
all, pardon not that." And now can it be well
understood that he does not belie the recognised
and very admirable national virtue of his race,

either since, or although he is a Jew, but that this
very virtue reconciles his character to that humanity
without which it had not been possible for a Shylock to have existed in the mind of Shakspeare.
His cruelty disappears before the greater and less
excusable cruelty of his judge. We hear only the
complaint of his injured heart trampled in the dust.
" When," says Heine, " I saw this piece in Drury
Lane, there stood behind me in the box a fair, pale
Briton, who, at the end of the fourth act, cried
bitterly, and exclaimed several times, ' The poor
man is wronged!' Her face was of the most noble
Greek type, and her eyes large and black. I have
never been able to forget them—those big black
eyes which wept for Shylock."

We do not, however, venture to believe that
the effect on Shakspeare's contemporaries could
be similar to that on Heine's "pale Briton" of
the nineteenth century. We might, indeed, doubt
whether Shakspeare himself had it in view. His
interest for the Jew may, so we ourselves imagine,
have had a purely pathological origin, but it
became more when he busied himself about him.
For it was impossible for Shakspeare to place
himself in the Jew's position (as, indeed, only
Shakspeare can place himself in another's position) without acknowledging with keen feeling

the utter injustice done to him, without, in accordance with the instinctive greatness of his spirit, taking part against the oppressor, and with the oppressed. Unintentionally the Jew rises out of his original baseness to the really great and masterly figure of the piece, whilst all others, Portia excepted, shrink into insignificance before him. It is true that Shakspeare invests his Hebrew with all the traditional horrors of the Middle Ages, and not to offend the illusive imaginings of the period, he is made to pant for Christian blood. But he has a bitter eloquence, before which no argument of his adversaries may hold ground, a fulness of keenest wit which pierces to the heart, not Christianity, but its believers in this play. Who may speak of Christian humility or Christian generosity, scrutinising the character of that fine, noble man ? But for the last consequence the despised, the slandered Jew—as he is the real hero of the drama—had also withdrawn from it in triumph. Regard, however, for the public opinion of his time, to which he had made several concessions, it may be, forbade the poet drawing this consequence. It would have been little according to its taste, and certainly not have found its approval, had the Jew, after he had lost his cause, retained any high and moral spirit. Much more popular and intelligible was the moral of the ballad of 'Gernutus the Jew,' which concludes with warning all Christian folk in common to beware of the wretches who, with cunning longing, desire our spoil, and to trap our innocence when they may—

> " From whom the Lord deliver me,
>   And every Christian too,
>   And send to them like sentence eke,
>   That meaneth so to do."

In accordance with this, Shakspeare overwhelms the utterly broken-hearted Hebrew with scorn, in which, as we may suppose, the groundlings of the Blackfriars and Globe Theatres strongly participated, and leaves him at the last the choice between the half of his fortune and his faith. What Shakspeare himself thought of the making of proselytes he has put into the mouth of the jester of his piece, Launcelot Gobbo : " This making of Christians will raise the price of hogs; if we grow all pork-eaters, we shall not shortly have a rasher on the coals for money." But the public at the beginning of the seventeenth century might well think otherwise, and Shylock becomes a Christian. So doing, by one stroke he forfeits, as a Jew, all those sympathies which formerly were his, as a human being; when the oppressed so deeply humiliates himself as to confess the faith of his oppressor, he overturns all his premises, and sinks back into a baseness greater than that from which he at first arose. This was no longer the true Jew —who at that very time in Spain and Portugal, with the praise of his God on his lips, mounted, rather than deny Him, the funeral piles of the Inquisition, or only escaped them by wandering in foreign lands a friendless exile.

Such a Jew who loved his God—the God of his fathers, Abraham, Isaac, and Jacob—more than his ducats, more indeed than his daughter, Shakspeare knew not, or if he knew him, yet dared not show him to his contemporaries. But not fifty years later such a Jew England saw.

III.

This Jew was Menasseh ben Israel,* a divine of Amsterdam.

England had gone through the frightful struggle of the Civil Wars. Charles I. had fallen on the scaffold, and Oliver Cromwell stood on the summit of his short, but, for all the future decisive career, which by one sharp stroke separated the Middle Ages from modern time. He, almost the first, proclaimed those two words whose echo was never more completely to die away, Thought-freedom and Toleration. His war against the dark powers of spiritual slavery and violence done to conscience—against the Papacy and its worldly ally—may have forced him to hard measures; but since we have lived to see something similar in our own time, and have learned to know afresh as our enemies those who were his also, we shall not be able any longer to reproach him for his hardness. His great heart appealed for the holy things of humanity, and his strong hand for those who had hitherto suffered on their account.

---

* Kayserling, ' Menasseh ben Israel.' Berlin. 1861.

His idea of a kingdom was that of a kingdom of
God, in which there could be no persecutor; but
the persecuted found in him at all times that which
was expressed in the only title which he would
accept—the Protector.

The fame of this powerful man, whose appearance must have had in it for his Bible-governed
contemporaries something Messianic, spread itself
across the seas to the Jews, who for now nearly
400 years had been barred the coasts of England,
and one of them, Rabbi Menasseh ben Israel, formed
a bold resolution to urge Cromwell for permission
to return. Born in Portugal, and belonging to a
family which, persecuted by the Inquisition, had
forsaken its native land, Menasseh had come, when
quite a child, to Amsterdam; and here, after he had
finished his studies, he became a Rabbi and teacher
of the Talmud in the Jewish institution. Spinoza
was among his pupils. The mounting star of Cromwell aroused Menasseh's observation, and when he
believed the time to have arrived he stepped forward with his plan, the execution of which was especially favoured through the acknowledged and far-
spread affection for the Old Testament in the then
ruling circles of the Independents. After many
steps of a preliminary and private nature, Menasseh
ben Israel at length, in the year 1650, acted openly,

by engaging himself in a petition to Parliament on the subject of the Jews.

Thus we see the question from this precise moment raised to the political ground, which henceforth, and until its complete solution in our own century, it has ever maintained. It was in the year 1653 that, on the occasion of a fresh petition from Menasseh, for the first time, amid lively debates in the English Parliament, it came into discussion, and in the following year an invitation, in diplomatic form, was sent to the Rabbi of Amsterdam, who meanwhile had personally appealed to the Lord Protector, in consequence of which he travelled to London, and there appeared as " Ambassador of the Jewish nation." He was treated with the greatest distinction, and was received by Cromwell at Whitehall in solemn audience. He presented his petition, which embodied the wishes of the Jews, and bore the title, " To His Highness the Lord Protector of the Commonwealth of England, Scotland, and Ireland, the humble address of Menasseh ben Israel, a divine and doctor of physic, in the name of the Jewish nation."* Cromwell received the address graciously,

---

* In the year 1868 a reprint of this Address, of which a copy lies before us, was published in Melbourne.

U

and sought with vigour to advance the cause therein propounded.

But there was not wanting a very heavy opposition, especially on the side of the Presbyterian clergy, which Cromwell had every reason to spare as much as possible; and also on that of the mercantile community, who saw, in the return of the Jews to England, an injury to their own interests. These sought to refer the unselfish and full-hearted benevolence which Cromwell exhibited towards the Jews to the impure motive of a monetary speculation, as though he would have drawn himself out of financial embarrassments by means of their wealth. So says Abraham Cowley, a contemporary Royalist writer in his ' Discourse on Cromwell's Government,' after he has spoken of the burden of the debts of the Protectorate :—" The other plan to raise a suitable sum which he unhappily followed, but could not carry out, was the recalling of the Jews into London. To this end, it is said, he intended to sell them St. Paul's as their synagogue, supposing their piety and purses to be strong enough to buy it. Had he done this to reward the nation who set the first noble example of crucifying their King, he might claim the merit of gratitude, but his prevailing principle was the love of their Mammon."

This hateful report, which was at that time set in circulation as a means of agitation against the friendly efforts of Cromwell for the Jews, and since then has been repeated innumerable times as a charge against his character, has nothing incredible in it, if it be considered that the Cathedral Church of London was then used as a stable,* and that during the naval wars with the Netherlands manifold Bills were brought into Parliament for empowering the Government openly to sell by auction some of the Cathedrals.†

Cromwell, however, had as little to do with these matters as the Jews, and Menasseh ben Israel refuted this directly in his 'Vindication of the Jews' (*Vindiciæ Judæorum*), where he expressly says there was a common report that the Jews had bought St. Paul's for a synagogue. Many other like fables were promulgated, which never for a moment entered into the Jewish imagination.‡

* Carlyle, 'Oliver Cromwell's Letters and Speeches.' Tauchnitz ed. ii. 136. "l'aul's Cathedral, we remark, is now a Horseguard; horses stamp in the Canons' stalls there."

† Guizot, 'Histoire de la Révolution d'Angleterre,' iii. 295. "Des *bills* furent aussi proposés pour la vente des forêts royales, et même de quelques cathédrales, qu'on se proposait de démolir."

‡ Deutsch von Moses Mendelssohn, in his 'Gesammelten Werken,' iii. 218. Leipzig, 1843.

On the contrary, the proposal was made by Harrington—whom we have learned to know in a former chapter as the founder of the first political club, the Rota Club—with all seriousness, in his 'Oceana,' that the kingdom of Ireland should be sold to the Jews, and England in this manner relieved at once of its National Debt and of Ireland. But the Jews were far too good tradesmen to entertain such a proposal, even if it had been made to them.

Besides these small insinuations, there were not wanting voices to bring forward again the old tales of murdered Christian children, which were already so well known to the English people by their ballads. Yet unwearied, during his many years' residence, Menasseh ben Israel carried on his battle against ill-will and prejudice face to face with his opposers. But he was never to attain the great aim which he set for himself, the recall of the Jews by a Parliamentary decree. For a measure that must have recognised the principle of Jewish emancipation, the time had not yet arrived : still, the word had been spoken, ever and ever to be taken up again after every defeat until its final accomplishment. The severe opposition which arose from all sides made Cromwell reflective. He summoned some of the most

esteemed members of the clergy and the legal
profession to a conference in the reception-room
of Whitehall, to sound opinions in some measure
before bringing the subject before Parliament.
Very meagre records have we of this remarkable
assembly; but so much we know, that Cromwell
interested himself with the utmost zeal for the Jews,
and an ear-witness relates that he had never heard
any man speak so well as the Protector did on this
occasion. It ended thus: Cromwell was convinced
that he could not carry through any legal decree,
and decided, therefore, for the practical way of
silent patience. What he could do personally to
the advantage of the Jews, and the honourable
champion of their interests, he did. He distinguished Rabbi Menasseh by a pension under the
State Seal; and had the learned son of the Rabbi,
Samuel ben Israel, made a Doctor of the University of Oxford, as its Chancellor—the first, and
till now only case in which any Jew in England
has received the four-cornered cap, the golden
ring, and the kiss of peace.

So, driven away by the kings, the first Jews
returned to England under the Republic; not,
indeed, by reason of any decree, but simply by
reason of Cromwell's toleration. This last, however, seemed to be itself quite sufficient, as

appears from a remark of the English diarist, Evelyn, who, under date of December 14, 1655, after the last conference at Whitehall, entered the following words in his day-book: "Now are the Jews admitted."

With this prospect for his people, and with high honour for himself, Menasseh ben Israel in the year 1657 returned to Holland, but not again to see his house in Amsterdam. He died after his landing at Middleburg, and was buried in the Jewish burial-ground in Oudekerk. The inscription on his tombstone runs thus: *

"The fame-crowned Menasseh rests buried under me;
　But through the style of iron and lead (that is, through printing)
　Is he in the whole world known as a glory and as an ornament,
　Since his works serve his head for a crown."

Under these lines in Hebrew, we find in the Spanish language, "He is not dead, but lives in the heights of Heaven in holy attire. Here upon earth, however, remain his performances for an eternal memorial." Also, in the Hebrew lan-

---

* I have to thank the kindness of Dr. M. Wiener, in Hanover, for the communication of the above inscription, and its interpretation; he borrowed it from the collection of old epitaphs in that churchyard by De Castro.

guage, round about the stone, we read : "Grave of the distinguished and learned man, Menasseh ben Israel, who died on the 14th of Kislew, 5418" (that is, the 20th of November, 1657).

When two years later his powerful friend and protector, Cromwell, in one stormy September night, followed him into that quiet land, for which, under the burden of the work that rested upon him he had so often longed, the Jews found themselves quietly settled in London, some in Bevis Marks (Aldersgate), some in and about Duke's Place, inhabited even to-day exclusively by Jews, and the seat of their great synagogue. They had received, under Cromwell, in the year 1657, a spot for the interment of their dead, in Stepney, precisely where their hospital is now standing. In the same year they erected their synagogue in King Street, in the neighbourhood of Duke's Place. Seven years later they established their first benevolent society for the study of the law, and for the care of poor Jewish children ; and ten years later their number was so strikingly increased that they elected their first Rabbi in the person of the great Talmudist, Jacob Sasportas, who had come over with Menasseh ben Israel. Up to this time, only Portuguese Jews had established themselves in London ; but

now came also German Jews, who soon formed a
community; and as early as the year 1692, an
equally wealthy and pious member, Moses Hart,
brother of the first of their Rabbins, erected, at his
own cost, a synagogue in Duke's Place, on the
spot on which a hundred years after this, 1791,
the synagogue was built which stands there
at the present day, the largest in London, and
the official seat of the "land and sea rabbin" of
England.

"The dream of a kingdom" of God, which had
had its leader and judge in Cromwell, the Protector, and its holy singer in Milton, the poet
of Paradise Lost and Regained, had disappeared
after ten years' duration, and, as in the Bible,
there followed after the kings.

The Stuarts, when they returned to England,
found the Jews settled there; and as they could
profit by them, did not care to drive them away.
From that time they fared neither better nor
worse in England than in most other countries.

Money transactions truly flourished, especially
in the days of the Restoration of King Charles and
his merry Court, the costs of which were mostly
covered through Jewish loans. Very profitable
this might be for the merchants of Duke's Place,
but they did not gain much honour by it. The

more that was gained by them, the more right there seemed to be to illtreat them. As no one could now take their wealth as in the more simple times of the Plantagenets, they were flattered when it was required, and when it was obtained laughed at. As Louis XIV. took Samuel Bernard, "his Jew," for an airing in his coach in the garden of Versailles when he meditated an attack on his cash, so did the Duchess of Mazarin, after she had fled from France in boy's clothes, and arrived in England, first make an assault on the heart of "her Jew" Moses, when she had need of money.

Saint Evremond, her confident and friend, wrote to his noble mistress, toward whom he indulged a Platonic inclination, while she lived in Charles II.'s castle : " Moses let me go half the way on foot, while he spoke of you in such a manner that not one of Solomon's eight hundred wives equalled you in intelligence or beauty. When he is the master of the shop we are likely to make good bargains." But as another of the country folk of the beautiful Duchess said, " It is much pleasanter to borrow than to repay." Their money was taken at high interest, and the borrower felt himself safe, while he cursed them as usurers and cheats. He increased their wealth, and at the same time covered their person with the stain of dishonour, in doing which he certainly did not reflect, that "where wealth exists, might must necessarily follow."

Since, in the past ages of chivalry and politeness, few had engaged in monetary business, and this business, indeed, had but an insignificant and not seldom a mean character, it was very willingly permitted to the despised race again to take chief possession of it. However, the influence and position of the Jews could not but rise as soon as their occupation itself rose out of its abject sphere, as soon as they increased to importance, as soon as they began to exert an influence in the organism of the State and lend a fresh support to it, which added to Capital its rightful share in the destinies of the State, and which sought to establish, in those youthful days of national economy, the relation of the State to the Capital, as to-day, on a much more advanced scale, the relation of Capital and Labour is sought to be established. Capital was then a power which, for its recognition, had no less to fight than Labour at the present time; one of the first who, to his great credit, did not refuse the recognition of Capital, was Marlborough, the great General.

It is true that the beat of that wonderful pulse, which has continued through five ages of men to show the alterations of the body politic, for the first time found expression, early in the year 1692, in the midst of that long-protracted war, which, to enrich France, devastated the provinces of the Continent; and that this pulse beat again in the year 1699, immediately before the end of that century and the beginning of the long-waged war about the Spanish inheritance. But yet was the great man whom we have named—Marlborough —an English Duke, and Prince of a German kingdom, if not the first, who, with the keen glance of a General, marked the connection between prosperity and the money-market, in any case, the first who opened that wide path for development, in which speculation has since moved, and moves to-day.

There·were joint-stock companies in the year 1692, and the first time-bargains were, according to Macaulay, made early in the year 1694; but the trade with State papers first arose through State debts, and for the last the Spanish war of succession provided. The English National Debt, for instance, which in the year 1689 amounted to little more than half a million, and now, indeed, amounts to some 750,000,000*l.*, was at the end of the Succession War, in 1713, grown to the respectable height of 53,000,000*l.* Marlborough seized on this contingency with skilful hand; and since he gave the element to the business, which up to the present day remains its chief stem and stock, the Duke may well be termed the originator of the new Exchange, on which daily, as F. C. Schlosser says, "in all great States the fate of Europe is bought and sold." But it must be added, for the honour of the Duke, that no one may venture to point to him as the originator of stock-jobbing. Johnson says in his dictionary that this word has no etymology; but we find it as early as two hundred years ago used as a cant phrase, and jobbery was then (ironically enough, if we think of the later destiny of the expression) synonymous with robbery. The word in its present use meets us in a comedy by Shadwell, performed in 1693, 'The Volunteers, or the Stock-jobbers;' and Macaulay resents it as an error that the existence of stock-jobbing should be ascribed to the National Debt, whilst the former preceded the latter by many years, and made use of it for its own interest with all its power as soon as it came into existence.

Meanwhile the position of the Jews in England had somewhat improved, especially since William's accession to the throne. Machado was his favourite, and another Jew, Suasso by name, had advanced to him the sum of two millions for his expedition to England, with these words :—" Si vous êtes malheureux, je consens de les perdre ; " an action, the nobility of which has been mentioned with praise by Frederick the Great in his ' Mémoires de Brandebourg.' * As William was thus fortunate, it may be supposed that he was also *grateful*. So remarks the " Voyageur en Angleterre " who visited England in the year 1698 :†—" The Jews of London (I know not whether it be the same elsewhere in England) have gradually ceased to wear the yellow hat which they were formerly engaged to wear, and at present have no distinctive dress."

It was about this time that a mania arose, which we have since had the opportunity of learning to know in its various forms as swindling.

A Scotch adventurer, of the name of John Law, had established himself in Paris, and there had

---

* Compare Grätz, Voltaire and the Jews, in Frankel's 'Monatsschrift.' 1868. Maiheft, p. 214.

† In Germany this engagement for the Jews endured far into the following century; in Frankfort - on - the - Maine, Charles VI. first released them from it.

founded a joint-stock company, known as the
Indian Company, for the purpose of gaining a
monopoly of trade with the Mississippi provinces.
Swindling. is always infectious, and soon all Paris
and the whole of France was attacked by it. The
shares rose to twenty times the price of their
original value, and the *chimerical* value exceeded
(Voltaire, 'Siècle de Louis XV.') *by twenty times*
all the money that was then in circulation in the
French kingdom. In the Rue Quincampoix, the
principal theatre of this affair, from break of
day an impatient and busy multitude thronged,
knowing, as it seemed, no other hunger than that
of gold, which let pass by the regular hours of
meals, a multitude which could not be dispersed
even at night, until after a bell had given the
signal for the close of business. The smallest
chamber in this street was hired for an enormous
sum. The commissioners were not in a position
to be able to take note quickly enough of the
buyers as they pressed forward, and Lord Mahon,
in his 'History of England,' relates that a little
cripple made not less than fifty thousand francs,
in lending his hump to the eager speculators for
them to sign their contracts on.

But this cripple was the only one who became
rich through all this monstrous speculation; for,

as the noble historian whom we have before mentioned says, " Although at first it was a farce, it afterwards became a tragedy."

Its end began when it appeared that there were, indeed, no countries about the Mississippi with which it was possible to carry on any commerce ; but this discovery was not made (for at that time, as is well known, there were no steamboats or telegraphs) before the disease had spread to England, but with this difference, that here it went deeper among the true populace, and again higher into the Government circles, and even to the throne itself, which George the First had ascended five years before—a good husband and careful father—so far, to wit, as high percentage was considered. This, under the new title of the South Sea Company, left nothing, indeed, to be desired. The shares which had stood at 130*l.* in the winter, in the following August stood at 1000*l.* The misfortune was that the riches of the South Sea, on which the English Company speculated, had, if possible, even less existence than those of the Mississippi, which John Law had monopolised. The double crash happened at almost the same time, 1720, and the blow was frightful in both countries. In Paris the people clamoured only for the head of John

Law, who saved his life by flight; but in London
rang the cry, "the swindle of the Prince of
Wales!" through Change Alley and the corridors
of the Exchange Buildings. Blood and confisca-
tion were demanded; an insurrection threatened;
the mistresses of the King were persecuted;—
Parliament ordered an inquiry, but thousands of
hitherto well-to-do families were ruined.

Like the cobbler in France, so in England, but
two people had gained by the general collapse—
a Minister and a Jew. The Minister was Robert
Walpole, who had sold his shares when they stood
at 1000*l.*, with the words "I am content;" and
the Jew was Samson Gideon, the son of a West
Indian merchant.

Samson Gideon had not enriched himself in *one*
campaign with Marlborough, or with *one* speculation as Walpole; he had chosen the more tedious
course. He had not drawn any profit from the
losses of others, like the Minister; with the exception of this one profit; namely, that he learnt
how one should *not* carry on such operations. He
had in the South Sea affair, and the hundred other
swindling transactions that were connected with
it, run through his curriculum, and the experiences
which he therein made were soon to bring him
good. An honourable, honest, and prudent man,

he knew how to make himself the friend of
Robert Walpole, who was tolerant enough to avail
himself of the help of a Jew, in those financial
complications with which he was always concerned.
One of the principal sources of revenue for the
State in those days were the class lotteries, and
in this department it was that Samson Gideon,
under the protection of the Minister, laid the
foundation of his future wealth. But he made his
master-stroke in 1745, when the great Jacobite
insurrection threw the British world, and the mercantile world especially, into the wildest consternation. Charles Edward, the last of the Stuarts,
had landed on one of the Scottish islands, and
calling the clans under arms, had proclaimed his
father, the Pretender, under the name of James
the Third, King of Great Britain and Ireland, and
was now, with his army of Highlanders, on the
march to London, and but a few miles distant
from the Capital.

The panic at the Exchange was universal. The
funds fell with incredible rapidity, and every one
wanted to sell at any price. Samson Gideon was
almost the only man who did not lose his head.
Instead of selling, he spent every penny he had or
could borrow in buying. This was in the month
of November. During the following month the

public mind oscillated between hope and fear. At
length, at the end of April of 1746, the news
arrived of the battle of Culloden, of the complete
defeat of the insurgent army, of the flight of the
Prince, and of the triumphant suppression of the
rebellion by the Duke of Cumberland. Now
Samson Gideon began to sell, and in a short time
found himself in possession of something like a
quarter of a million—a sum which in the course
of fourteen or fifteen years quadrupled itself.

During the first half of the last century, Samson
Gideon's was one of the greatest houses, if not the
greatest house in the City of London, distinguished
especially, and deservedly so, not merely for correct
accounts, but for its ever-enduring superiority in
its promotion of assurances and revenues. But
Samson Gideon's ambition culminated in the effort
to form an *English* house. He was too old, he said,
to change his religion, but he had his children
baptized; and, through Walpole's instrumentality,
his eldest son was made a baronet when in his
eleventh year. The worthy man gave himself
especial trouble to make the presumptive successor
to his house firm in his new religion; and on one
occasion tried to catechise him on the most important points. " Who made thee?" was his first
question. " God," answered the boy. " Who re-

deemed thee?" he further asked, without his conscience presenting any difficulties to him. "Jesus
Christ," was the answer. But what was the third
question? Gideon could not remember what he
ought to ask in the third place. "Who—who,"
he stammered, and when absolutely nothing better
occurred to him, he asked, "Who has given you
this hat?" The young catechumen, Samson
Gideon, Jun., Baronet of England, was more sure
of his business than his father, and answered,
"The Holy Ghost." *

Gideon, senior, died in the faith of his fathers,
1762. He left behind him, as heirs of his immense fortune, a son and a daughter; and legacies
amounting to above 100,000 thalers, which were
to be divided in equal shares between Jewish
and Christian benevolent societies and poor. It
seemed as if on his death-bed he was unwilling
to injure himself with either of the two faiths.
"Gideon is dead," we read in the letter of a contemporary, "and his inheritance is worth more
than the whole of Canaan."

Samson Gideon belonged to that portion of the
Jews which, under the name of "Sephardim," or

---

* H. R. F(ox) B(ourne), 'The Merchant Princes of England.'
'London Society,' vol. ix. 1866.

" Portuguese " Jews, differs only in a few almost
immaterial ritual points (as, for instance, the pro-
nunciation of the Hebrew) from the Aschken-
esim, the German, or Polish Jews. The Portuguese Jews, under the ennobling influences of the
sunny south, and centuries passed in friendly
intercourse with the highly-cultivated Moors and
chivalrous Spaniards, became the nobility of the
Jewish people, whose beauty, knowledge, and
poetry they preserved, and took with them in their
second exile, when they fled from the Inquisition :
while the other branch of the Jews, more numerous
and enterprising, after its wandering through the
less cultivated lands of the north, and its residence
among rude inhabitants of Russia, Poland, and
Germany, brought with it the traces of its natural
and spiritual impress.

To say that these two branches were two sects
would be too much, although we have almost as
much as considered them so already. At the present time the best understanding exists between
the two in London and elsewhere, but thirty or
forty years ago, the bitterest animosity reigned
between their synagogues, of which the Portuguese held itself by far more important, and indeed
was so in its connections, than the German, and a
marriage between the followers of the one and the

other was regarded as a family misfortune. Nowhere did this separation appear to have developed itself more sharply and more completely than
in England. For these Sephardim, or Children of
Israel, were only too pleased, perhaps influenced
by a feeling of dislike towards their less preferred
brethren, to turn from the faith of their fathers in
order to make the nobility, of which they considered themselves the supporters, of importance
in a social and acknowledged sense. " They had
never," says the Right Hon. Benjamin Disraeli, in
the noble and simple biographical memorial of the
meritorious antiquarian, his father, Isaac D'Israeli,
" they had never left the coast of the Mediterranean
till Torquemada drove them out of their fair
palaces and rich possessions in Aragon, and Anda-
lusia, and Portugal, to seek even greater blessings
than a clear atmosphere and a glowing sun in the
marshes of Holland."

There remains no doubt that many of the
greatest and most important families of the second
Jewish migration, from the time of Cromwell,
belonged to this Portuguese branch; but it is
just as certainly a mistake, when the Right Hon.
B. Disraeli says that *all* of them were Sephardim,
and that they had closed their synagogues to
the Hebrews of Northern Europe, who occasionally

had stolen into England, as from a lower caste. As we have noticed long before, a synagogue had been built by the German Jews in Duke's Place early in the year 1692; and if the Portuguese were considered superior to the Germans at first in number, cultivation, and rank, the comparison of the two branches of the Jewish community would certainly in the course of the eighteenth century have resulted to the discredit of the Portuguese, after their great families became untrue to them : such as the family of the Villa Reals, which has brought wealth to these shores almost as great as its name, although it is but the second in Portugal, and which has twice connected itself with the English aristocracy; or those of the Medinas, the Laras, and the Mendez da Costas, members of which last family I have known in London, and now know in Manchester, and who have never changed their religion.

To the Sephardim family, who came to England at the time already mentioned and in the manner before described, the family of D'Israeli belonged. This family also, about the end of the fifteenth century, had been obliged by the Inquisition to emigrate from the Spanish Peninsula. Like so many others of their fellows in faith and suffering, they sought an asylum on the then tolerant soil of

Italy, and found it in the Venetian Republic. Here they laid down their proudly-sounding name which they had borne in the land where, until their fall under Ferdinand and Isabella, it had not been unusual for Jews to be the ministers and the physicians to the King; and thankful to the God of Jacob, who had supported them under unparalleled trials and preserved them through unheard of dangers, they gave themselves the name of D'Israeli, a name never before or since borne by any other family, by which their race should be known for ever after.

Unchecked and unimpeded, they flourished as merchants during two centuries, under the protection of the Lion of St. Mark; and early in the time when the rapid rise of Samson Gideon's house drew the eyes of the Jewish mercantile world towards London, the then representative of the D'Israelis at Venice, sent thither the younger of his two sons, Benjamin, " the son of his right hand," the grandfather of him who has been three times Chancellor and once Premier of England.

With the elegance which has always distinguished the pen of the last named, he has related to us the story of the conversion of his family to Christianity, rich in typical features and motives, which indeed generally in similar cases have been

similarly influential. His grandfather had little
intercourse with his fellows in faith, and at most
was indifferent to them. The motive power of his
final rupture with them was his wife. " My grand-
mother," says the late Prime Minister of England,
"the fair daughter of a family who had suffered
much from persecution, had imbibed that dislike for
her race which the vain are too apt to adopt when
they find that they are born to public contempt.
The indignant feeling that should be reserved for
the persecutor, in the mortification of their disturbed
sensibility, is too often visited on the victim, and
annoyance is recognised, not in the ignorant
malevolence of the powerful, but in the con-
scientious conviction of the innocent sufferer."

This feeling of personal injury, so truly described
by a man in whom family tradition has preserved
many of its features, contributed, and contributes
yet more and more, to drive irritable natures, such
as the Jews possess, to a resolve which other worldly
advantages would have wrung from them only in
the most exceptional cases. Yet the battle lasted
seventeen years in the family of D'Israeli.

At the beginning of the year 1782 their conversion to Christianity took place, and Benjamin
D'Israeli, the grandfather, was now a man who,
richly blessed with all good things, gained for him-

self an estate in the neighbourhood of London, laid
out a garden in the Italian style, " entertained his
friends, played whist with Sir Horace Mann, who
had known his brother at Venice as a banker, eat
macaroni, which was dressed by the Venetian con-
sul, sang canzonettes, and notwithstanding a wife
who never pardoned him for his name, and a son
who disappointed all his plans, lived till he was
nearly ninety, and then died in 1817, in the full
enjoyment of prolonged existence."

This son, " to the last hour of his life an enigma
to him," was Isaac D'Israeli, one of the most
amiable of bibliographers and searchers into the
byways of history, whose books contain an
amassed treasure of anecdotal knowledge, and will
long form pleasant reading for the English, and a
compendium of inestimable worth for the curious
of that nation. Isaac D'Israeli died, aged eighty-
two, in February 1848, on his estate of Bradenham,
in Buckinghamshire; and here, amidst memorials
of John Hampden, whose daughter was once
Countess of Bradenham, Benjamin Disraeli developed into the great Member of Parliament and
teacher of Constitutional Opposition, the eminent
statesman and novelist, whom we all know. It may
well have been the aristocratic bias of his forefathers that induced him to fight out for himself a

place among the great feudal nobility which he reflects in all his novels. But, to his honour let it be said, never has he been ashamed of his origin or denied it, either in his romances, in which he knew how to combine the glorious romance of the Middle Ages with a fanciful enthusiasm for Judaism, or in his Parliamentary course, in which he, a bold champion for Jewish Emancipation, contributed no little to bring this question to a happy issue under the second Derby Administration to which he belonged.

Little had the grandfather of the Chancellor of the Exchequer foreseen this position and aim of his successor, when he turned back from business on the eve of that great financial epoch with which his talents enabled him so well to wrestle, and, when the war and the loan of the Revolution began, to form those families of millionaires, among which he would gladly have seen his own enrolled. "But that was not our destiny," says, with a modest laugh, the recognised Tory leader.

Indeed, the "Gold Principality in Israel" had now passed from the Portuguese branch to that of the Germans in London. During the whole of the eighteenth century, in England's large towns, especially London and Bristol, a constant increase of the Jewish element was perceptible, and it

made a great stride at the end of the before-named
period, when the war with France, and the Continental embargo brought about by Napoleon, provoked smuggling to the greatest extent. Now
came that concentration of Jews, chiefly from North
Germany, Hamburg, Hanover, the Rhine, and Holland, in which last country their position had
become especially precarious, as being shut off from
all lawful trade, they were restricted to diamond-
cutting—a business in which some became rich, but
most went to the ground.

More firmly hanging upon old traditions, these
wanderers from the North had to suffer doubly,
from the reserve with which their fellows in faith,
refined by their residence in the South, looked down
upon them, and from the religious prejudice of the
English. To be sure, a happy effort had been
once made in the middle of the century to give
them a home-right in that land, in which they
now for nearly a hundred years had peaceably
lived. A Naturalisation Bill passed in 1753, by a
great majority, through both Houses of Parliament; but the City of London, with the Mayor
at its head, bore the matter so impatiently, that it
nearly brought about an insurrection. Great
masses of people thronged the streets of London
with the cry, " No Jews, no wooden shoes ;" and the

effect on the country did not fail. The witty Horace
Walpole wrote to his friend, Sir H. Mann, British
Ambassador at Florence : " You feared the fulfilment of the prophecies which announced misfortune and eternal dispersion to the Jews would be
hindered by an Act of Parliament, and their zeal
but wanted the presentation of a petition to both
Houses to determine the fulfilment of those prophecies. The country parsons preached against
the bishops for making the Gospel untrue, and
aldermen got drunk in country clubs in the honour
of Jesus Christ, as they had done formerly for the
King of Jacob."

The Bill was obliged to be withdrawn ; but the
Jewish question had run its second course, and
shown what progress it had made since the
debates in the year 1655, when the subject had last
been openly treated. The intelligent portion of
the nation, its legislators, and highest clergy, were
won over to it. But how greatly the people were
opposed to it was to become manifest, and at one
time most menacingly, on the occasion of the Gordon Riots in 1780, in which the rioters, though
certainly first of all intent only on the Catholics,
taking advantage of the favourable opportunity,
began also as they passed along to demolish the
houses of the Jews, who, in order to protect

themselves, wrote on their window-shutters, " This is a true Protestant house." In the meantime the community, which at the beginning of the century had in London numbered no more than sixty or seventy families, with one synagogue, had increased so much by immigration, that it had in 1770 three synagogues.

The great man of this time—the era of George III. —was *Aaron Goldsmid*. He was not so rich as Samson Gideon, but he was the better man, and certainly a stricter Jew in the inviolable traditions of his Church. Goldsmid had come from Hamburg, and established himself in London as a merchant in the middle of the century. His house arrived at its highest prosperity after his death, under his four sons, and the *coup* which every house must at some time make when it wishes to raise itself at one effort above others, this firm made at the time of the French Revolution. At the head of the business were then the two brothers, Abraham and Benjamin ; men of acknowledged integrity, and allied in friendship with Newland, the then chief cashier of the Bank of England. He also was a self-made man, who had risen from a baker's shop to his enormously influential position ; in which his administration was of so much service, that his likeness at the present day adorns the so-

called " Bank parlour," the sitting-room of the Bank
Directors. By means of Newland the brothers
Goldsmid were brought into connection with the
Government, which, since the year 1793, was compelled to have recourse to continual loans in consequence of the Continental War. But it was not
only what was won through a conspicuous share in
these operations that raised the wealth of the
brothers, but rather this, that they did *not* lose at
a time when, through war and revolution in all
corners of Europe, great houses broke in numbers
from day to day. One of the most noticeable
characteristics of Benjamin was his astonishing
knowledge of firms, which was not confined merely
to England, but embraced the whole money
market in and out of Europe. He valued with a
certainty bordering on the marvellous every name
which he found on the back of any bill. The firm
had to thank this circumstance that in the dangerous year 1794, when through the increasing
war of the Revolution the foundation walls of the
whole commercial world tottered, and great firms
fell like card-houses round them, the entire loss of
the brothers Goldsmid came to no more than 50*l.*
sterling. At the beginning of the present century
there was no house in London greater, more
brilliant and universally esteemed than this. The

magnificence of its undertakings was no less famed
than its solidity. The benevolence of its members,
especially towards their fellows in faith, knew no
bounds. Their hospitality, offered with open hand,
was eagerly and willingly received. They had
splendid houses in town and rich possessions in the
country, where they not seldom collected around
them the most distinguished men and the leaders of
the society of that period.

But a sad end was destined for this house, which
had been in every respect so great and esteemed.
One morning in April 1808, the youngest brother,
Benjamin, was found dead in his bedroom. In a
fit of melancholy, to which he was more and more
subject in the latter part of his life, he had hanged
himself to his bed-post.

His elder brother, Abraham, did not long survive
him. Ever afterwards he mourned the loss of his
brother, to whom he had been deeply attached
during the whole of his life; and it seemed as if
with that brother the star of the house of Goldsmid
had paled. No undertaking would prosper, as in the
old fashion; and at last, in the year 1810, Abraham
embarked his whole fortune on a fresh Government loan of 14,000,000*l.* sterling, which he discounted with the house of Baring. The business
failed. The house of Baring, also of German

origin, and now of European fame, survived the crash; but its chief, Sir Francis Baring, died, and Abraham Goldsmid—shot himself.

In the gap which two such powerful men had left in the city of London a new name appears, *Rothschild*. The house of Rothschild, or, as the English will persistently call it, "Ross-scheild," established its world-wide power on the ruins of the house of Goldsmid.

When we speak of Rothschild, every one knows what that means. Greater than Gideon, greater than Goldsmid, the house of Rothschild rules not only the money-market of the City, but that of the whole world. It was left for our age to observe the accumulation of riches, to which those of Crœsus bear the same relation as the hanging gardens of Semiramis and other wonders of the ancient world, to, let us say, the Crystal Palace at Sydenham, the railway over the Semmering, the Mont Cenis tunnel, and the Transatlantic cable. And yet it is but a hundred years ago that a very unpretending little man, in a very unpretending house, and behind a very unpretending counter, sat under the sign of the Red Shield in the Jews' Street of Frankfort; no more than seventy-five years ago that the French marched into Frankfort, and Meyer Amschel fled with his gold and silver to Cassel, and

entrusted it to the keeping of the Landgrave of
Hesse; not more than sixty-six years ago that the
Landgrave, in the meantime advanced to the Elec-
torate, flying before the French, entrusted *his* gold
and silver to his business friend in Frankfort; and
no more than sixty years ago that this Meyer
Amschel Rothschild, who was born six years
before Goethe, died at the age of sixty-nine years,
leaving behind him 12,000,000 florins. To be
sure at the present time, under the new conjunc-
tures and constellations in the financial world, the
house of Rothschild no longer holds, as it did
ten years ago, an uncontested power. Other
powers, the great Credit Institutes, have grown
up near it and forced it into the shade: Association has broken its isolated rule. But we all
remember the time when the name of this dynasty
was connected with every great operation in the
money market; and by the side of many other
deposed princes of the last ten years the house of
Rothschild will always maintain an historical
interest.

With what emotion did Börne lead the young
Heine, one winter evening of the year 1827, through
the Jews' Street of Frankfort, which, so dark
by day, was then gaily illuminated, because " the
children of Israel on that evening, as my cicerone

Y

told me, celebrated their joyful Feast of Lamps."
They stood before the house of old Madame
Rothschild. "Do you see," said Börne ('Hein-
rich Heine, on Ludwig Börne,' p. 35), "here in
this small house dwells the old woman, the
Lætitia, who has borne so many financial Buona-
partes; the great mother of all loans, who, in
spite of the magnificence of her kingly sons,
the rulers of the world, will never leave her
small family castle in the Jews' Street, and has
to-day adorned her windows with white curtains
in honour of the great feast of joy. How pleasantly sparkle the little lamps, which she has
kindled with her own hands to celebrate the day
of victory, in which Judas Maccabæus and his
brethren so bravely and nobly delivered their
fatherland, as in our days Frederick William,
Alexander, and Francis II. While the old lady
looks on these lamps the tears start in her eyes,
and she remembers with a sad delight that younger
time when her dear husband, the sainted Meyer
Amschel Rothschild, celebrated the Feast of Lamps
with her; and her sons were yet small babies, who
planted their little lamps on the floor, and jumped
over them here and there in childish ecstasy, as is
the way and custom in Israel."

Upon his death-bed Meyer Amschel made his

five sons bind themselves by an oath that they
would never separate, but would carry on the
business in company; that they would augment
the property as much as possible, but never divide
it. Every one knows how conscientiously this
oath has been fulfilled; and the consequence was
that the house of Rothschild, increasing with
each year, grew powerful, not merely in its
riches, but in the number of its sons, sons-in-
law, nephews, and grandsons; a house which
divided within itself the principal exchanges of
the world, which was diplomatically represented
in foreign parts, and finally which regulated its
affairs, its marriages, its dowries and inheritances
by its own family laws. The principal of this
new dynasty was, so long as he lived, the London
Rothschild, Nathan Meyer, the third son of the
old Amschel.

Nathan Meyer came to England in his twenty-
first year, towards the end of the last century,
with a starting capital of no more than 20,000*l.*
sterling. He first went to Manchester, where the
calico trade had risen to a height before unknown.
The young man understood how to pursue his
advantage; and whilst his modest competitors
were satisfied with being either manufacturers or
sellers, Nathan Meyer was both, and acted also as

banker for all. His exertion repaid itself so well, that in about six years his fortune had increased tenfold. With this 200,000*l.* he betook himself, in 1803, to London, the theatre of mercantile greatness, in which he in a very short time became of such consequence that Levi Barnett Cohen, a Jewish City magnate of the first rank, gave him his daughter in marriage.

It is said that he almost repented entrusting his child's fate to a young man whose speculations grew daily more bold and hazardous, but Nathan Meyer consoled him with the remark, " You have only, Mr. Cohen, given me one of your daughters, but you could have made no better financial speculation than by giving me the lot."

The War of Independence was the great event for Nathan Meyer and his house. First appearing as a rival of the then sovereign house of Goldsmid, he expected the restoration of the Bourbons. He reckoned that the last day of the Revolution would be just as decisive for the fortune of the Rothschilds as its first had been for the fortunes of the Goldsmids. He set himself in readiness for the war, taking the opportunity of the Government loan of 1810, in consequence of which the two greatest banking-houses of the time, Gideon and Baring, fell. Upon this, Nathan

Meyer opened *his* campaign. He bought up the bills which Wellington discounted in the midst of the Spanish war, and which the English Government had no money to pay. Through the prolongation of these bills, Nathan Meyer accredited himself to the Government, and made a good business. A direct relation between him and the Government was now set on foot. It found him very necessary because of his Continental connections, and made use of them repeatedly as its agents. Through his hand the moneys passed to the army, and the subsidies to the Allied Powers. Supplied with the most accurate news which were to be had, through his brothers on the Continent, he learnt more, by means of his relations to the English Ministry, of its home and foreign politics than any other man in England. And he was never wanting to the occasion. He became suddenly a breeder of pigeons. His acquaintances, who had not been hitherto aware of any bucolic tendencies in the bold financier, were astounded, but the root of the matter was that he was educating carriers. His pigeons soon flew to south and east, whilst fast-sailing vessels on the shortest route which he could discover by the aid of sea-charts, carried his messengers, and sacks of gold, to and from the coasts of Germany, France, and

England. It does no little honour to the keen-wittedness of this wonderful man, that the packet-boats which ply at the present day between Folkestone and Boulogne have selected as the shortest passage much the same way which Nathan Meyer first discovered for his own sailing-vessels.

Whilst in this manner Nathan Meyer made his movements, the great armies made theirs. The victorious fires of Leipsic, the entrance of the Allies into Paris, Elba, the Hundred Days—all this drove Wellington and Blücher, but also Nathan Meyer, to the crisis, to the battle of Waterloo. At this battle Nathan Meyer was present in person. From his lurking-corner, in the neighbourhood of the Castle of Hougoumont, he followed the fluctuations of the 18th of June with no less anxiety than did Wellington or Napoleon. But when towards evening he understood that the Prussians were there, and saw Wellington and Blücher at sunset greet each other on the heights of Belle Alliance, he said, "The house of Rothschild has won the battle!" and mounted a horse which during the whole day had been standing ready saddled for him. He rode through the whole night, and arrived early in the morning at Ostend. The sea

was so stormy that no sailor was willing to take
him across. At last he succeeded in inducing
a fisherman to make the attempt for 80*l*. By
evening he was at Dover, and on the Exchange
in London early on the 20th of June. Reports of
the gloomiest nature had meanwhile been spread
over the City, and Nathan Meyer took particularly good care not to disperse them. In the
sole possession of the secret, he was as eager
to buy, by means of his agents, as all others
were anxious to sell. When on the 21st of June
the Exchange closed, the paper chests of Nathan
Meyer in St. Swithin's Lane were crammed, and
an hour later arrived the Government courier
with despatches from the field of battle. The
whole of London rang with shouts of victory,
and the next morning the Exchange opened with
fabulous prices. On an English ship of war
the mighty son of the Revolution, the captive
Emperor, was carried to his rocky prison of
St. Helena. Louis XVIII. once more ascended
the throne of the Bourbons, and Nathan Meyer
stood under his pillar in the south corner of the
Exchange Buildings of London richer by about
a million.

From this day dates the lustre of the house of
Rothschild. Enterprises of moderate, or perhaps

unfortunate results, like the English loan of 1819,
or the French of 1823, were more than compensated by other enterprises, which like the gain of
the mines of Almada in Spain, and of Idria in
Illyria, made the Rothschilds monopolists of the
whole quicksilver traffic of Europe. By degrees
the house became the agent of almost all Govern-
ments, and all great loans were concluded in great
part by its means. But the brothers, mindful
of the oath which they had made to their dying
father, maintained faithful partnership; and by the
marriage of male and female cousins, almost without exception, the colossal fortune remained over
the second generation, not only in an unlessened,
but in a continually, by its own power, increasing
bulk. How rich Nathan Meyer became for his
own part no one knows. Some estimated him
at three, others at ten millions sterling. But both
calculations are probably below the mark. He
left to his widow an annuity of 20,000*l.* besides
his residence in, and a landed estate near London.
Each one of his four sons as soon as he attained
his majority had to receive 25,000*l.*, and was to
possess, further, 75,000*l.* upon his marriage. To
his three daughters, besides the 25,000*l.* which
each one received on arriving at her majority,
he left by will 100,000*l.* ; one half as a marriage

gift, and the other half to remain in the business, and with interest at four per cent. It was on the wedding day of his eldest son, Lionel, who in the year 1836 married one of his Neapolitan cousins, that Nathan Meyer was suddenly taken ill. A few days later, on the 28th of July, he died, not sixty years of age, and on the following morning one of his carrier-pigeons, which flew over Brighton, was accidentally shot. It was to bring to London the news of his death. On its neck was found a slip of paper with these three words, " Il est mort."*

---

* H. R. F. B.   'The Merchant Princes of England,' &c.

IV.

The day had now arrived in which Macaulay's proverb was to be verified, namely, that power must necessarily follow wealth. For the third time in the course of two hundred years had the Jews' question been brought before Parliament, and this time to disappear from it no more until its complete solution. The battle lasted for twenty-eight years, but its conclusion was a decided victory.

It was in the year 1830, that Mr. Robert Grant made a motion, to be allowed to bring into Parliament a Bill which removed the civil disabilities of the Jews. The motion was carried through its first reading by a majority of eighteen voices, but fell in the second by a majority of thirty-six. Upon this Macaulay, in January in the year 1831, wrote his classic essay on the civil disabilities of the Jews. In it he says: " The points of difference between Christianity and Judaism have very much to do with a man's fitness to be a Bishop or a Rabbi. But they have no more to do with his fitness to be a magistrate, a legislator, or a

minister of finance, than with his fitness to be a
cobbler. Nobody has ever thought of compelling
cobblers to make any declaration on the true faith
of a Christian . . . Men act thus, not because they
are indifferent to religion, but because they do not
see what religion has to do with the mending of
their shoes. Yet religion has as much to do with
the mending of shoes as with the budget and the
army estimates." Again : "He said it would be
impious to let a Jew sit in Parliament. But a
Jew may make money; and money may make
Members of Parliament. Gatton and old Sarum
may be the property of a Hebrew. An elector of
Penrhyn will take 10 pounds from Shylock rather
than 9 pounds 19 shillings and 11 pence three
farthings from Antonio. . . . That a Jew should
be a Privy Councillor to a Christian King would
be an eternal disgrace to the nation. But the Jew
may govern the money-market, and the money-
market may govern the world. The Minister may
be in doubt as to his scheme of finance till he has
been closeted with the Jew. A Congress of
Sovereigns may be forced to summon the Jew to
their assistance. The scrawl of the Jew on the
back of a piece of paper may be worth more than
the Royal word of three Kings or the national
faith of three new American Republics."

In the year 1833, Mr. Grant brought forward his motion again, and this time, supported by the warm eloquence of Macaulay, it passed through with *éclat*.

Parliament was opened to the Jews. The only thing now was to set foot in it. But this was not so easy. In the first place a Jew must be elected. It was to be shown whether the people in a body were as enlightened as their representatives in Parliament. For a hundred years, from 1653 to 1753, Parliament had not given a favourable regard to the subject. Now it was to be seen what progress the people had made in the next hundred years, from the eighteenth to the nineteenth century.

As early as 1836, the first Jew, Mr. Salomon, presented himself before an English constituency at Shoreham, but without success. In 1841 he again appeared before that of Maidstone, and this time with no better result. But in the year 1847 two Jews were elected at the same time for the City, Mr. Salomon at Greenwich, and Baron Lionel Rothschild, the son of Nathan Meyer. When, however, both of them, using their rights, were about to take their seats, there was still a last hindrance in their way, the formulary of the oath. This excluded them for another eleven years. It was the last stage in the two hundred years' battle.

The words of the oath, "upon the true faith of a Christian," had also so far excluded the Jews from the acquisition of any municipal freedom, and thereby from any municipal honours. But it was now, after the Church and State had long made good what they had done against the Jews in the days of Cromwell, that the City which had declared itself against them, even to the times of the Pelhams, itself first opened for them a way into Parliament. The impulse in favour of the Jews was universal. The whole population of England, of all classes, was prompt to recognise in them fellow-citizens. As a significant token of the change of feeling must be noticed the gigantic success of a piece which had been written with the express object of pleading for the long-despised race, 'The Jew,' by Cumberland. Brought out in the last decade of the foregone century (1793) at Drury Lane, this play remained for more than a third part of our own a favourite of the British public. It was also familiar on the German stage, and even at the present time it occasionally appears upon the boards. A piece with a particular purpose, in the best sense of the expression, its

poetical worth was not sufficient to conquer prejudice; but the hardest part of the task was,
just the reverse of what is seen in Germany,
accomplished already on political ground. To
begin the contest a Lessing was necessary. In
England it had prospered so far that a Cumberland was sufficient. On the other hand, the difference between Shakspeare's and Cumberland's
Jew, between Shylock and Scheva, shows the
great distance which public opinion had travelled
during two centuries. Scheva, though without
any civil right, has yet a sort of acknowledged
existence as a citizen. He lives in Duke's Place,
is the broker of a rich City merchant, Sir Stephen
Bertram, and "no man's character stands higher
in Change Alley," the then Exchange of London.
Though in his outward appearance not much
better than Shylock, his injured feeling does
not erect itself stubborn, proud, and revenge-
ful against his persecutor, but his heart is
tender and gentle, and "flows," as Börne says,
"abroad in a sea of beneficence." A niggard
in the satisfaction of his own wishes, he is a
spendthrift in fulfilling those of others in hard
battle with himself, he converts his enemies into
friends. "Speak not of my goodness, I give
nothing for the sake of goodness. When pity

is loosed from my heart, whether I will or not, I give—what can I do else?" The end of the piece does not exhibit the poor Scheva humbled and ashamed, but the rich City merchant and baronet of England. "This is the man," exclaims Ratcliffe, as he points to his benefactor, "the widow's friend! the orphan's father! the poor man's protector! the universal philanthropist!" Upon which Scheva, who had promised to his young Christian friend his entire fortune, replies, "I do not bury it in a synagogue, or in any other pile; I do not waste it upon vanity or public works, I leave it to a charitable heir, and build my hospital in the human heart."

Not all Jews are Schevas, but, as this one says to the rich City merchant, "so are not all Christians Bertrams."

"It is curious," says Lamb, in his analysis of Marlowe's 'Jew of Malta' ('Specimens of English Dramatic Poets.' Bohn's edition, p. 28), "to see a superstition wearing out. The idea of a Jew, which our pious ancestors contemplated with such horror, has nothing in it now revolting. We have tamed the claws of the beast and pared its nails, and now we take it to our arms, fondle it, write plays to flatter it: it is visited by princes, affects a taste, patronises the arts, and is the

only liberal and gentlemanlike thing in Christendom."

We have heard similar pious ejaculations in Germany from over-anxious minds; but neither here
nor in England have they hindered the Jew's quiet
and steady progress; and after the good citizens
of London had wondered at the noble Scheva for
thirty-seven years on the stage of Drury Lane,
they gave to him the long-sought right of citizen-
ship. It was in the year 1830 that, after the
alteration of the formulary, the first Jew was
allowed civic honour, and in 1835 Mr. David
Salomon became Sheriff of London and Middle-
sex. In the year 1845, under Sir Robert Peel,
the Act passed through Parliament which permitted, on the installation into office, the addition
" on the true faith of a Christian " to be dispensed
with, and immediately we see two Jews as aldermen of Aldgate and Portsoken.

They had now passed through the great City
gate, and it could not be long before they might
venture to step into Parliament. A precedent
was established, and the stream of public feeling
was too strong for the last hindrance not at last
to yield. Meanwhile the Jews did everything on
their side, and in respect to this matter no name
will have a more honourable recollection attached

to it through the future than that of *Sir Moses Montefiore*. One of the first Jewish Sheriffs of London, he was one also of the first to whom Queen Victoria awarded the honour of knighthood in 1837, in the early days of her prosperous reign. Three years later, the frightful persecutions of the Jews in Rhodes and Damascus gave to this singular man the opportunity of displaying the whole grandeur of his humane disposition. It will ever remain in grateful remembrance how then, in the universal horror which stunned the world at this relapse into the barbarities of the Middle Ages, this one man arose with energy of action to carry rescue and help. Six hundred years had flown by since, on this English ground, the debt of Christian bloodshed had been charged against the Jews; now it was charged again in the far East, and now it was England which prepared a Government vessel, under the flag of Great Britain and Ireland, for the oppressed.

It is well known, and will never be forgotten, how Sir Moses Montefiore carried on single-handed his mission, and how his return resembled a triumph. It was no longer one of Cumberland's characters speaking as Scheva on the stage of Drury Lane, but in the Mansion House, the palace of the Lord Mayor of London, before a large

z

and splendid assemblage of all most distinguished
and noble in England, these words were heard :
" None of our fellow-citizens is more jealous to
promote humanity, to help the poor and needy, to
protect the orphan, and to favour literature and
science, than yourself; your benefits are not confined to those of your own creed, but Christians
rejoice in them as well as Jews." Queen Victoria,
inspired by the desire of " giving our true and
beloved Sir Moses Montefiore an especial mark
of our Royal favour for his continual labours on
behalf of his sick and oppressed brethren in the
East and the nation in common," allowed him an
heraldic decoration, which was formerly permitted
only to peers, and persons of the highest rank.
She gave to him the so-called " supporters," which
were designed to immortalise his services, viz., a
lion, a stag, and a banner, with the Hebrew
inscription " Jerusalem."*

So stood the Jews on the threshold of Parliament for fifty years; while only the Tories
hindered them from crossing it, by refusing to
yield to any modification of the form of the oath,
after the precedent of the City. Then out of
their own ranks stepped forth a champion, to

---

* Grätz, 'History of the Jews,' xi., 535, 552.

whom it was destined to bring the cause he represented to a glorious issue. It was in the year
1851 that he, in the 'Political Biography of Lord
George Bentinck,' for the first time eloquently
and expressly pleaded for the admission of the
Jews into Parliament, after having exhibited
long before in his romances a glowing preference for them. The composer of this biography, no other than *Benjamin D'Israeli*, then
merely a gentleman without any title, had the
gratification of seeing his cause gradually carried
through by his party, and in the year in which
his work reached its fifth edition, and himself
became for the second time Chancellor of the
Exchequer, the decided victory was proclaimed,
and on the 26th of July, in the year 1858, the
first Jew, Baron Lionel Rothschild, entered the
English Parliament, whilst for the first time
the words of the form of the oath " on the
true faith of a Christian," were omitted; and
soon after, six other Jewish Members followed
him.

In relating the history of the Jews in England
we have handled a theme which already almost
entirely belongs to the history of the past. But
of all the interesting, indeed wonderful features
which it has brought under our notice, this last,

which through D'Israeli brought about the crisis,
is perhaps, in its whole bearing, the most interesting and the most wonderful. In fact, it was a
phenomenon, significant not merely for England
but for the whole modern world, that he, by birth
a plebeian, who reconstructed the Tory party, and
as its head, struck at the Whigs with their own
weapon, viz., the Reform Bill, to conquer in that
moment in which the Reform Bill, carried through
by him, came into operation; that he, if not a
born Jew, was at least a Christian only since his
twelfth year, the 31st of July, 1817,* and the son
of parents, who both (his mother was a Basevi†)
had been members of the Portuguese Jewish
community of London.

On the day, in the year 1868, in which he
was seen Prime Minister at the head of Her

---

* "Baptized 31st July, 1817. Benjamin, said to be twelve
years old, son of Isaac and Maria D'Israeli, King's Road,
Gentleman." Baptismal Register of St. Andrew's, Holborn,
London. 'Athenæum,' 12th September, 1868, p. 336.

† "A Basevi flourished at Prague in the seventeenth century, and was raised by the German Emperor to the rank
of nobility under the title of "Basevi von Treuenfels;" afterwards, being entangled in the fall of Wallenstein, he was
crushed, together with that mighty Duke, and died in
misery."—Julius Rodenberg, in 'Deutschen Landen.'

Majesty's Government, he expiated that other day in which, in the year 1290, a Plantagenet drove his unfortunate banished ancestors over the sea, after they had been pillaged and plundered; and, with four English dukes on his right hand and on his left, D'Israeli then wiped away once for all the robbery of half a thousand years.

The whole number of Jews settled in Great Britain and Ireland amounts to 40,000, of which the greater number live in England, and 25,000 in London alone. Of these latter 5000 may be reckoned as belonging to the higher, 8000 to the middle, and 12,000 to the lower classes.

In the higher class of Jews we find English baronets—Sir Francis Goldsmid, 1841; Sir Moses Montefiore, 1846; Sir Anthony Rothschild, 1846; and Sir David Salomons, 1869: seven Members of Parliament, and finally, a large number belonging to the professional callings of gentlemen— lawyers, physicians, merchants.

From various and evident reasons, to which we will return, the circle of trade among the Jews of England is always relatively contracted, although it has a tendency to enlarge itself, and already embraces in London the following occupations:— goldsmiths, watchmakers, cigar manufacturers, smiths, and locksmiths. It is a remarkable circumstance that the Jews, especially those from Poland, devote themselves by preference to glass-works.* The women employ themselves in the manufacture of shirts and umbrellas, bonnets and slippers. The sale, too, of fish and fruit is followed largely by the Jews of London.

Whilst the upper and middle strata of the Jewish population in England enjoy in rich abundance the blessings of this enlightened period, the same cannot be said of the mass of the lower Jewish class. No greater difference can be imagined than between the fine and aristocratic Jewish inhabitants of the West End and their fellows in faith crowded together in musty corners of the City. There they may be seen sitting thickly packed in the old grimy and unhealthy quarters in which their fathers and forefathers dwelt. Their exchange is the rag-exchange of Houndsditch, and their principal street is Petticoat Lane, a narrow, evil-smelling alley, in which, from early to late, bartering and cheapening, baking and roasting, are carried on. The blind alleys and courts around are stuffed with old clothes and lumber. The door-steps and gutters exhibit a truly Oriental

---

* Cracroft, 'The Jews of Western Europe,' vol. ii. (Essays). London, 1868.

fertility, peopled with little, dirty, dark-eyed, dark-haired, crawling beings; and with the squalls of children is mixed the scolding of their fat mothers, the laughter of pretty, carelessly clad girls, organ-playing, singing, and the eager, loud talk of chaffering men, who have for ever some old thing —now an old coat, now an old watch—in their hand. Everywhere German is spoken; not the German of Sanders' Dictionary, but a *Gemauschel*, or Jewish German slang, which only the initiated can understand.

Between this class of Jews and their Christian neighbours a wall of division always stands, which could not have been firmer even in the times of the burning and demolishing of their houses in the Middle Ages; but neither the religion of the one, nor the prejudice of the other, is in fault. Such division is just as much in the nature of things as the contempt with which the Christian Londoner looks down on the Christian Irishman, who carries on, not far from that neighbourhood which we have described, much the same employment as his neighbour, the Jew of Petticoat Lane, poor and dirty as he, but in a far worse state of moral abandonment and decay. The difference lies in this; that the cultivated and wealthy Jews take care of their uncultivated

and poor brethren in faith, in another and more
magnanimous manner than either is, or perhaps
could be, the case with any other religious community. If we could not be assured of this upon
its own showing and experience, the testimony
might be summoned of one who knows perfectly
well the circumstances of the poor in London, and
has lately published the result of his researches
upon this subject in an ample work.*

That the greater number of the new arrivals
are without means scarcely needs especial mention. The Jewish immigration into England,
especially London, is continually stronger, and
Holland, North Germany (Hamburg), and Poland,
supply the greatest share. The new-comers either
help to enlarge the originally not very extended
circle of poverty among the Jews, or they join
themselves to their brethren of Petticoat Lane,
and increase the number of traffickers. Towards
both, the tendency of Jewish benevolence extends
itself in London. The effort is made to draw away
the lower class of the Jews more and more
from traffic and lumber, and to educate them for
hand-labour, manufactures; and in one word, for

* Dr. Stallard, 'London Pauperism amongst Jews and
Christians.' London, 1867.

work. `But manifold obstacles oppose this design.
The indigenous Jews of the lower classes are universally so strong adherents to the Mosaic law that
it is not possible, or at least, not easy, to put them
under the instruction of a Christian master, on
account of the Sabbath festival, the laws with
regard to food; and of Jewish masters there are
none, or very few. An endeavour was made to
procure labour for them in the docks, but this was
decidedly the worst place for the commencement
of any civic activity among the Jews. The dock-
men soon enough abused and beat their Jewish
rivals out of the docks. But for these immigrants
there are even more formidable obstacles. They
arrive, for the most part, in a miserable condition; they can neither speak the language, nor
are they of the age when it is most easy to learn
anything. The progress of reform in this direction
will therefore be very tedious, and must naturally
be contented with small results for the present,
and hope for greater in the future. Yet the chief
part is done already by the recognition of the
need of internal reform to realise a complete
emancipation, and to render that not the privilege
of a few, but the right of all. And in England
people seem to have attained to this view. " The
great Jewish families," says Dr. Stallard, "literally

vie with one another in liberality and personal regard for the welfare of their less-favoured brethren. Schools and establishments contribute to this object, not merely by removing poverty, but also, and especially for the rising generation, by awakening a desire for regulated occupation, and, together with the position of the poor, to improve the educational standard of the lower Jewish classes generally."

It deserves to be mentioned with praise, that even this lowest class of the Jews in London (as, indeed, do the Jews generally) enjoys, in respect of morality, the highest reputation, and that it is one of the greatest exceptions to find a Jewess, either old or young, in a London prison. Further, no poor Jew may make any claim for help, unless he declares that—supposing he has children—he sends them to the school in which instruction is imparted gratuitously.

This is the way to make those prejudices, which in the higher classes of society have already been wholly laid aside, disappear also from the great masses of the population. More and more will the Jews turn from the sole art of gain— which begins in the sublime regions of the Exchange to end in the sordid shops of the lumber market—from this gain, to which, indeed, the shortsightedness of earlier ages had condemned them, to busy themselves with other employments; and, labouring and wrestling in all the domains of public life, to share in the fate of nations, with which the holiest interests have inseparably connected them.

PICTURES OF ENGLISH HIGHROADS.

I.

UP to the present time England is far more than Germany the land of railways. To say that in England there is scarcely one village from which you may not travel to another by means of the railway is as nothing, when we reflect that in London there is scarcely a house from which one may not proceed to any other by the railway, be it either by that which runs beneath the foundations of the houses, or over the roofs of the same. It is therefore no easy task to depict the peculiar life of English highroads. The difficulty is to find any highroad that has not yet been superseded by railways. Where such an one exists, however, there are we certain of perceiving pictures and features which belong to the bygone century, and with themselves carry us back at once to that period. But there are a few spots in England from which the highroads will never disappear— those in which it is impossible to construct a railway. First, because of its romantic charms, ranks amongst these railroadless neighbourhoods the so-called "English Lake District," in the far

North, close to the Scottish border, in Westmoreland and Cumberland. Here the mountains tower
around like the wall of a fortification, and wild
and riven precipices bar any entrance to the
steam-horse; at most permitting him to set down
on the borders those strangers whom he brings.
Once entered, the traveller has at his disposition
the good old English highroad, and upon this
do I entreat the honoured reader to follow me, in
order to show him all its beauty.

That which attracted me in these English
lakes, long before I had ever seen them, was
their names, which I had sometimes read on the
walls of railway-stations, and more frequently
in my Bradshaw, the guide-book, *par excellence*,
of the English. Some of them, it is true, were
simply designated as waters; as, for instance,
Coniston Water, the first of the lakes which we
reach in coming from the south; but by far the
greater number of their names are formed from a
combination with "mere," as Windermere, Grasmere, Buttermere, &c. Now this "mere" is no
other than our German "meer," a circumstance
which has often made me wonder that it should
have disappeared from the language of those of
our family stock, who are most connected with it
and all belonging to it. But the truth is that the

English in their sense of "meer," as we call it, are more thoroughly German than the Germans themselves, since our old poems, as for instance the 'Gudrun,' always speaks of *See*. We recognise two kinds of "*See*." The great *See* (feminine), or ocean, and the *See* (masculine), or lake. Our German sailors to this day call the Mediterranean the Mittelsee. The Englishman knows but one See which washes around the islands and the world. The word "meer" he has either never had or has lost, except in this retired district of the lakes, and then, contrary to the present German use of the word, it implies an inland water.

With Coniston Water the panorama of these lakes opens when, as already stated, the traveller comes from the direction of the south. It is the last piece of railway on this side, and a wild piece of railway it is, wrested from the mountain which towers above it more and more boldly, with indescribable obstacles. The journey from Furness Abbey, the last station, is a continuous clatter over bridges and ravines, accompanied by a thundering echo from the abysses and bottoms of the opening mountain-world, till the train suddenly stops immediately on the border of the lake. Here we have the first glimpse of the Lake country, the first narrow track of water, which, seen through a

2 A

vista of trees, sparkles up as out of a goblet of mountain stone covered with green. Coniston Water is a modest beauty, and by no means so gifted with charms as its more preferred neighbours. Nevertheless, with its quiet deep blue, and in the silent environment of its chain of hills, it affords an interesting picture when beheld from the hotel, which, not far from the station, is built on a projecting tongue of land, and is surrounded by a garden of brightly-smiling colours.

Under the stone portico stood Mrs. Atkinson, the hostess, and Miss Atkinson, the daughter of mine host—the former plump, well-favoured, with brick-red cheeks, the latter slight, elegant, and fair. This scale of figure and complexion is peculiar to the race of landladies in Great Britain. Of landlords I speak not. I believe, indeed, that such persons as landlords must exist, but they are never visible. The landlord of an English hotel concerns himself about everything except his guests. He is generally a robust sportsman, an angler, and horse-amateur; but the cares of entertainment devolve on the women. The only places in which one is likely to have a glimpse of him are the drinking-room, in which he assumes the manners of a guest, or the stable, in which he shows those

of a connoisseur.   Life in these country inns is
peculiar, old-fashioned, and comfortable.   In these
remote nooks and corners of England a good
deal of the olden time is retained, both as regards the journey and the hotels.   There is an
atmosphere of comfort around, and a smattering
of solid humour which refreshes the heart after
the dry hotel prosers with their long stiff collars,
and still longer reckonings.   Every hotel, too,
here has its sign-board, very charmingly painted
with this or that fine scene, to which is sometimes
added some very pretty and religious sentiment ;
as, for instance, the following, or something like
it, which I have seen on one of the sign-boards
of this neighbourhood.

> "O son of man, that livest by bread alone,
> What gives thy jolly nose so red a tone?
> Come in and take a drink, O donkey's head,
> No one for nought need show a nose so red!"

But to return to Mrs. and Miss Atkinson, still
standing beneath the portico.   Horses, coaches,
and coachmen, were arrayed before them in vast
numbers.   Let no man imagine that these coachmen are children of men not more uncommon
than ourselves!   In these mountain-districts of
England, where the railway has not been able
to put down from its position the coach, the

2 A 2

good old coach, there remains for its driver some
of the glory of the coaching days of Old England,
when discontented parish priests, officers on half-
pay, and misguided younger sons, "took to the
highroad," as was the expression at that time,
that is, became coachmen; but did not thereby
cease to be "gentlemen," and were called "gentlemen of the whip," in contradistinction to those
other gentlemen who also practised on the highroads, and were called "gentlemen of the road,"
and "captains;" and translated into the language
of the present day would be termed *robbers*. Highway robberies were then a recognised resource
for "gentlemen in distress," or "under a cloud,"
i.e. "for people of position who had no means of
support for their wives and children, or for themselves; as, for instance, was the case with the
highwayman who, in Fielding's romance, attacked our friend Tom Jones and his companion,
the schoolmaster Partridge, "about a mile from
Highgate."

This "highwayman" was but a novice in his
profession, and his pistol was—unloaded. Amid
crying, and importunate imploring entreaties for
mercy, when Tom Jones had cast him on the
ground, he confessed that he had been driven by
"distress, the greatest indeed imaginable," to

this step, since he had five hungry children and a wife, who was already confined with a sixth. The noble-minded Jones not only gave his conquered enemy life, but in addition, the unloaded pistol and a couple of guineas, whereat the poor sinner was so touched that he reforms in the course of the romance, and under the eye of the reader. Those who engaged seriously in their calling kept their pistols carefully loaded, and stationed themselves, as soon as darkness grew in, upon some one of those hilly heaths over which the road to London lay. The heaths of Hounslow and Blackheath, and Highgate and Primrose Hill, were especial favourites for this purpose; for though highway robberies abounded in all parts of the kingdom, yet they were most rife, from very evident reasons, within a circle of thirty miles round London. Here the gentleman held himself concealed in night and dusk, till the heavy wheel of a carriage or the tramp of a horse was heard, and then stepped out on to the path of the belated travellers, and, if they were not better armed than himself, soon compelled them to stand by presenting a pistol.

The ingenious Horace Walpole, who lived scarcely a mile from London, on his estate at Strawberry Hill, wrote, even in the year 1782, in a

letter to the Earl of Strafford, that he could not
after sunset venture twenty minutes' walk from
his house without having one or two servants with
him armed with blunderbusses. People had become
so accustomed to this warfare on the highroads,
that from both sides it was regarded as a sort of
accomplishment; and as there were very famous
highway robbers, so were there not wanting
great noblemen, who gained a name for themselves by their manner of getting rid of them.
To these belonged Earl Berkeley, of whom Lord
Mahon, or Earl Stanhope, relates in his 'History
of England' the following amusing anecdote:—
One day, so goes the tale, the Earl, who, after
darkness had set in, was travelling over Hounslow
Heath, was aroused from his slumber by a strange
face at his carriage-window, and a loaded pistol at
his breast.

"Now, I have you at last, my Lord," said his
assailant, "after all your boasting that you would
never let yourself be robbed."

"Nor would I now," replied the nobleman,
whilst he thrust his hand in his pocket, as if with
the object of drawing his purse from it, "if it were
not for the cursed knave who is looking over your
shoulder."

The robber turned himself hastily round to see

the pretended second person, who might, perhaps,
dispute his booty with him, but at this moment
the Earl substituted his pistol for his purse, and,
less magnanimous than Tom Jones in the romance,
shot his opponent dead upon the spot.

All this was done with the greatest good-
nature, and the newspapers of the time referred
to it in a similar and quite business-like tone.
" Last Saturday evening," says the 'St. James's
Chronicle' of 1762, " was Mr. Sims, the architect,
of Edgeware, set upon by a well-dressed highwayman, on Dollars Hill, near the sixth milestone on
the Edgeware Road, and robbed of his money and
his watch." Or, " On Saturday the post-chaises
on this side of Dartford were stopped by three
men in ambush, who were armed with pistols and
whips, and robbed of a considerable sum. The
three men were afterwards seen on Blackheath
on their road to London."

It was not, however, the rule for highwaymen
to associate in this way, and to work in company.
They exercised their profession, for the most part,
each for himself, and at his own peril.

Many a reader may here well ask how it could
possibly be, that a solitary pistol should accomplish
such deeds of bravery. Now this doubt has been
already settled by our before-mentioned friend the

schoolmaster Partridge, who during the pugilistic
combat of his master, Tom Jones, with the faint-
hearted highwayman, had buried himself in a
ditch, from which, after the conclusion of the
battle, when safety was reassured, emerging again
into view, he thus soliloquised over the uncer-
tainty of fire-arms. " A thousand naked men are
nothing against one pistol; for although it is true
that it can only kill one at a shot, nobody can say
whether he may not be that one."

. But " the road " was not only the last resource
for honest people with wives and children to get
food, "the bloods," aristocratic "good-for-nothings,"
who had gambled or betted away all their fortune
at White's, made use of this same means to re-
cover their money, and rendered highway-robbery
in one period of the last century a very fashionable means of livelihood. They gave to it the perfection of better birth and finer education, which
was removed beyond the narrow horizon of people
of the lower class. And under their hands it
changed its original character of a trade for
that of a liberal art, for the exercise of which
a great portion of grace, generosity, and gallantry, was necessary. Out of this class arose
the " Captains," whose knightly adventures and
noble deeds inspired the story-tellers of that day

with so much enthusiasm for murder and assassination. Some of these—for instance, a certain
Defoe, a lineal descendant of the writer of 'Robinson Crusoe,'—brought the pursuit to a high pitch
of popularity ; and to see these men, with all the
graces of their virtuous mode of life, carried to
their end at last on the gallows at Tyburn was
an enjoyment for the people, for which they
hired places long beforehand, as for a cock-fight
or boxing-match. The biographer of Oliver Goldsmith, Mr. John Forster, relates in reference to
this that in that time scarcely a Monday arrived
which was not a "black Monday" for Newgate
(the criminal prison of London). An execution
was as regular as any other weekly exhibition,
and if it should happen that a shocking spectacle
of fifteen condemned to be hanged was reported,
the interest was naturally so much the greater.
George Selwyn, one of the most famous wits of his
day, spent quite as much of his time in Tyburn
(where the gallows stood) as in his fashionable club
at White's ; and Boswell, Johnson's biographer,
had a dress of execution black, so that he might
appear at the scaffold in good taste. Indeed, there
was a kind of *terminus technicus* for this species of
delinquents, describing them as "hanged for the
highway." "The Flying Highwayman" seems

to have obtained great celebrity in this line;
of him the old newspaper out of which I have
taken some extracts (the 'St. James's Chronicle'
of 1762), often makes mention, and always with
becoming reverence. "Some days ago" (it says
in one place) "'the Flying Highwayman,' known
under the name of Campbell, robbed the postil-
lion of a gentleman in Colebrook of 1 guinea,
3 shillings, and 6 pence in coppers. He asked the
fellow how far he had to travel, and was answered,
'A good way, with 3 turnpikes to pay;' whereon
the robber returned him the silver and copper,
saying, 'When you reach home, say that the
"Flying Highwayman" is not taken, as has been
reported, and, as a proof, you can tell how you
met him to-night,' and thereon he bade the lad
good-bye."

The false report about "Captain" Campbell, as
this old newspaper informs us two pages further
on (such stories of robbers are its principal
themes), originated in the seizure of another
"Captain" named Walter, or Samuel, or Norris
(he went by all these terms in turns), who, after
he had served in Bourgoyne's light cavalry, decided upon the highway as a more profitable mode
of getting money. Like the greater number of
his comrades, he at last had his "payment in full

at Tyburn;" and his appearance at the foot of the "tree" is described by the same paper as "that of a good-looking young man with an honest face."

Whence came, will the German reader ask, not only this condition of extreme insecurity, but much more the popularity of the robbers of England? It is a characteristic which is deeply implanted in the English national character; and Henry Taine, in his 'History of English Literature,' calls attention to this characteristic when he mentions Robin Hood, the monarch of the woods, who even to this day lives in the peoples' songs and plays, and quotes of a later date, in the fifteenth century, the Chancellor, Sir John Fortescue, who expresses himself in the following manner :—" C'est la lâcheté et le manque de cœur et de courage qui empêche les Français de se soulever, et non la pauvreté. Aucun Français n'a ce courage comme un Anglais. On a souvent vu en Angleterre trois ou quatre bandits par pauvreté, se jeter sur sept ou huit hommes honnêtes, et les voler tous; mais on n'a point vu en France sept ou huit bandits assez hardis pour voler trois ou quatre hommes honnêtes. C'est pourquoi il est tout-à-fait rare que des Français soient pendus pour vol à main armée, car ils n'ont point le cœur de faire une action si terrible."

With a sort of malicious joy the honest Chancellor goes on to tell, that from the above-named causes more robbers had been hanged in England in one year than in France in the course of seven years. Indeed, the national opinion of the superiority of English robbers was still so uncontested at the end of the last century, that in a letter which the well-known Philipp Moriz, in 1785, wrote from England to the Dean Gedike in Berlin, we read: "Our fellow-passenger in the waggon began to maintain the honour of English highway robbers against French, the latter only robbed, he said, but the former murdered also." A celebrated and learned French traveller, M. Pierre Jean Grosley, Member of the French Academy and of the Royal Society of London, who visited England in 1765, made the passage from Dover to London one Sunday. Owing to the reigning quietude of the Sabbath, he found nothing to eat on the way, but, and with this he consoled himself, he found also no highway robbers, who on other occasions abounded on that road; from which it follows that these gentlemen, besides their other virtues, possessed that of religion— they rested from their labour on the Sabbath. If, however, for this reason, the pleasure was denied to the French Academician of making their personal acquaintance, he was yet able to see some specimens of them here and there—on gallows by the roadside. There they figured, he tells us, in wigs, and clothed from head to foot.

Highway robbers formed then so much a standing article in every correct book of travels and sketch of English people, that Seyfart also, in his 'Present State of England, 1757," has devoted to them an entire chapter, in which he (characteristically enough), after the definition of the word "gentlemen," immediately passing on to robbers, says that the number of English highwaymen was the result of too great liberty. "They are quite different," he says, "from our footpads (*Buschkleppern*). Their excursions are generally on horseback. They are met in woods and highways generally with masks. One of these 'gentleman of the highway,' as the English call them for honour's sake, will stop your coach, put a pistol to your breast, and demand a certain sum, or strip you of everything if he is an unpolite specimen; but generally they are good enough not only to leave you enough to continue your journey to the next stage, but to allow you afterwards to redeem your property."

One sees the profession had its rules and its laws, which could be found laid down in the

handbooks of the period, just as to-day we are
instructed in a 'Bädeker' or 'Berlepsch,' about
behaviour towards landlord, waiter, or boots, with
this difference only, that the highwaymen always
considered themselves " gentlemen," and took
what they desired only as " knights'-alms."

II.

This chivalric race, which enlivened in such an extraordinary manner the monotony of the highways and the romance of the last century, is now, alas, utterly exterminated, but the " coaching gentleman " still remains. He wears as of old his red coat with brass buttons, his red waistcoat, his white felt hat, and his pair of yellow calf-skin gloves on his hands. The horses only are his concern, and these only when they stand ready harnessed. Their attendant, so long as they find themselves in the stable, is the ostler, and the boundary where the duties divide is the pole. As soon as the horses are ready for departure, the coachman gives the signal, with his horn, for the passenger's ascent troubling himself, little about his freight, which he leaves to take care of itself, and the passengers clamber up the wheels and spokes as best they can to find their places. He himself takes up his position with a noble repose, as if all this did not concern him, on his lofty seat in front; on which like a king he sits enthroned above the passengers, receives whip and reins from the ostler, four horses start, and the coach flies away as in a storm.

The noble steed, and all connected with him, stable and ostler, has a quite different appearance in England from that which it has in Germany. Everything is dignified and well-to-do. The Englishman has not forgotten that Hengist and Horsa were his ancestors; he considers, there-fore, his coachman not as one of his other ser-vants, and does not pay him like them a "salary," but an "honorarium," and treats him with the same politeness that he shows to his physician or his lawyer. Although the veneration for the English coachman is now great, yet was it once far greater,—it was, indeed, almost a worship; it cannot, therefore, surprise us, that at the same time in which reduced gentlemen took to the highroad in order to improve their circumstances by highway robbery, other "gentlemen" in like conditions seized on the whip, a position not less honourable, and far more honest. Among the coachmen of those days were numerous officers on half-pay, members of learned societies, and men of rank.

The 'Athenæum,' in an article of the year 1860 (we know not the number, as we do not unfor-tunately find it in our notes), says, that such a

coachman was sometimes the best man, as well by
birth as by cultivation and learning, on the outside
of his fully-packed coach. "In the days," adds
the same-mentioned article, "in which coach proprietors were as great men as railway contrac-
tors now, when Richard Ironmonger represented
Stafford, and William Chaplin" (this firm of carriers
is still great in London) "sat in Parliament for
Salisbury, their best ' whips' were not infrequently
first cousins and younger brothers of landed proprietors, through whose parks they had driven
their foaming teams. Proben, the handsome youth
who drove the Reading coach for years, was a
captain of the royal army who had sold out, and
he left ' the road' only to betake himself to a
handsome property which he had inherited. So
Dennis, who concluded his career by driving
the Norwich coach, was a clergyman, who gave
up the post of vicar in Berkshire when he mounted
the box of the ' White Hart,' which went from
London to Bath."

This worship for "the whip" reached its climax
in the days of George IV., who was himself an
accomplished coachman, as even Thackeray in his
"Four Georges" admits, and he seldom finds much
to praise in him. "He drove once," he there says,
"in four hours and a half, from Brighton to

Carlton House, a distance of fifty-six miles."
Those were the sunny days of the "Four-in-
hand Club," *i.e.* of driving from the box with four
horses. The *élite* of the youthful aristocracy of
that time belonged to this club. Those who had
their own team made an arrangement with the
drivers of the stage coaches, whereby they might
once a week "finger the ribbons" and "tool
the team," just as the young noblemen of our
own time find a pleasure in standing in sooty
smock-frocks near the engine-driver on the loco-
motive, to direct the engine all day from London
to Edinburgh and back. But the members of the
" Four-in-hand Clubs" went farther. A certain
Hon. Mr. Ackers, a rich and distinguished young
man, allowed one of his front teeth to be extracted
for no other object than that he might be able to
spit in the right manner like a coachman! And
in a book which was very popular at that time,
and which Murray has lately re-published in his
railway library, viz., Nimrod's ' The Road,' we
read : " When so great a person as Sophocles did
not think it beneath him to expose his wisdom
before the public in playing at ball, wherefore
should an English gentleman not' practise his
talent on the coach-box ?"
    Although to-day we find neither the scholars of

Sophocles, nor the first cousins or younger brothers of the great landed proprietors upon the above-named seat, yet the seat next the coachman is still regarded as the place of honour, as much on the country coach with four horses as on the London omnibus.

I, with my contracted German views, had certainly preferred a place on the back seat near a friendly young lady with a blue veil drawn down; but in the forepart, near the coachman, there had grouped themselves the following: a "reverend" with a long coat and a white necktie, a corpulent farmer, a man in a mackintosh, a young married couple, a photographer with a camera obscura, a "volunteer" with his gun—which is always carried by these soldiers of peace as a walking-stick on all their pleasure excursions—a London attorney with the 'Saturday Review' in his pocket, and a dentist who frequented the neighbourhood. Behind these people, and on the roof of the coach, sat an old woman, a little child, and a dog, which was tied to the rail. The interior of the coach was used partly as luggage room, and partly as an asylum for invalids and aged travellers, for every healthy traveller prefers the outside, especially as it is cheaper. Here the luggage was so closely packed together that there was only space for two old people and two dogs, the former of whom were constantly crying out that the boxes were falling on their feet, and the latter were perpetually yelling, apparently from the same reason.

Of such a journey, amid such noise and circumstance, it is scarcely possible to convey an idea to a German reader. How one goes up-hill and down-hill, and how madly one goes up. No sensible man would expect such a thing of a German horse, but the power and endurance of English horses is truly amazing. They are fed also in a totally different manner. The oats which they eat stand to them in the same relation as the roast beef which their masters are accustomed to eat. This it is which gives to both their well-nourished and compact appearance, and causes the fearless dash round sharp corners and edges, over water, rocks, and precipices, which to a German who sees it all for the first time, give actual heartache. One passenger falls on another, as the coach, whirling this way and that way, deposits the lady and myself in each other's arms, her in mine or me in hers, whilst we are powerless to prevent it. At first I attempted to apologise, but she merely said, " Never mind."

But to proceed thus at a continual gallop, however much packed the coach may be, or however mountainous the district, could not, with all due praise to English horses and coachmen, be possible, if the way, the highroad, were not splendidly even.

The English highroad is the best of the kind anywhere. In the English highlands and the far off mountain-districts of Cumberland it is of the same strength and solidity as in the low country of Kent and Sussex. It is everywhere as smooth and even, as dry and firm, as the floor of our sitting-room, and there are no obstacles in the ground. The English highways are the triumph of road-construction, and as such are extolled by the poets and prose-writers of England. Thus Dr. Johnson, England's oracle, says that there can be no earthly pleasure greater than to travel in a mail-coach over a good highroad, at so many miles an hour (I cannot exactly remember how many); and Byron, in his ' Don Juan ' (x. 78), sings thus :—

> " What a delightful thing 's a turnpike road !
> So smooth, so level, such a mode of shaving
> The earth, as scarce the eagle in the broad
> Air can accomplish, with his wide wings waving."

The perfection of the English highways is due to the system of macadamizing, which, long known and employed by ourselves, has made the name of its originator immortal, although we daily tread him under our feet. Mr. M'Adam (MacAdam) was an old Scotch gentleman (living from 1755–1836), who, as he dwelt in the neighbourhood of the most frightful roads, hit on the fortunate idea that, could a road be strewed with a quantity of small stones, it might be kept dry and hard, and free from ruts. He also made the economical calculation that the necessary process of gradual trituration might be accomplished, not by the makers of the roadway, but by the wheels of the vehicles of those who made use of it. People smiled at first at the whim of the old gentleman, but before he died he had realised 10,000*l.* in one year alone, by superintending the several post-roads constructed upon his own plan.

But the English highways were not always what they now are. After carriages had been introduced under the first Stuart who sat upon the English throne, it was necessary to have masses of brushwood strewn whenever the King wished to go to Parliament, so that his coach might not remain sticking in the holes. In the time of the civil wars under the second Stuart, 800 dragoons were taken prisoners on their horses, having stuck fast in the mud of the road. Travelling, therefore, at that time, and until the time of George I., was principally on horseback, and carriages were used only on great occasions in town or country, when neighbours made solemn calls.

Coaches were then regarded as signs of great wealth or great extravagance, however far removed from the comforts of the present day. They had, for example, no glass windows. These were introduced from France, after the Restoration (1660), and the coaches were called " glass coaches." Till then, the windows were only closed in by linen curtains with French borders; and in a day-book kept by Sir Harry Slingsby, one of the most loyal and unfortunate adherents of the King in the time of the civil wars, the diarist complains (1641) that these had been stolen from him in a journey during the night, and that for the rest of the way, since they were fortunately in the neighbourhood of London, they were obliged to fasten a pair of curtains with pins before the windows.

Worse, however, than the coaches were the roads; and a journey, however short, always required the most careful preparations. The members of the then " upper ten thousand " who went to the dinner of some neighbouring nobleman in their carriage, sent out people early in the

morning to repair the deep tracks of former travellers. Then to render them distinguishable in
the night, they threw great heaps of lime on
the road, or laid down white casks in a double
row, between which—just as now in the road
from Schevening to the Hague, the trees by their
white appearance at night point out the approach
to the country houses—the intoxicated coachman
might steer back his master and family in com-
parative security to the haven of their home.

But such far-seeing preparations manifestly
could not be carried out on long journeys; and
so it happened continually that coaches, adorned
with golden coronets, lined with velvet, and
drawn by six horses (the Sovereign alone dared
have eight!) in clear day, and on the open road,
remained sticking in the mud. Amusing in a
high degree are the accounts of the sufferings
which travellers of that olden time had to experience. Macaulay, in his unparalleled ' History
of England,' gives us one of the most charming
pictures of the adventures of these first " martyrs
of the highways," how they were in the habit of
making half a mile in six hours; how they continually lost their way; how they sometimes ran
into danger of being carried off by streams that
had overflowed, or of being beaten by carriers

sticking in the mud like themselves, and how in order to save their lives, they had to swim through broad streams; or if they wished to save their coaches, were obliged to take them to pieces, and carry them a great part of the way themselves. " On the best lines of communication," says the great historian, " the ruts were deep, the descents precipitous, and the way often, such as it was, hardly possible to distinguish in the dusk from the uninclosed heath and fen which lay on both sides. . . . Often the mud lay deep on the right and the left, and only a narrow track of firm ground rose above the quagmire. It was only in fine weather that the whole breadth of the road was available for wheeled vehicles. But in bad seasons the traveller had to encounter inconveniences and disasters which might suffice for a journey to the Frozen Ocean or to the desert of Sahara."

So the Commission sent by the Parliament, in January 1646, to the King at Newcastle, as appears in the memoirs of Sir Thomas Herbert, one of the adherents of Charles I., who kept true to the unfortunate monarch even to the scaffold, took nine full days to accomplish a distance that amounted to little more than thirty miles.

This difficulty frightened most from riding in

coaches. People used the saddle much more, and rode " post," as it was called in that time.

Our friend Tom Jones, and his companion, the schoolmaster Partridge, rode thus, when they sought the "lovely" Sophia; and she herself, with Mrs. Fitzpatrick, who had left her husband, together with Dame Honour, of rich eloquence, rode from one inn in the kingdom to another on saddle-horses. A universal shout of revolt went through the British nation, when about the beginning of the last century the improvement of the roads began, and " post-chaises " came into use. Some declared that the national courage would be destroyed, if a man, who had been in the habit of riding on horseback through the country, and of maintaining at any time a struggle with a highway robber, should now allow himself to sneak along in coaches. " The health of the public will suffer," cried the philanthropist, who could not stomach the thought of seeing people shut up in hot and dusty coaches, instead of breathing the fresh air on a fiery steed. " Health and trade will go to the ground," bewailed others. During the old usage each journey needed a fresh suit. In a coach, however, any one might journey for a whole year without benefiting his tailor by a penny. Saddlers, spur-makers, horse-dealers,

united in a petition to Parliament, that in its
wisdom it might bridle the velocity of such
"flaming meteors," whose unheard-of haste
threatened important trades with complete ruin,
and the art of riding with decay.

"Whither is the sun of England going?" was
the almost universal cry; but most angrily of all
wrangled the package carriers, who hitherto had
had nearly sole possession of the road, and who,
when the weather was especially bad, and they
were in especially good temper, allowed the foot-
passenger, overtaken by the rain, to creep into
the straw of their carts; in which manner, for
example, Roderick Random, and his trusty friend
Strap, travelled part of their way from Scotland
to London. "The way was made for their carts,"
they cried, "and people of position had no right to
use it." Much more recently have we heard a
similar cry in Germany, where the States brought
a complaint before the Imperial Diet (1790)
"against the manifold injury" done through the
Post Office, by which the "old and hitherto well-
conducted city and country messenger delivery"
was destroyed. They entreated, therefore, the
Diet (Hausser, 'Hist. of Germany,' i. 127) either
to put a stop to the "post-carriages, supported to
the greatest prejudice of the citizens," or else to

confine them to the simple transport of travellers and their baggage.

But over the troubles of the German States, as of the English tailors, saddlers, and carriers, the coach and four rode triumphantly. On the highway, which improved daily, it soon appeared, though at first meanly equipped and at a very tardy pace, stopping for the night at every inn where it was allowed to do so, and spending a whole day upon the road between places which may now be reached, the one from the other, in an hour.

In the Bull Hotel at Cambridge, one of the most noteworthy of the old inns which I have seen in England, full of all kinds of curiosities, art relics, old prints and engravings, I found under a glass frame, in the entrance hall, close to the door, an advertisement of the year 1706, in which the coaches were advertised which were to travel from London to Cambridge, and *vice versâ*. These " stage-coaches " travelled three times a-week, and devoted four days to a distance which now the railway would accomplish six times in five hours daily. "If God permits," adds the page, in parenthesis, as we now see the great steamer which goes to places over sea announce its departure under the given condition, " Wind and weather permitting."

But the better the road, the quicker the coaches; and the time soon came of the wonderful Brighton 'Age,' of the 'Butterfly,' and of the 'Highflyer,' with thoroughbred tits, and coachmen with red coats. How bright must the English highroads have then appeared, with all their carts, coaches, and carriages! Now and then among them, at the time when Parliament opened in London, might be seen the venerable, broad, gilded vehicle, in which my Lord and my Lady jolted to town. In the carriage of the nobility the whole family found room; while on the back seat in the so-called "boot" or "well," the page, chaplain, and chambermaid, were seated. This Noah's ark was drawn by six horses, and before it trotted the runners, clad entirely in white, adorned with the arms of their master's house, stitched in silver on the left arm, and a long staff in their hands to clear the road for my Lord's coach, of pack-carts and other ignoble vehicles, just as they at an earlier time had been used to set the "landship" (as the first coach was called) afloat again, when it had stuck in a bog. Without this class of servants (which has now naturally died out, though the long stick yet remains in the hands of the foot-men) at the beginning of the eighteenth century no great household was complete. Generally it possessed about half-a-dozen of them. They ran in front of, and beside the fat Flemish mares to which the carriage was attached, and their speed was so great that they always arrived in sufficient time at the various inns, either to prepare the dinner for the family, or to arrange for quarters. They were light-footed, strong youths, chiefly French or Irish, who regularly, and without any especial effort, ran their five German miles a day, " to the tune of the coachman's whip," and to the accompaniment of his reproach. They received when in service, so as not to overload the stomach, nothing but barley-bread, ham, and butter-milk.

Many noble people of that period allowed these poor fellows to run in this manner from Scotland to London, and what a " runner " could do on ordinary occasions he could double if necessary, *i. e.* he could accomplish ten German miles daily. The household rode behind, armed because of robbers; and so, between his runners and his armed servants, the British nobleman of the last century arrived at London.

The glory of the English highroads is certainly gone, and the cry, " Hurrah for the road !" will no more be heard from any gentleman. Yet there is nothing more enjoyable in the world, than such

an old-fashioned coach journey as one still has in
some districts of England, on a vehicle packed
outside and inside with trunks, travellers, and
dogs, with a variety of legs everywhere hanging
down, and a variety of figures which jump up in
the air, while the coachman in his red coat makes
his "Hiss! Hiss!" and the four gallop along,
till they steam again. Yes, the highway of England still retains something of its former charm.
No moment passes but we meet a small cart, or
a merry wanderer, or a pretty shepherdess with
naked legs, in the midst of her herd of goats, or a
member of the noteworthy company of tramps,
known among ourselves by the name of *Land-
streicher*, who have made the highroads their
hunting district, sleeping under hedges, and roam-
ing over the kingdom at the expense of those
who are settled in it. These merry wanderers
have great resemblance to gipsies, mend kettles
with them, and are regarded by cooks and
bulldogs of the courtyard with not much more
favourable eyes.

But they would themselves reject with contempt
a comparison with these dark foreigners. They
pride themselves on being Britons, native-born
subjects of Her Majesty, and their life is, indeed,
one of the happiest which the world can ever

grant. The tramp has a good appetite, gratifies it at the expense of other people, smokes his pipe, and sniffs the clear morning air earlier and fresher than any one else. It is true that he is liable to rheumatism and cold if he lies on the damp ground all night, but he is the last romantic relic of the English highroad; and to see him creep with his little ragged household, out of something like a shepherd's cot, to station himself by the side of a meadow-brook behind an inn, and under the shelter of some high hedge, or at night lay himself down by a fire in an open stubble-field, these are, indeed, picturesque sights which one may sometimes enjoy by the side of the English highroads.

The vehicle—alike waggon and dwelling—in which these nomadic kettle-menders pack together, wife and children, kitchen and cellar, reminds the traveller of their common descent from German forefathers, who, some thousand years ago, passed in similar house-vans the classical morass which Tacitus describes.

But this is a reminiscence which lies pretty far from us all, especially the Englishman. Nearer to them lies that other reminiscence of the "coaching days of old England," when people said, "at every inn which God has given us we will stop and have a drink." The present generation clings yet to this fundamental rule, and particularly the Reverend in front, by the side of the coachman, was never weary of shaking the hands of the stout landladies who appeared at the door, and stroking the cheeks of their sprightly daughters who served him, tasting it beforehand, with his "bitter ale." He seemed to know every inn on the way, every Hebe of the highroad, and emptied his pewter at every station without appearing to suffer the least harm from it, except that, at the end of our journey, the ostler gave him his honest right hand, supported on which he, by means of a ladder, descended from the roof of the coach.

This was at Ambleside, after a two hours' journey, which I regard as one of the most enjoyable I can remember. As in a great panorama, mountain prospects, houses, gardens, and clear streams of water, had constantly varied; and it was a pleasure only to see the general prosperity, the wealth of the landscape, the comfort of the villages, and the glad countenances of the people.

Yet more. In these two hours I had travelled in the spirit over two hundred years; had seen the changing shapes of the highroad during that long period, and had allowed all its horrors, as well as all its cheerful follies to pass in review

before me, all its splendour and all its happy
cheerfulness, and only first awoke to the life of
the present, when under the last of the trees along
the Ambleside road, the majesty of the Lake of
Windermere shimmered out under the glorious
sunlight of an autumn afternoon. Here I took
my farewell of highwaymen and gentlemen-
coachmen, to steer towards new objects in a
pleasant little steamboat.

AUTUMN ON THE ENGLISH LAKES.

(1862.)

". . . . . et hæc olim meminisse juvabit.—*Æn.* i. 203."

I.

FURNESS ABBEY.

BESIDES including the north-west border of England, the "Lake district" surrounds part of the counties of Lancaster, Westmoreland, Cumberland, and reaches to the forerunners of the mountains of Scotland, and that "border land" upon which (highly celebrated in the old songs of both peoples) was decided the most bloody and romantic of all combats between Scotch and English. The earth around is rich with warlike traces of the past; the last remains of the Roman stations, overgrown with nettles and holly-trees, as well as the numerous castles that partly lie in ruins, and are partly inhabited by the later descendants of their first builder, give information of that wild spirit of feud which here raged for more than a thousand years, and which first emerges in history connected with the dark name of the Picts, and outlasting the days of intestine slaughter, the Wars of the White and Red Roses, first found its end in that Statute which bound both kingdoms in *one* name and *one* Parliament.

But apart from this scene of uninterrupted quarrel, Nature has secured all that she possesses of beautiful, lovely, and peaceful, in a circuit of mountains which with blue, soft contours, enclose a neighbourhood plentifully adorned with all the charms of a landscape, with forest and meadow, with hills and slopes, above all, with that which is the soul of the landscape, and which lends to it its spiritual expression ; with water, with lakes! This is the land of the Lakes—a holy relic of English olden time, of which the remembrance is here united with the remains of Celtic Druidism in so many still valleys—a holy relic of English poetry which is dedicated to the remembrance of Coleridge, which conceals the grave of Wordsworth, and in the name of " The Lake School " has received an imperishable memorial in the history of English literature.

It may be said that the " old romantic land " begins with Lancaster, an hour (by the railroad) from Preston, the cotton town, and two from Liverpool, the town of ships and of universal commerce. Here, in Lancaster, stands an old weather-grey castle, with old weather-grey towers ; one of which was built by the Emperor Adrian of Rome in the year 122, and another more than a thousand years later by the knightly Plantagenet,

Edward III. Years ago I stood once, on a mild autumn afternoon, upon the highest of these towers, my eyes fixed on the extensive view around; of the town itself, which with its grey lead roofs, in the form of a terrace, stretches up to the mountain; of field and forest, green in the blue autumn air; of the stream which peacefully meanders through the plain; of the Irish Channel, with its slowly travelling sails and masts; and of the Westmoreland hills, behind which the Lakes lie. My look followed a column of smoke which streamed thin through the blue autumn atmosphere—it was the railway which goes to these Lakes and to Scotland—and a sensation seized upon me similar to that which the poet describes, " seeking the land of the Greeks with the soul."

Of this autumn afternoon I thought when I, four years later, passed by the same castle and under the same tower. It was, as the former, an autumn afternoon, but fuller, more sunny, after a series of heavy dull days, and my soul was also riper and fuller, seized by the joy of again being free. From a short wandering through the English weaving districts, at that time heavily oppressed, I had taken a sorrowful impression of heavy weight and icy coldness. I cannot reflect without pain upon those pictures of human misery which I saw there,

and they mingle themselves in my memory with
the fog, tough and yellow, with the rain and the
wind, which, sharp and cutting, floated upwards
from the neighbouring sea, and made those days
the gloomiest I ever passed in England.

But here, by Lancaster, where the roads divide
themselves, the sun returned. It gilded with its
late beams the tower upon which I had stood
before, and the surface of green and blue, which
I knew so well. An indescribable feeling of a new
pleasure in life was awakened by this glimmer of
departing day, which sparkled upon the green
grass and stalks yet wet with great raindrops,
which at times, glittering like diamonds, fell to
earth. I had never seen the sun set so warm
in colour, and so full of promise for a long time,
as on that evening over the shore and water of
Morecambe Bay. Morecambe Bay is a deep inlet
broken by the Irish Sea in the coasts of Lancaster
and Westmoreland. A broad girdle of sand, glittering like silver against the dark blue of the
water, which now waved in the rosy golden tints
of evening, spans this bay, and close to its edge
lie the rails of the railway. There is nothing
so sublime to the soul and eye as the aspect of the
sea in such moments of solemnity, when over it
shines poured out another sea of light and colour,

of glow and glory. Then it has something of that glitter and fabulous enchantment which transports the imagination of man, and shows it in the great purple clouds pictures of fantastic mountains and palaces, as if the sunken islands emerged for a moment from out of the depth of the sea. Now the sun stands like a fiery ball upon the shuddering edge of the water. Now a vapour flies over it—as when one breathes upon a polished mirror—its pure beauty is troubled, the fire is extinguished, the red melts into grey, clouds ascend, the sea is cold, the enchantment is at an end, the sun is gone. It is dark, and we travel through an unknown land, for twilight and night are scarcely separable over the water.

Such travel in a dark unknown land gives some extraordinary foreboding to the soul, one knows not where it will end and whither it will lead. In the midst of the monotony of the rattling railway it still preserves to us something of the good old sort, when travelling was still in itself a delight, where not only the eyes but the mind was busy. Scarcely had the last sunbeam died away, when out of the mountain-passes the evening lights flashed forth, as will-o'-the-wisps out of the mountain clefts. Soon there was a hollow roll and smoke to the left,—the sea, soon

a low whispering and waving to the right,—the
forest, which at times extends even close to the far
flat bank, at times climbs high above the steep
surrounding rocks.

At last the train stopped, and we were in the
Abbey, or rather at the station which takes its
name from it, Furness Abbey.   But both are wall
to wall, and under *one* roof.   What a wonderful piece of romance is that which introduces
us by railway into the midst of an old abbey!
But so it is.   Here, where the train stops, surrounded by hedges of autumn roses and ivy-
clad ruins, still stands the old Manor House, in
which 700 years ago the Abbot of Furness resided.
The cloister and the church are fallen to pieces,
but in this manor house the present has made
itself again a habitation; and famed, as formerly
for the holiness of its monks, is now this valley
for the comforts of its hotel and the picturesque
grandeur of its ruins—the " Valley of the Deadly
Nightshade," so named after a plant which
formerly bloomed here in abundance, and may
yet be seen in the broken seal of the old Abbey.

It was, till a short time back, the custom with us
to hold England as the land of prose, and it seldom
occurred to any one to travel there except for
business.   And yet England is not only one of the

fairest, but also one of the most poetical lands, rich in lovely landscapes as in mighty wild moor and forest scenery. Nowhere in such a narrow space are so many objects united, nowhere such a variety is offered to the view. Out of one town, black with the smoke of manufactories, we pass into another of silent mediæval appearance, with gables and venerable cathedral. The sea which unites two worlds breaks on its coasts, and gathers in its roomy havens the fleets of all nations. Baronial halls surrounded by wide deer-forests, and ducal castles overgrown with ivy, rise in its interior. On the slopes of its mountains pasture the fat flock, and on the flat plain the well-to-do farmer prepares the fruitful soil. As through a carefully-tended garden we pass through all England, and the traveller participates in the feeling of prosperity which everywhere reigns. He participates in the blessing, the smiling grace and contentment spread around him, and finds in the smallest wayside inn some portion, however minute, of that comfort which the Englishman thinks necessary for life's enjoyment; and even in that most decried race of mortals, waiters, some of that stiff demeanour and measured dignity which in a higher class characterise the " gentleman."

Such an honest man, with white necktie and

black coat, received me as I alighted, and not without an inner fight against my native German awe
of such articles of attire, I allowed him to possess
himself of my travelling effects, and followed him
through an open hall, around which were the
whispers of late roses and verbenas, up the stone
steps of the old residence of the Abbot of Furness.

At once, as by a touch of magic, I was set in
the midst of mediæval romance—not of that kind
which we are wont to wonder at in museums and
scientific galleries—no, it lived around me, and I
lived in it.   Yesterday in sad, misty Liverpool,
but to-day in the poverty of the distressed weaver-
districts of Preston, and now in the lovely peace
and delicious repose of the "Nightshade Valley!"
What a name! But nothing tore the pilgrim from
this strange illusion.   I stood in a high hall,
roofed with embrowned rafters.   On both sides
cross-ways opened themselves, with those pointed
bay-windows and massive pillars known to me so
well from that old cloister school in which I passed
my youth.   All, to the smallest detail, was in the
style of that long dead past; the windows, the
carved wood-work, the staircases and floors,
the chairs, the house furniture, even the lamps,
candelabra, and chandeliers, which, though lighted
with gas, were yet very old-fashioned, and made

of brass. A large, lean greyhound was the second
to greet me, after the man in coat and cravat. He
came stalking from the staircase when I entered,
laid his beautiful head confidentially on my knee,
and looked up at me tenderly with his brown eyes,
just as was the way in old times, when the dogs
failed not to be present at the solemn welcome of
the stranger in the abode of knight or priest.

A sweet smell from the autumn flowers, stocks
and mignonette, was wafted towards me, without
from the beds of the verandah, within in the hall
from the lofty nosegays, and mixed with many
other perfumes not unlike the strong smell of in-
cense, gave new nourishment to the conceit of a
cloister.

But this illusion happily now proceeded no
farther. For out of the "culina," or "kitchen"
in the speech of the modern host, appeared some
very pretty girls, whose cloisterlike habit consisted
of a clean, snow-white kitchen apron, and from the
"refectorium," alias "dining-room," came some
young ladies, no less lovely, who, however, had
broken conventual regulations so far as to lean on
the arms of young gentlemen, and vanished with
them through the door into the garden. One of
the very loveliest nuns took a brass candlestick
out of the kitchen, ornamented with ever so many

wonderful flourishes and caricatures, and led me
up all kinds of staircases and through all kinds of
galleries, which were covered with heavy green
and red plush carpets, into a cosy little room, with
a small pointed bay-window, of which the panes
were set in lead, and through which the wild vine
from without climbed in. The trees and the waterfall rustled, the stars twinkled in the sky, but
I gave only one glance into this glimmer, tingling
and whispering, only drew one breath. Then I
turned around—but my little nun had vanished.

As well as I could, I sought to follow in her
steps; but it was not easy to find one's way aright
in this labyrinth of nooks and corners, of steps
and little steps. Not her, but the entrance I
found again, and came into the garden, which,
by the side of a splashing brook, led to the ruins.
There they stood in the gloom of the night,
huge, venerable, a little awful, as if at any moment a ghost might step forth out of them. But
all was still. Only two brooks prattled; the one
briskly splashing, the other, somewhat farther off,
dull, mysterious, as the voice of a time long past,
and become unintelligible.

Upon the turf, under the verandah and behind
the cloister-wall, in the broad, shadowy walks
of high dark chestnuts, it was much livelier.

Here walked and tittered many a gay pair. There was much wandering in dark, remote paths; here many women's dresses rustled over the turf; and there in the background before the door, glimmered once more the white aprons of the nuns .... Suddenly rose the moon over the dark forest-mountain, clear, light, all silver; a wonderful contrast to the golden comet by its side, to the dark blue wood opposite. What a scene was that! The whole garden bathed in light; the trees, the bushes, spreading broad deep shadows; and in the background, as very ghosts, the high, open bays of the windows and portals through which the moonlight streamed. Nature's voice, with all her sweet welcome tones, spoke here continually to the heart of man; and into a late hour of the night I sat listening to the whispering, rustling, and dropping of the wind and shrubbery and water which surrounded this solitude.

Suddenly I heard, as it were, another note in the magic monotone. I roused myself, and went again to the ruins, which now appeared silver-white, surrounded by large, thick masses of shadow, under the moon. Once more came over me that anxious feeling, as if an unknown something was about to step forth out of the ruins, and this time I was not mistaken. It was but a song, yet a sweet song, and sung by the soft voice of a young girl. As I listened I heard the Scottish ballad, ' Corn-rigs are bonnie, oh!'—lively and clearly it reached me out of the midst of those awful ruins :—

> " It was upon a Lammas night
> When corn rigs are bonnie, oh!
> Beneath the moon's unclouded light
> I held awa' to Annie, oh!
> The time flew by wi' tentless heed,
> Til 'tween the late and early ;
> Wi' sma' persuasion she agreed
> To see me through the barley."

Slowly the melody died away, in the manner peculiar to Scottish ballads, but only to be again taken up by a strong manly voice :—

> " I hae been blithe wi' comrades dear ;
> I hae been merry drinkin' ;
> I hae been joyfu' gath'rin' gear ;
> I hae been happy thinkin' :
> But a' the pleasures e'er I saw,
> Though three times doubled fairly,
> That happy night was worth them a',
> Amang the rigs o' barley."

Then the two voices joined pleasantly in the chorus:—

" Corn rigs an' barley rigs,
An' corn rigs are bonnie, oh !
I'll ne'er forget that happy night,
Amang the rigs wi' Annie, oh ! "

The verse was not yet ended, when there was a rustling in the ruins, and a figure came forth in bright, light raiment—the figure of a woman, slim, elegant, delicate, and pretty, as the moon which, now full, irradiated her face, showed me.

She did not see me. Coquettishly she fastened her garments together, and turning to the tower, cried, " Harry, now I shall run away." But before she could carry out her threat, " Harry " appeared upon the lowest step of the tower, embraced her, held her fast, and said joyfully, " Now try it, Jessie ;" and then kissed her heartily.

Willingly would I have remained in obscurity, but they had now observed me. " I beg your pardon," said I, whilst I made room for them. Jessie appeared much disturbed, and cried, " For God's sake!" But Harry comforted her and me with a " never mind;" and was even so amiable as to beg a light from me for his little pipe. My burning cigar might well have betrayed me to them.

Then we returned together, and on the way Harry related to me that they were a newly-

2 D

married pair, and were here at the Lake spending their " honeymoon" (at which word Jessie tittered). For the rest, they were two handsome young people, and appeared to have a good deal of love for one another.

In the Manor House all was now quiet. The only one still to be seen was my friend, the greyhound in the hall, who licked the hands of both the young married people, and ran after them to the door of their chamber, whereat he turned back, and looked after me as I withdrew, in order to seek my own. Moonshine and shadows of the wild vine danced upon the wall as I opened the door—and what a clear, lovely morning, when I awoke to the next day! All was bathed in golden sunshine, the turf sparkled, over the trees lay the coloured glow of autumn, and high above in the warm blue heaven still stood the pale crescent moon. Before me, surrounded by green, rising earnest and holy out of the emerald carpet of turf, stood the ruins of the Abbey; wonderfully sublime ruins, so wide, so spacious, everywhere fallen to pieces, and yet everywhere so magnificent! Here for the first time, in this lovely light, clearly enlivened by the background of the blue heavens and the foreground of green turf, I surveyed them in their real connection. Imagination

easily supplies the missing parts, and peoples the
stately building with forms of past time. The little
brook sings its song, and the ever-moving trees
and bushes join in, rustling as the sound of the
organ and the choristers. What a song was it
which I here heard! How it murmured to me in
the holy, sunny stillness of the morning! I sat at
my little arched window surrounded with wild
vine, and looked through the leaden casement.
Nothing but this song of the brook and the trees,
—the hum of the insects,—the trilling of the
lark,—the far-off sound of an axe in the forest,—
the whetting of a scythe in the meadow;—and
anon a hollow noise, and rolling from afar, coming
continually nearer, and now, with a cloud of smoke,
breaking forth in a long row out of the green
hill and puffing past—the railway with its coal-
waggons, which run through the midst of this
territory, the once consecrated ground of the old
Abbey! Already all is again still—the new time
is over; the old time, with its sun and its dreams,
rises again, and stands alone before the devout
soul.

This is the threshold to the district of the
English Lakes. Here where I now sit, once sat
the Abbot of Furness, and the noble lords of
Preston followed him in the Manor House. Half-

monkish, still half-knightly, is everything in it—
the gay, glass windows, the high roofed halls,
the stately fireplaces . . . . But I look dreaming
into the forest and the sky, and the little brook
from below murmurs and whispers . . . .

When later I went into the breakfast-room, I
had the pleasure of seeing all the young lovers
and married couples (for in the first stage of marriage both seem to be the same) who yesterday
wandered through the gardens in the moonshine,
assembled at little tables, at which they fed with
uncommonly good appetites. Here I found again
"Harry and Jessie from the ruins." They sat at
a table under the great garden window, half in
shadow of the shaking leaves, half in the small
streams of sunny light which stole through the
leafy branches. They had taken good care to
have their table well provided with all the good
things of a "substantial" English breakfast, and
invited me to partake. After the meal was
finished, Harry filled his little wooden pipe.
Jessie put on her great straw hat, took a beauti-
fully-bound copy of Moore's 'Loves of the Angels'
under her arm, and so they withdrew with a
cheerful greeting, clomb the hill behind the ruins,
and disappeared under the forest.

But my friend, the greyhound, associated with

me. Even he, however, left me in disgust on the turf before the Abbey, when I was for going farther; for he was spoilt by the peace of this monastic abode, and no friend to fatiguing walks, and so stretching himself close to a bank under a rose-bush at his ease in the warm autumn sunshine, he let me go my ways alone.

" Quærite primum regnum Dei." These words, which I read on an old stone over the staircase as I left the coffee-room, had deeply impressed themselves on my memory; and therefore I went into the ruins in order "first to seek the kingdom of God." Oh! how still the courts were! How the rustling wind preached, whispering through the cloisters, the nothingness of all earthly things— all without exception, worldly as well as spiritual, love as well as its renunciation!—the familiar rooms full of silent happiness, the high vaulted roofs full of fervent devotion! See, here once stood a lordly cloister, with proud portals, strong pillars, and high towers. It was founded in the year 1127, under the patronage of Stephen, Earl of Montaigne and Boulogne, afterwards King of England, by the monks of the convent of Savigny, in Normandy, who had come to England under the guidance of Evan, their first abbot. Three years and three days they stayed in Tulkett, near

Preston, before they settled in Nightshade Valley,
and founded this cloister, which they dedicated to
the Virgin Mary. Here, in deepest desolation,
had monks prayed for hundreds of years. On
their seal they bore the image of their Saint.
There is the Virgin under a starry canopy,—on
her left arm a baby,—about whose head is a halo
woven, and in her right hand she holds a ball, as
Queen of the World. On both sides is a coat-of-
arms, with the three Norman leopards, above them
a branch of nightshade, beneath a monk in the
full habit of his order. The flying dragon was
assumed in honour of the second Earl of Lancaster,
the relation of the royal Plantagenet, encircling all
were the words—

SIGILLUM . COMMUNE . DOMUS . BEATE . MARIE . DE . FURNESIO.

To what a distant time is the imagination
brought back by this seal! Yet with all which it
possessed for us holy, affecting, and honourable,
it was broken in pieces as the walls of the cloister
itself, when in the sixteenth century Henry VIII.
of England left the creed of Rome, and con-
fiscated all monastical possessions. Since that
time the old glory is turned to dust; only these
ruins are here to tell the sad history of its fall.

Through the fair indented windows pours in by

turns sunshine and rain,—the lofty pillars standing erect on the turf cast their lonely shadows over desolate halls and walls; buttresses and pointed arches lie around in ruin. The artistic work of stonemasons, long dust, lies in pieces in the grass; two heads look down from the chief entrance, the heads of King Stephen and his wife, the friends of the Abbey while they lived. But kingly favour, like all else, passes away. Even monarchs must turn to dust and ashes, and only of a very few will posterity preserve the names. What mean these upright figures without heads, but with folded hands holding a breviary? What signify these stone pilgrims lying flat upon the ground? What these gravestones with the crook on the burst slab, these illegible inscriptions, these crosses fallen asunder? They show us the striving of a past period to preserve their recollection in that to come; they show us how they strove in vain, when their names were not written elsewhere than on slabs of stone.

Nature herself destroys these names with inexorable finger. She sows her green seed in all joints and clefts; she clambers over the highest towers, and leaves her green scaling-ladders waving in the air; she covers the churchyard with her growing green; she buries one generation after another ; but her smile and her beauty belong to all.

A sharp whistle rang through the stillness. The enchanted kingdom disappeared, the loco-motive was hissing by. It was the train for the Lakes. It waked the pair sunk in the wood there above in the ' Love of the Angels.' Hastily they passed me with a short farewell : they were off to the Lakes in this very train. A second whistle a little later, told me that Harry and Jessie had left Nightshade Valley. For awhile echoed the hollow roar of the departing train amidst the ruins, and then the former still-ness returned. Softly above me waved the leaves of the ivy, low out of the distance whispered the water under the old bridge covered with foliage, and nothing more interrupted my meditation and my dream.

II.

THE LAKES OF WESTMORELAND.

The Lake of *Windermere* is the most comprehensive and varied of the Westmoreland Lakes. It is the " diamond of the Lake district," and the " Queen of the Lakes." Its length from Ambleside to Newby Bridge is some eleven English miles, its breadth one. It is deeper than the other lakes, and numerous islands, luxuriantly wooded, lend its shape the appearance of a greater variety. The characteristic of its landscape scenery is a tender and graceful beauty. It has nothing of the savage grandeur of the neighbouring lakes of Cumberland, which in this respect almost vie with those of Scotland; and here only, at Ambleside, the mountains attain a reasonable height, whilst on the other parts of the coast they are but gently-swelling hills, on whose tender line the eye willingly hangs. A surprising view is it where the road from Ambleside opens on the lake. In the foreground, the varied *staffage* of coaches, boats and steamers, with men embarking and disembarking; in the background, the mountains, whose

unparalleled magnificence suddenly discloses itself,
and between these the lake, so still in the sunset!
We go aboard the steamer, 'The Fairy Queen,'
which is just departing, whilst the other, 'The
Firefly,' arrives. The golden water is our cradle.
In the background are the mountains with their
tops one above another in tender aerial contours,
with the colours and shapes of light vaporous
clouds, at last disappearing, and surrounded by a
tender mist, melting into the distance, so that the
eye almost loses the distinction between earth and
air. All dissolves into a blue vapour, in which
we recognise fanciful and soft figures, of which
it scarcely can be told whether they be those
of mountain or of cloud. Around us glows the
water, in whose dark depths are mirrored in the
late sunset all the colours of the cloud-mountains,
the mountain-clouds of heaven, which with all its
azure, with each of its rosy cloudlets, arches itself
below the wave. Here and there is one of the
blooming islands of the lake, like a flower-pot
of porphyry, filled with thick, gold-green, luxu-
riant underwood, which spreads a shine of the
same hue in the water around. A dream-voice
overpowers the soul—and yet it is not too weary
to turn back to the presence of life which is here
so indescribably beautiful—to the meadows lying

in the mist of the sunshine, to the woods, which
seem blue in the purple shadows of the afternoon,
and to the white houses on the shore, the " villas "
and " cottages " which, lightened by the red gleam
of fuchsias, offer pictures of peace and domestic
happiness, almost more lovely in their reality than
in dream. Oh, to dwell in these houses around
which flowers bloom, and the lake whispers, under
the mountains, on the meadows—and here in
entire seclusion to devote one's life to contemplation and the monitor within! Here have poets
lived—poets whose names the English people
mention with pride and love. Here by this lake,
and under these hills, was Wordsworth born; here
Southey settled and Coleridge sang; here was the
home of the Lake School named after the lakes, on
one of which we now gaze, and which blossomed
alone, undisturbed by the travelling swarm, till
the end of the last century.

Rich in the remembrances of these is the surrounding scenery, and celebrated through their
poetry is each wood, each mountain, each brook,
each lake. It is impossible to walk in this neighbourhood without thinking of them, without being
reminded of them and their famous circle of friends,
in which one of the most interesting men was
De Quincey, the opium-eater. Yes; something like

an opiate seems to be in the air and the beauty of
this Lake district; something like a gradual dissolu-
tion, a pleasant soporific, a dreamy captivity. Such
a character is peculiar to the Lake School. Most of
their great poems have the formlessness, at times
the disconnection of dreams—of dreams, moreover, of an uneasy sleep, an opium drunkenness
(Coleridge died from opium-drinking); but they
have also the fanciful boldness of these, and their
entire scorn of earthly limits, of possibilities which
lie in time and space. We can scarcely call
them spiritualists, for they have much more of a
strong, if not exactly healthy sensitiveness; but
" their kingdom lies in cloud-land, and their world
is only too often a visionary world;" says Freili-
grath, our German poet, who translated some of
their most important poems, and published those
of Coleridge in the " Tauchnitz edition." I can
imagine how those indistinct fancies of far unknown lands and seas attracted our poet—him
who *dreamed* of the wonders of the Tropic Zone,
of the mirage of the desert. But he dreamed of
the *actual*, the lion with his claws in the Giraffe's
back, the tiger fighting with the white man;
whilst their dreams are *phantasmagorias*, which
float like Coleridge's phantom ship *over* reality. It
is true this entire neglect of that which we consider

definite order makes sometimes a childish, but
still more often it makes a gigantic impression,
as if the whole despair of genius was struggling
against boundaries which no power is in a condition to destroy. One immediately feels a certain
relationship with the *Sturm und Drang-Periode*,
or dawn of German classic literature, in which
Goethe wrote his 'Werther's Leiden,' and soon
after, Schiller his 'Robbers;' only with this difference, that one strove after earth, and reached it
in fact, with firm feet; while the other, the Lake
School, strove after heaven, and remain fixed in
the clouds. Yet is it these who freed English
poetry from the fetters of a formalism of style
and matter inherited from Pope and Dryden, and
prepared the way for the appearance of the great
romancists, Byron and Scott.

But we Germans must not forget that it was
our own poetry and philosophy on which those
poets leaned; that they formed their ideas in
Germany, and were instructed under the influence
of German doctrine and teachers. Their two heads,
Wordsworth and Coleridge, came to Germany in
1798 to study the German language, German
poetry, German philosophy, and German theology;
to visit the singer of the Messiah, and to hear from
him that Bürger was a true poet, who would live,

and Schiller, on the contrary, would be soon
forgotten. Nevertheless, two years after, in 1800,
appeared Coleridge's translation of Schiller.
Would Goethe's introduction into England by
Carlyle have been possible, had it not been preceded by the Lake School? This it was that,
through the philosophy of Kant, Fichte, and Schel-
ling, threw the yeast of the present movement into
the clammy theology of England and America;
and to this, above all, are we indebted for that
mighty exchange of ideas and movements, which
now—profiting both shores—" streams to and fro
over the German Ocean."

In the meantime we have reached Bowness, and
our little bark lies at anchor. Bowness is on the
left bank of the lake, nearly in the middle of its
whole extent. It is quite a charming little spot,
—half village half town, like most in this neighbourhood. Here lies a little heap of houses together on a hill, like Swiss chalets; there are two
more with wooden carved-work, and all kinds
of creeping plants by the waterside. Streets
properly there are none, every path leads to
the lake below, or from the lake above.

From Bowness extends a pretty mountain path,
between wood and country seats, to the little
village of Windermere, and to a stately hotel

with broad terrace, from which we enjoy a truly charming prospect over the lake and its banks. There, immediately under the terrace, wholly covered with flowers and trees, ends the railway from London ; and in this secluded idyl of sea and hill, where one lives as in another world, every afternoon letters, newspapers, magazines, and books, come fresh from town, with a convenience only perhaps possible in England.

Best was it up here in the forenoon after breakfast. Out on the terrace sat, perhaps, some gentlemen, and read the ' Times,' or enjoyed a walk under the verandah, smoking a cigar. Then one conveyance after another drove off; the large house on the hill-top was empty, the terrace still, and I remained alone with the sun and the laurel-hedges. Over these shining hedges, through whispering tree-tops, over glimmering roofs of the village and soft hills, the glance travelled away to the dreaming lake, and the vapoury purplish blue of its woody bank.

Sweet was it then to wander down the path to the hill-side under the majestic vaulted chestnut-trees. It was quiet as on a Sabbath, as if Nature was here occupied for ever in prayer ; only now and then came a solitary conveyance, or a dog barked, or a bell rang through the air. So still was it that

one could distinguish the trembling and whispering
of each leaf, the light sighing of the wind, and
every voice in the chorus of the birds.   Still
houses with shadowy gardens, in which to *live*
itself must be a happiness, lay at my side ; dark
groups of trees, varied with green meadows and
vapoury wood-paths, which led deeper into the
mountain ; and over all through the leaves
trembling in the sun, I caught a glimpse of blue
water or blue sky.   Such an indescribable peace,
such a holy calm, was around !   And my heart is
full of a sentiment like home-sickness when I think
on those days so fair and golden, so sunny and so
silent.   Then and there, when I sat myself down
by that English lake, on one of the mossy stones
under the thick chestnuts, in the balmy air of the
morning, I had a feeling as if life had no purer
joy to offer than such a moment of blessed in-
toxication and absorption in nature.   Then speaks
the spirit in us with that spirit which blows in
the bloom, and whispers in the whisper of the
wind.   It feels itself one with that spirit in pure
harmony, and the soul begins to speak in its own
language with every leaf that stirs.   The gloomy
veil which the impure alloy of day breathed over
its mirror passes away, and clear again therein
shines the sunny picture of the outer world, with

all its outlines, its vapoury colours, and its quiet life.

The lower part of the lake from Bowness to Newby Bridge, where it seems to lose itself in a rustling waterfall, is of a more simple beauty, yet retaining the character of the beautiful. It was in one of those long autumn evenings, full of colour, which have so tender and sad an influence on the spirits, that I took a boat at Bowness to travel over the lake in this direction. The mountains of the background had already lost themselves in the deep lilac of the evening, and left the eye only the weak outlines of their contours; all else seemed to grow brown in vapour,—ravine, height, valley, and mountain-top, a strange grey picture of mist. But before me and around me was light. On the right the sun sank behind the high hill-tops, sometimes flaming out fiery from a mountain cleft; on the left glimmered his varied reflection. Over the wood hung the double purple of the autumn and the sunset,—the leaves so crisp, so brown, so golden, moved by the wind—here and there a soft, sloping meadow with cows grazing on it,— a comfortable quiet house by the edge of the wood or of the water. Now the sun shone forth once more, now it disappeared for the last time behind a wall of hills, and the lake darkened into a deep

2 E

steel-grey,—growing ever darker and more quiet,
till I was quite alone on the wide water, black
with the shadows of the mountains, and nothing
was heard but the strokes of my boatman's oars.
Once, indeed, a steamer passed us,—the ' Fairy
Queen,'—with music, which died away over the
lake, soft and dreamy, in the evening stillness.
Then the loneliness of the night and of the water
was no more interrupted; and by the time our
boat reached the margin of the lake, the heavens
were golden with those great stars, the mountains
had taken that colour of deep dark blue, which
give something so unspeakably solemn to the night
landscape.   We had still to go a little distance
under trees, whilst the roar of a great water
seemed continually to come nearer, before we
reached the ' White Swan ' inn, in which Mrs.
White hospitably rules.

I had brought with me a card of recommendation to this lady from a friend of the house at
Preston, and I must say, that I have never been
more heartily welcomed or more hospitably cared
for than in the ' White Swan ' at Newby Bridge.
I had scarcely sent in my card, before Mrs. White,
a stately woman of forty years, with quite a
morning glow on her cheeks and nose, entered
the little room in which I had laid down my knap-

sack. There followed her, in round numbers, half
a dozen most charming girls, all of whom she
presented to me as her daughters, and who, after
confidingly shaking hands with me one after
another in descending order, were all sent off to
make things comfortable for me in the 'White
Swan' at Newby Bridge. One went away with
the order to prepare my bed and bedroom; another
was to look after my tea and supper; the third to
dismiss my boatman; the fourth to fetch boot-jack
and slippers; the fifth—but what say I? Never
in my life was so much trouble taken for my
comfort, and the whole half-dozen had plenty for
their hands, large and small, to do, while Mrs.
White reclined in an arm-chair by my side, to
have a chat with me about her friend. The arm-
chair in which Mrs. White had established herself
was the most colossal piece of furniture of the
sort I have ever seen, and so old that one must
think himself a hundred years older when sitting
in it. All the little room was a marvel of old-
fashioned comfort, with couch and arm-chairs,
brown, and with wolf's heads carved on the arms.
The lamp on the table was as large and heavy as
a small lighthouse. The low walls were decorated
with pictures of country-seats, sporting dogs, races,
and noble gentlemen and ladies of the last century

in long perukes. Over the looking-glass, which
was of an oval form, and had the peculiarity of
giving every one who looked into it an appearance
of suffering from toothache, hung a fish, very
ingeniously carved in wood, and painted and
varnished with exquisite neatness. In short, here
I was in one of those good old English "country
inns" which some of the novelists of the last
century describe for us in such an incomparable
manner. I wanted nothing but my friend Squire
Western, in 'Tom Jones,' to smoke a pipe and
empty a tankard, or perhaps even two, in his company. I thought of him enough on that evening ;
also of his daughter, the lovely Sophia, though this
last thought may have been a little unjust towards
Mrs. White.

The sign of the house was a swan, which sat
up high above the door in painted wood. On
another part of the house hung a blue bunch of
grapes, probably as a counter-demonstration, and
for the better information of those travellers,
who with the representation of a swan involuntarily associate that element on which this poetic
bird lives.

The 'White Swan' of Newby Bridge lies quite
alone in this valley, and nothing could be heard
but the roar of the waterfall opposite. Just on

the other side of the bridge, which leads across
the water, was a forge, before which a couple of
lads stood and sang Scotch songs; and somewhat
farther on was a "mansion," that is, the country-
seat of one of the gentry, with a park and high
wall. That was all; besides only mountains, woods,
water, and the magnificent starry sky, and solitude.

By ten o'clock all was quiet at the 'White
Swan,' and I found myself alone in my chamber
just above the waterfall. It was so cozy there.
Again I might have imagined myself in the inn at
Upton;—and I should not have been astonished
if the door had suddenly been burst open, and the
Irish gentleman, with a cudgel in his hand,
had rushed in to seek his wife—but nothing
of the kind occurred. Then there were so many
mysterious nooks and corners in this room, cup-
boards built in the wall, wooden seats nailed to
the floor, washhand-stands of incalculable length.
And then there was the bed, such a colossal huge
bed as I had never hitherto seen even in England,
that land of wonders in the way of beds—a little
dwelling-house, with roof, walls, and pillars,—
what do I say?—with four mighty posts like
boundary posts, a kind of small German Principality. Into this bed one gets by means of port-
able carpeted steps. It was of a completely square

form. The length and breadth could therefore
not be distinguished from one another, and the
intention of top and bottom could only be guessed
at ; so I thought to myself of the " bed of Ware,"
which appears to have been the English normal
bed of Shakspeare's time, and of which Sir Toby,
in ' Twelfth Night,' says it measured twelve feet
square, and twelve men and twelve women could
sleep in it. Wonderful things can one dream in
such a bed. And moreover there was the rushing
of the waterfall, which filled the loneliness of the
night with a strong roar almost like thunder. I
had shortly before heard sung a song by Tenny-
son. Now the waterfall appeared to have appro-
priated the words of the Laureate, and it hummed
unceasingly in my ears :—

> " For men may come, and men may go,
> But I go on for ever."

At last it was morning, and at an early hour
lively, especially in the stable. Horses and coaches
were brought out and washed, the honest " ostler "
appeared on the scene, and Dame White, with her
pretty daughters, began again to conduct domestic
concerns in the kitchen and courtyard. Here also
I made the acquaintance of Mr. White, that is to
say, on the bridge opposite the house, where he

was standing with two large, wild-looking hounds, and "smacking," as he expressed it, a new whip. Mr. White was so good as to call my attention to the beauties of the neighbourhood. As he could not take me for much of a "sportsman," he informed me about the fish which were caught in the river, and recommended me as bait a particular kind of worm, which I could find at a certain place in the bank, farther up. After this he turned again to his hounds, and went away to "smack" the new whip, while I walked along under the gently-moving trees by the water-side, drinking in with perfect delight the fresh perfume of the morn. It was such a genuine picture of an English landscape; the little inn with the white swan and the blue bunch of grapes; the small windows with the vine-leaves creeping round them; and the hospitable column of smoke which rose quietly from the wide chimney; the grooms with the horses and carriages at the stable; the girls with buckets at the well; now a coach-and-four rolling up, stopping, and filling the space before the house with figures of all kinds of colours—among which, naturally, the red of the "coaching gentleman" was especially prominent; the quiet mansion, like an enchanted castle concealed in green, with a high wall surmounted by trees and bushes, without any sign of life; the forge; the waterfall; the neat quiet path between the meadows, on which cows pasture, and a child stands minding them; and around, almost touching these, the wooded mountains which picturesquely inclose the little valley of Newby Bridge.

It was nine o'clock in the morning when, after an excellent breakfast, I shook the respective hands of Dame White and her daughters on my departure, and betook myself to the steamboat which was to bear me back again across the lake to Ambleside. It was a day without sun,—a melancholy sky, the lake veiled in mist. The air was soft, and full of the sweetest autumn aroma; but a deep sadness lay spread over the watery mirror, and each tree on its banks let its feathery foliage hang down as if in sorrow. There was nothing of light, but the one variously-coloured green displayed by wood and meadow;—that wonderful wealth of colour of the woods in autumn, filled with beeches now green, now yellow; with oaks, which, like strong natures, pay but slowly the tribute of existence; and with firs and pines, that description of coniferous trees which in the more southerly countries of Europe and in England, akin to them in the mild vegetative force of climate, has somewhat supplanted our wild pines. The islands in the water too—my bouquets of flowers in porphyry vases—glowed now, free from light and shade, in the complete splendour of their own light yellow and dark green. All that adorned the margin of the lake—the woods, each meadow, each house grown over with ver- dure, each little villa encircled by gardens—was reflected dreamily in the depth of the waters, as though intoxicated by its own native beauty. And this reflection was almost more beautiful than the reality itself, for the water was of such wonderful clearness that the green of the moun- tains and meadows glittered in it with the peculiar brilliancy of coloured jewels. Closing the view of the lake stood the shadows of the mountains like dark gigantic forms; as yesterday, in the clear sky, clouds could scarcely be distinguished from mountains, so to-day, in the dark sky, could clouds and mountains scarcely be distinguished from their reflection in the water. Such a mist of clouds and vapour, and damp breath from wood and water, surrounded us—it was like a dream! Then a boat passed by with two ladies in white dresses and round hats—one held the rudder with both hands, the other lay back in the red cushions and dreamed. Then came a boat with sails;

others rocked near the shore. Everything was so
subdued; the light, the shade, every sound in the
air, every plash of the wave, the beating of one's
own heart. There was such a harmony in this
sunless day that the soul imperceptibly changed
into the same tone. It was a day to visit graves,
and celebrate feasts of remembrance!

And to such an act of piety this day was consecrated, for I wished to visit the dwelling-places of
the poets, those which they inhabited as long as
they lived, and those which they now inhabit
since they left life—their graves. The coach
which runs in this true land of poets, awaits
at Ambleside those who come from the lake.
Here, where now dwells the grey authoress, Miss
Martineau, a charming hilly district opens, through
which the road gently leads upwards. Behind
me on the outside of the coach sat two young
English ladies, with their equally youthful hus-
bands. One of the ladies had a pleasant, noble
countenance, pale, and with a pair of eyes as
melancholy as this day. Waterfalls murmured
down—subdued—here and there on each side of
the road. The noise of water accompanies us continually in this Lake country; now it resounds
from the height, now it resounds from the depth.
Before long even the coachman began to speak of

Wordsworth and Coleridge. That is no wonder. Everyone speaks of them here.

Here, where the mountain rises up even from the road, where the park, half wood, half garden, leads up to the old castle, where the waterfalls murmur, and where, through the veiled trees beneath the gloomy sky, a new lake becomes visible. Here is, indeed, a land for the poet! There is in it a beauty so rich in sentiment, so much soul, so much harmony! For, to repeat what I have said already, water is the soul of the landscape. What says our Goethe?—" The soul of man is like water. It comes from Heaven, and to Heaven returns. Again it comes back to Earth, and so alternates for ever."

Therefore our soul feels a sort of affinity to this soul of the landscape, and with a quiet aspiration it follows for hours the graceful windings of a stream, or subsides into blissful dreaminess in the sympathetic obscurity of a mountain-inclosed lake.

The park, with the castle-like residence in it, close to our road, is that of the old Norman family le Fleming; the lake which we see glittering through the trees is Rydal Water. Rydal Water, or Rydal-Mere, is as lovely a piece of water as can be found in all the Lake district; so small, indeed, that one can survey the whole of its banks, but even on that account so much the more lovely. Like a little jewel it lies in the rich casket of this happy land. And on the mountain above the lake and the park, called Rydal Mount, still stands the house in which William Wordsworth dwelt.— Immediately after this little lake comes the not much more extensive one of Grasmere; and in a small house resembling a cottage, on its extreme verge, lived Coleridge, and after him, De Quincey. Dreamy enough for an opium-eater! High rushes grow on the margin of the water. Swans glide about on its drowsy expanse. Dim hills allow their floating images to mingle in the scene. All slumbers, all dreams by this lake of Grasmere.

In the court and garden of the hotel, before which the coach stops, it was no whit more animated. I sat—I know not how long—close to the brink of the lake, where the late autumn roses shed their fragrance. It was so quiet here! One heard the beetles hum, and every bird in the air sing. Mountains and meadows among the woods inclosed the motionless water;—a red gondola passed along with a young couple in it, and three swans, as in the national song, swam slowly behind.

At last, late in the afternoon, I ascended from the lake. By hilly paths, which lead along the slopes between high hedges, here apparently losing themselves, there reappearing, I wandered through fields, past quiet country houses. I saw no man, I only now and then heard a cart. Far below, where the lake ends and the hills open out a little, lies Grasmere, the village; in the fore-part the church, one of those of which the modestly-religious exterior invites the heart not only to devotion but to humility,—and behind this church is the churchyard with the grave of the poet. If the dead felt every step that is made on their graves! I have a remembrance of my childhood, that we were strictly forbidden when we went into a God's acre to tread on the graves. Since that time it has been impossible to me to set my foot on a grave, and it always grieves me if I see any one else do so. Of the poets only *one* rests here in Grasmere—William Wordsworth. Hartley Coleridge, who sleeps near him, is not the poet who was called Samuel Taylor Coleridge, but his genial, though, unfortunately, somewhat disorderly son. He himself, the poet, died at Highgate Hill, in London, and in the house of Dr. Gillman; to whom he had intrusted himself that he might cure him of the use of the deadly opium. There, above the noise and smoke of the roaring Capital, in the pure air of the suburban hill, he rests in his grave. Southey, who lived not far from this lake, in the neighbourhood of Keswick, also lies interred in the churchyard of his village. On Wordsworth's grave rises a very simple iron tablet. In this one grave rest together the poet and his wife, and on this tablet there is nothing to be read but the words: "William Wordsworth, 1850; Mary Wordsworth, 1859." But how much these words say! How much of that faithfulness which surrounds a whole life, and of that love which believes in a reunion after death! How pleasantly from their common grave they guide our look beyond it! Pyramids and urns, in which even this little village churchyard is so rich, may be for others; the poet and his wife have only this simple tablet but—their immortal names are upon it. And down below the meadow-brook murmurs away to the lake, that same lake which the poet in life so loved to greet and sing. A little bird trills in the evening air, and the pine trembles gently over his grave. Oh! to sleep like this poet in his own land, surrounded by all which had been the glory of his life, his mountains, his woods; sung to rest by the chorus of familiar trees, the friendly brook, and native bird! If any dead man is to be envied, it is William Wordsworth! Nothing disturbs the solitude of this place but the reverence of his people, when now and then a traveller comes to rest by the singer's grave. Nothing is there but the little grey church, the grave-digger's house, the pine-tree, the solitary bird, who sings over the churchyard his twilight song, the brook, which gently plashing, kisses its walls, murmuring " for ever, for ever, for ever." It was here at the grave of the poet that I saw the English lady with the melancholy eyes once more; for the last time, for she remained when I went. She entered the churchyard with her party as I was about to leave it. After a little while, when I looked round from the road, I saw her still sitting on the graves—with her light garments in the deepening twilight—not unlike the spirit of resignation.

The day had worn away into grey evening, and the night lay soft and heavy, and dark as velvet upon the hills, when, after long wandering, I reached the lake.

III.

THE LAKES OF CUMBERLAND.

It was again a morning of glorious beauty, that morning on which I bade farewell to my darling Lake of Windermere! The landscape, the water, the hills, beamed in a true golden autumn splendour. Under the hot, midday sun I drove away in a little cart, with a horse as thin as a spindle, but powerful to go and to ascend hills, and with a very discreet little man in a coat of green frieze, who acted as coachman. For the pride of red coats and of coaches and four had an end here, upon coming to the narrow, stony paths in the mountains and to the lakes of Cumberland.

It was one of the warmest dâys in this year, and at this altitude all was blue with mist and shimmer. Directly from the hotel the road ascended almost uninterruptedly, and with the road I myself had to ascend. For the little man in the frieze coat had much more compassion for his horse than for his passenger, and for the greatest part of the difficult way all three—coachman, horse, and traveller — walked along peaceably side by side. We left below us Windermere, the lake, the village, and at last the mountains, which there had appeared to me so lofty; and from our height had a wonderful view down, where all at last vanished in a kind of transparent blue, in which here and there the white glittering bands of the lake appeared to be woven. At last a hot vapour concealed this also, and the air above us grew cooler; here, on the desolate mountain-crest, we had reached the border of Cumberland.

This county is, with Northumberland, the most northerly in England. It reaches to the edge of Scotland, and much resembles it in appearance. This wilder character of Cumberland encountered us immediately in the high, bare, stone rocks, which, only lightly overgrown with the green of heath or moss, cast their colossal shadows on the broad sunny surfaces of the opposite precipices. I was also reminded many times of Irish scenery and loneliness; and in the midst of this unusual glow of autumnal sunshine there was something strange to the soul, something stupefying in the almost immediate change from the shores of the lakes, fragrant with wood and meadow, to the vast monotony of these treeless and shrubless table-lands.

Here on these plateaux, which in some places, with their rugged, scarcely accessible precipices, resemble natural fastnesses, has long been the refuge of the first inhabitants of England, the so-called Cymri, and even to our time their name is retained in that of the county, " Cumberland," whilst their old Celtic language, even the nation itself, has merged into the English. The Britons of Strath-Clyd, and Ryed, and Cumbria, melted away by degrees into the surrounding people, and, with the loss of their language, ceased to be recognisable as a distinct race. But it is very probable that this process was accomplished at a comparatively recent time. In the bishopric of Glasgow, which includes the greatest part of the old Cumbrian kingdom, the "barbarous " language of the Britons gave way to that dialect of Saxon-English which is called " Lowland Scottish," somewhere about the thirteenth century: in some remote districts the language continued until the Reformation, but was then entirely destroyed by the ecclesiastical government of the Protestant clergy. But the broad " u," which the traveller encounters on the shores of the lakes of Cumberland, reminds him of the heavy kind of tone of the old Celtic tongue which is still spoken by the inhabitants of the principality of Wales, as is

indicated in Cumberland by several British traditions of that especial land of the Cambrians, Wales.
Pendragon Castle, while it recalls to his thoughts
the fabulous Uther, the father of Arthur, conjures
up at once before his sight the whole of the
poetry of Merlin. "King Arthur's Round Table,"
one of the countless Druidical remains in these
secluded mountain districts, the last asylum of
that gloomy form of heathenism, at once, if only
by its name, causes to rise before our eyes the
knightly King and his brave traditional companions, with all the memories of Guinevere and
the Holy Grail. Some of the mountains which
lend to this landscape an appearance at once so
gloomy and so sublime, have preserved the desig-
nations given to them by the primitive population, and "Skiddaw" and "Helvellyn" stand now
as mighty monuments of a whole race which has
passed away.

For a long while no man, no carriage met us;
and as in a country dead and forsaken of all
living beings, we wandered on under the silent,
burning sun, always ascending and ascending,
until we reached a gate which closed the way,
with a cottage close by, out of which at our call
came an old woman to open the wooden barrier
for us. Every vehicle stops before the door of this

cottage; because, as a board over it says, " This is the highest inhabited house in England." The old woman brought some water for the horse, and some beer for the man, and they both—untroubled by the almost ghostly sensation which the loneliness of the scene caused—drank with much relish. Grey and bathed in sunlight the stony mountain stood before us in the dark blue afternoon sky, without a tree, without a shrub, without a trace of life. Only the purling of a spring close by the house could be heard, and the cackling of a couple of hens which ran about on the scanty grass down in the hollow. There seemed to be no one in the house besides the old woman; and when she appeared at the door, with her face looking as gloomy and wrinkled as the rocks opposite, I thought involuntarily of the story of the wicked fairy and the runaway bairns. .But the man—my coachman—was not assailed by such ideas; and after he had drunk his beer, and mine as well, he harnessed his little horse again, and we drove forward in the now lessening splendour of the sun, which already held its afternoon position over the mountains. Deep hollows full of blue shadows opened before us, while in the purer height of ether the summits of the rocks took all kinds of fantastic outlines.

" This is the Church," said the man, whose mouth had been opened by the two glasses of beer, " this is the Giant," " this is the Cross." I took the man's word for it, but saw nothing of it all, on account of being obliged to hold fast to the rail of the little cart, so as not to fall out. For as we formerly had ascended in an alarming manner, so now we flew down hill in a manner still more alarming; often so close to a precipice, or turning so sharply round projecting ledges of rock, that an upset seemed almost the sole possibility in our advance. But the man told me to hold fast, to have no fear, and to let the horse go; and as I fulfilled these three directions as much as in me lay, all went off very well.

Now the country began to be somewhat more lively, after the long monotony through which we had hitherto come. On the declivities of the still bare mountain-sides clambered sheep—those modest animals for whose support the fruitfulness of stones appears to suffice—and above all, water-falls ran and roared from the granite, and curved about in long silver bands, glittering down from the height, or rushed in broad cascades over blocks of stone and rubble, filling the silence with their lovely music.

Cattle-keeping is the only employment that

remains for the inhabitants of this angry district, which reminded me of the "inhospitable heights" of Horace's Ode. Their grey stone huts are to be seen scattered here and there, lying under a sheltered declivity, scarcely to be distinguished in this blinding sunshine from the rocks on which they hang. Stone walls divide off the several lots, and where the road winds along the boundary barred gates are erected, around which lie in wait whole troops of children from the neighbouring cottages, who, as soon as a carriage approaches, get up to open the gate, and expect their "ha'penny" as toll for so doing. But they do not beg like their relations in Wales, still less do they refuse passage to non-payers, like those in Scotland, where this kind of compulsory levying of tolls has survived as a remainder of the "black-mail" of the old times of the clans. No; these children of the Cumberland mountains are certainly very dirty, running barefoot and clothed in rags, but, nevertheless, very modest and pleasant children. One of them, a girl of ten years old, with very pretty dark blue eyes, sprang up on the board behind, and drove on with us over stock and stone, allowed me to stroke her hair, her forehead, and her cheeks, and looked at me, constantly smiling so bashfully, as if she desired more. At last I kissed her mouth.

She continued, however, to smile, and at length, after half an hour, sprang from the carriage. Unfortunately I only learnt from my coachman when it was too late, that the fulfilment of her modest wish had nothing to do with a kiss, but with a "ha'penny," of which, in fact, with such a pretty child I had never even thought.

Gradually as the road descended, the character of the landscape became softer: trees again appeared, at first only pines and other coniferous trees, then leafy trees mingled with these, the foot of the mountain was clothed with shrubs, and the cheerful evening sunshine illumined soft grassy levels and lovely woods, between which red roofs shone out, and somewhat farther off, a new lake. It was the little village of *Patterdale*, which nestles almost on the margin of the lake of *Ulleswater*, one of the most famous in Cumberland. What a pleasant change was this cheerful landscape, in which the bee roves from rose to rose, and the bird sings its evening song in more serene air and a more cloudless height, from the stony desolation through which I had just passed! Here, too, the lake was to be seen in its full evening glory. Rocks with bold summits, rent by wind and storm, formed the shore on the other side, which is only bordered with green wood and

turf round the foot, where it sinks into the lake.
But upon our side wooded mountains dipping into
a dark hollow, surrounded the water, now glittering in the evening sun. And here on a large,
broad plot of grass, which is spread like a carpet
on the shore of the lake, stands the inn. One
can think of nothing more charming than this
inn, with its flower-beds and its lawn lying right
in the woody hollow and close to the lake, as it
appears with its lighted windows here in the
cool leafy twilight, and there on the mirror-like
water. It is tranquil—but with a different tran-
quillity from that above in Windermere. It is
more the rest of a conscious self-contained happiness, free from every sorrowful alloy, a fresh
joyful view of the present. Without knowing
why, I thought much in distant Cumberland
of Berthold Auerbach; thought that here, among
these dark trees, it must have been as quiet
as in his own Schwarzwald. But now, while
I walked on the lawn, redolent with all the
perfume and cool freshness of the evening, there
appeared suddenly at one of the windows, which
reached to the green ground, a female figure,
which immediately upon perceiving me uttered a
loud laugh, and then disappeared. This laughter
troubled me much, and brought me almost entirely

out of my wonderful evening mood. What could there be so laughable about me? I thought, as I walked to the lake carefully to inspect my appearance in its clear surface. I discovered nothing, however much I twisted and turned; till at last I saw the lady at the window again, but this time with a gentleman by her side, giving themselves much trouble to make themselves recognised by the unceasing waving of both their handkerchiefs, and, when this appeared to be of no use, they began to sing with their fresh voices :

> " Corn rigs, an' barley rigs,
>   An' corn rigs are bonnie, oh!
>   I'll ne'er forget that happy night
>   Amang the rigs wi' Annie, oh! "

Now I knew them again, the two ghosts from Furness Abbey, who here by the lake of Ulleswater were to be again charming spirits of amusement to me. Immediately I hastened across the lawn, entered to them by the window, and found to my joy that Harry and Jessie, although they had been married now over a week, still loved each other very much. We had no ruins and no moonlight this evening as on the former, but we had a good tea and an excellent piece of roast beef to console us instead. I also found this evening . that matrimony has no more zealous advocates than those youthful beings who are still on their wedding journey. Later indeed, when life wears its everyday face, and there are no more mountains, lakes, or honeymoon, they are in the habit of thinking and speaking somewhat more quietly on this point. But that is only quite right, for "true happiness is silent." The following afternoon, shortly before my departure, Harry and I exchanged cards in the hope of seeing one another again, if not in this district at least in this life; and for a long time after I was on board the little steamer which slowly moved off from the shore, I saw them both at the window signalling to me, with their white handkerchiefs, farewell.

The lake of Cumberland is less varied than the lakes of Westmoreland, and in form and substance its shores are decidedly more sombre and grotesque. They are naked rocks, which tower up peak over peak. But at this hour, when the splendour of the sun polished their sides like dead gold, they had a cloudy softness, as if one range of cloud stood behind the other, and a twilight of soft, and everextending blue inclosed the glassy water of the lake, which was light to the last. After an hour we reached the end of it at Pouley-Bridge, where

once more a red coat and a coach-and-four awaited
us. This was my last coach drive in the district
of the lakes, by night-covered meadows, borders of
fields, and quiet villages as far as the little town
of *Penrith*, which received the coach rattling
briskly in right joyfully, with flickering gas-
lights and cheerful street noises. Of the little
town itself, although it is considered very pretty,
I could not see much, notwithstanding the gas-
lights; but I saw so much the more of the smoking and drinking-room of the 'Royal George,' as
my hotel was called. In the said room the talk
was very high upon a cattle-market which had
been held that day in Penrith. There sat the
well-to-do farmer in leathern gaiters; there sat the
crafty cattle dealer from the Scotch Lowlands; and
there sat also the worthy host of the ' Royal
George;' all three with great hats on, with long
clay pipes in their mouths, and with silver cans
and a rum bottle before them, to which they dili-
gently applied themselves. Near them under the
chair each one had his " spittoon," into which once
in every ten minutes he knocked out his clay pipe,
and before them on the middle of the table a tin
box with black tobacco, called "shag," from which
each as frequently refilled his pipe. They drank
and smoked with very grave countenances, and

carried on at the same time very grave conversation about the price of oxen, and other useful
animals. There was no lack of pretty, giggling
girls; but like the angel with the flaming sword,
the stout landlady with the red nose had posted
herself on the threshold of the kitchen, and let
none of them come much into view. On the sofa
in the coffee-room was stretched a "commercial
man," as in this country the "commis voyageur"
is called; so that after all memories of rippling of
lakes and moonlight nights, nothing remained for
me as a last rest but the bed, which comfortably
received me under its red silk canopy, and
encircled me with its red, though somewhat faded
hangings.

When the sun rose the next morning I found
myself already on the road. But one more last
farewell look at the romantic was to be granted
me before the land of the Lakes closed to me
completely. There stood a stately castle, silent in
the virgin morning scent of the trees, on a broad
lawn fresh with dew, its mighty battlements and
pinnacles clearly outlined in the ever-increasing
golden light of dawning day. This is the family
seat of the Musgraves, and the name of the
castle is *Edenhall.* Who does not think of one
of Uhland's most beautiful ballads, 'The Luck

of Edenhall,' when he hears this name? It came upon me as a strong home remembrance, as a perfect echo from the time of my youth, when I saw before me this theatre of one of my favourite poems, and involuntarily my lips moved, as I remembered the young Lord rising at the head of his table in the midst of music, and roaring amidst his drunken guests for the cup which was called the ' Luck of Edenhall.'

The tradition, as it is told on the spot, runs thus: " The butler of Edenhall came once in the olden time to the spring of St. Cuthbert, which is near the castle, just as a troop of fairies were dancing in a ring upon the grass. These airy beings flew frightened away, but left their drinking-glass behind them. One of them came back to fetch it; but when she saw that it was in the hands of the cup-bearer, she flew sadly away and sang :—

> " If that glass should break or fall,
> Farewell the luck of Edenhall."

Or as Uhland has it :—

> " Kommt dies Glas zu Fall,
> Fahrwohl dann, o Glück von Edenhall."

The Musgraves are one of the oldest families in England : they trace their pedigree from one of

the companions in arms of William the Conqueror.
From that far time they have continued valiant
in war and peace, have been sheriffs of their
county and Members of Parliament, and afford
us at the same time an example of those families
which, older than the oldest house of the English
nobility, still only belong to the gentry. One
of their ancestors, Thomas de Musgrave, in the
time of Edward III., commanded in the victorious
engagement at Durham, and took David Bruce,
the young King of the Scots, prisoner. Later, in
the civil wars the Musgraves stood true to the
Royal banner of the Stuarts, the first of whom had
created them baronets. The second baronet, Sir
Philip, fought at Marston Moor, and under the
heroic Countess of Derby, for King Charles I., and
at Worcester for his son, the Charles II. of aftertimes : another Musgrave, of a collateral line, Sir
Edward, sold his possessions to raise a regiment
for the same purpose. The brave Royalists were
overthrown, and King Charles fell on the scaffold ;
but in the battle of Worcester, Sir Edward was
again present, together with his cousin, to fight
once more for the throne. It was here that
Charles II. had his horse shot under him, and Sir
Edward gave him his. After the unfortunate
issue of the battle, Sir Edward fled to Scotland,

where he hoped to find shelter with the noble
Duke of Gordon; but his refuge was discovered,
and the Duke received a message from Cromwell,
" that if he did not at once give up Ned Musgrave,
that arch rebel, he, Cromwell, would send a band of
troopers to storm the Duke's castle." To the unfortunate Royalist no choice remained but again to
take flight; he betook himself over the sea to the
Isle of Man, and there he died before the Restoration, which reinstated his family, and that of his
cousin, in their property. Still a patent which
would have made the Musgraves, these true
cavaliers, barons, was never issued; they were
and still are to the present day plain baronets.
But proud of their family traditions of more than
eight hundred years,—an antiquity with which
none of the titled families in England can even
remotely compare,—they still remain in their
family castle of Edenhall among the mountains of
Cumberland; and there with other relics is the
celebrated drinking-cup, celebrated in song and
tradition, "the luck of Edenhall," carefully kept
as a palladium of the family. It is preserved in a
leathern case, which is decorated with branches
of vine-leaves, and has upon the lid the letters
J. H. C. The drinking-cup itself is of green
glass, adorned with leaves and enamel of different

colours; it is deep, narrow, holds about an English pint, and from the style of its ornament, appears to date from the fifteenth century.

In our Uhland's ballad the glass suddenly cracks at a banquet, and immediately the vaulted hall cracks also, flames start out from the rift, the guests are dispersed, the enemy rushes in and murders the young lord, who still holds in his hand "the shattered luck of Edenhall." In the morning the butler wanders alone seeking the shards of the drinking-cup :—

> " ' The stone wall,' saith he, ' doth fall aside,
> Down must the stately columns fall ;
> Glass in this earth's luck and pride ;
> In atoms shall fall this earthly ball,
> One day like the Luck of Edenhall.' "

Thus, with a thought of the German poet, little then imagining how soon he was to be taken away from us, I closed my autumn days at the English lakes.

———

Ten years have flown since then, and like a dream, when I look back, these days stand before my eyes, dipped in all the charm and perfume of romance. But more especially dreamy appears to me that idea, that feeling which vividly possessed

me when I read again my yellow journal about
the English lakes,—that feeling, divided between
unquiet impulse to wander, and strong desire
for home, which once governed Germans when
abroad, as is so strikingly expressed in the beautiful song of Justinus Kerner :—

> "Love follows him, Love leads him by the hand,
> Makes him a dear home in most distant land."

With these lines,—God knows,—we have often
comforted ourselves when, hundreds of miles
away, it would not have been well for us to have
been seized by sore aching after the home which
we had left in dejection and discontent . . . . .
That is now all past. No more need we seek
our home in the "most distant land ;" we have
found it, and will lose it no more, thanks to you,
O faithful dead, whose song accompanies us cheer-
fully, a last invisible link between hearts abroad
and in the parental home! What we wanted
when away was Germany; but it was Germany
also that called us back! Its new birth in war
and victory has again shown to him, who long
remained away from it in solitude, his place
where he can feel at home, and make himself
useful to the great whole. No more out into
the distance, but homeward throngs every wish

and every thought; and with a full feeling of happiness and love we embrace the dear ground of that fatherland, on whose threshold the wanderer, returning, now lays down with fervent thankfulness his staff of pilgrimage.

THE END.

LONDON: PRINTED BY WILLIAM CLOWES AND SONS, STAMFORD STREET AND CHARING CROSS.

BENTLEY'S
BURLINGTON LIBRARY

OF USEFUL AND ENTERTAINING WORKS.

GUIZOT'S Life of Oliver Cromwell. In Roxburghe binding.

MIGNET'S Life of Mary Queen of Scots. In Roxburghe binding.

FIGUIER'S The Day after Death.

Dr. McCAUSLAND'S Sermons in Stones. In Roxburghe binding.

——————————— Adam and the Adamite.

——————————— Builders of Babel.

JOHN TIMBS' Lives of Painters. In Roxburghe binding.

——————————— Lives of Statesmen. In Roxburghe binding.

——————————— Wits and Humourists. In Roxburghe binding. 2 vols. 12s.

*——————————— Lives of the Later Wits and Humourists. In Roxburghe binding. 2 vols. 12s.

*——————————— Doctors and Patients. In Roxburghe binding.

*LORD DALLING AND BULWER'S Historical Characters. In Roxburghe binding.

*THE BENTLEY BALLADS. In Roxburghe binding.

Dr. DORAN'S Table Traits, with Something on Them.

SOUTH SEA BUBBLES. By the Earl and the Doctor.

WILKIE COLLINS' Rambles beyond Railways.

EARL DUNDONALD'S Autobiography of a Seaman. In Roxburghe binding.

BESANT and PALMER'S History of Jerusalem.

CROWEST'S The Great Tone Poets.

AMÉDÉE GUILLEMIN'S The Sun.

An Asterisk (*) is attached to the latest additions.

RICHARD BENTLEY & SON, New Burlington Street,

Publishers in Ordinary to Her Majesty, and to the Palestine Exploration Fund.

1

BENTLEY'S FAVOURITE NOVELS.

*Each Work can be had separately, price 6s., of all Booksellers
in Town or Country.*

By MRS. HENRY WOOD.

East Lynne. (55th Thousand.)
The Channings. (25th Thousand.)
Mrs. Halliburton's Troubles.
The Master of Greylands.
Verner's Pride.
Within the Maze.
Lady Adelaide.
Bessy Rane.
Roland Yorke.
Lord Oakburn's Daughters.
Shadow of Ashlydyat.
Oswald Cray.
Dene Hollow.
George Canterbury's Will.
Trevlyn Hold.
Mildred Arkell.
St. Martin's Eve.
Elster's Folly.
Anne Hereford.
A Life's Secret.
Red Court Farm.

By MISS AUSTEN.
(The only Complete Edition.)

Sense and Sensibility.
Emma.
Pride and Prejudice.
Mansfield Park.
Northanger Abbey.
Lady Susan and The Watsons.

By MISS RHODA BROUGHTON.

Nancy.
Good-bye Sweetheart!
Red as a Rose is She.
Cometh up as a Flower.
Not Wisely but Too Well.

By MRS. ALEXANDER.

The Wooing O't.
Which shall it be?

By ANTHONY TROLLOPE.

The Three Clerks.

By MRS. ANNIE EDWARDES.

Ought we to Visit her?
Susan Fielding.
Steven Lawrence : Yeoman.

By BARONESS TAUTPHŒUS.

| The Initials. | At Odds. |
| Quits! | Cyrilla. |

By LADY G. FULLERTON.

Constance Sherwood.
Too Strange not to be True.
Mrs. Gerald's Niece.
Ladybird.

By MRS. AUGUSTUS CRAVEN.

A Sister's Story.

BY ANONYMOUS AUTHORS.

| The Last of the Cavaliers. | Johnny Ludlow. |

Comin' thro' the Rye.

RICHARD BENTLEY & SON, NEW BURLINGTON STREET,
Publishers in Ordinary to Her Majesty.

2

Beattie (James)—Poetical Works of, with Life, portrait and illustrations, crown 8vo, cloth extra, gilt edges (pub 2s 6d), 9d. A neatly got up edition ; very suitable as a gift.

The New Library Edition of
The Works of Robert Burns, large paper copy, edited by W. Scott Douglas, with Explanatory Notes, Various Readings, and Glossary, illustrated with portraits, vignettes, and frontispieces, with India proof plates, by Sam Bough, R.S.A., and W. E. Lockhart, R.S.A., all newly engraved on steel, woodcuts, facsimiles, maps, and music, 6 vols, royal 8vo, cloth extra (pub £8 8s), £2 15s, W. Paterson, 1880.

Lyndsay (Sir David, of the Mount)—A Facsimile of the ancient Heraldic Manuscript emblazoned by the celebrated Sir David Lyndsay of the Mount, Lyon King at Arms in the reign of James the Fifth, edited by the late David Laing, LL.D., from the Original MS. in the possession of the Faculty of Advocates, folio, cloth, gilt top, uncut edges (pub £10 10s), £3 10s.
Impression limited to 250 copies.

Also Uniform.
Scottish Arms, being a Collection of Armorial Bearings, A.D. 1370-1678, Reproduced in Facsimile from Contemporary Manuscripts, with Heraldic and Genealogical Notes, by R. R. Stodart, of the Lyon Office, 2 vols, folio, cloth extra, gilt tops (pub £12 12s), £4 10s.
Impression limited to 300 copies.
Several of the manuscripts from which these Arms are taken have hitherto been unknown to heraldic antiquaries in this country. The Arms of upwards of 600 families are given, all of which are described in upwards of 400 pages of letter-press by Mr Stodart.
The book is uniform with Lyndsay's Heraldic Manuscript, and care was taken not to reproduce any Arms which are in that volume, unless there are variations, or from older manuscripts.

Wilson (Professor)—The Comedy of the Noctes Ambros-ianæ, by John Skelton, Advocate, with portraits of Wilson and Hogg, crown 8vo, cloth (pub 7s 6d), 3s, Blackwood & Sons.
"Mr Skelton has erected what is perhaps the most durable monument to Wilson's fame that we possess. In it we find the immortal trio at their best throughout. From beginning to end their meetings are inspired and sanctified by Bacchus and Apollo."—*Academy.*

Younger (John, shoemaker, St Boswells, Author of " River Angling for Salmon and Trout," " Corn Law Rhymes, &c.)— Autobiography, with portrait, crown 8vo (457 pages), cloth (pub 7s 6d), 2s 6d.
"'The shoemaker of St Boswells,' as he was designated in all parts of Scotland, was an excellent prose writer, a respectable poet, a marvellously gifted man in conversation. His life will be read with great interest ; the simple heart-stirring narrative of the life-struggle of a highly-gifted, humble, and honest mechanic,—a life of care, but also a life of virtue."—*London Review.*

Sent Carriage Free to any part of the United Kingdom on receipt of Postal Order for the amount.
JOHN GRANT, 25 & 34 George IV. Bridge, Edinburgh.

Historians of Scotland, complete set in 10 vols for £3 3s.
This Grand National Series of the Early Chronicles of Scotland, edited by the
most eminent Scottish Antiquarian Scholars of the present day, is now completed,
and as sets are becoming few in number, early application is necessary in order
to secure them at the reduced price.
The Series comprises :—

Scoticronicon of John de Fordun, from the Contemporary
MS. (if not the author's autograph) at the end of the Fourteenth
Century, preserved in the Library of Wolfenbüttel, in the Duchy
of Brunswick, collated with other known MSS. of the original
chronicle, edited by W. F. Skene, LL.D., Historiographer Royal,
2 vols (pub 30s), not sold separately.

The Metrical Chronicle of Andrew Wyntoun, Prior of St
Serf's Inch at Lochleven, who died about 1426, the work now
printed entire for the first time, from the Royal MS. in the British
Museum, collated with other MSS., edited by the late D. Laing,
LL.D., 3 vols (pub 50s), vols 1 and 2 not sold separately.
Vol 3 sold separately (pub 21s), 10s 6d.

Lives of Saint Ninian and St Kentigern, compiled in the
12th century, and edited from the best MSS. by the late A. P.
Forbes, D.C.L., Bishop of Brechin (pub 15s), not sold separately.

Life of Saint Columba, founder of Hy, written by Adamnan,
ninth Abbot of that Monastery, edited by Wm. Reeves, D.D.,
M.R.I.A., translated by the late A. P. Forbes, D.C.L., Bishop
of Brechin, with Notes arranged by W. F. Skene, LL.D. (pub
15s), not sold separately.

The Book of Pluscarden, being unpublished Continuation
of Fordun's Chronicle by M. Buchanan, Treasurer to the Dauphi-
ness of France, edited and translated by Skene, 2 vols (pub 30s).
Vol 2 separately (pub 12s 6d), 8s 6d.

A Critical Essay on the Ancient Inhabitants of Scotland,
by Thomas Innes of the Sorbonne, with Memoir of the Author by
George Grubb, LL.D., and Appendix of Original Documents by
Wm. F. Skene, LL.D., illustrated with charts, out of print (pub
21s), 10s 6d.
In connection with the Society of Antiquaries of Scotland, a uniform series of
the Historians of Scotland, accompanied by English translations, and illustrated
by notes, critical and explanatory, was commenced some years since and has
recently been finished.
So much has recently been done for the history of Scotland, that the necessity
for a more critical edition of the earlier historians has become very apparent.
The history of Scotland, prior to the 15th century, must always be based to a
great extent upon the work of Fordun ; but his original text has been made the
basis of continuations, and has been largely altered and interpolated by his continuators, whose statements are usually quoted as if they belonged to the original
work of Fordun.   An edition discriminating between the original text of Fordun
and the additions and alterations of his continuators, and at the same time trac-
ing out the sources of Fordun's narrative, would obviously be of great importance
to the right understanding of Scottish history.
The complete set forms ten handsome volumes, demy 8vo, illustrated with
facsimiles.

*Sent Carriage Free to any part of the United Kingdom on
receipt of Postal Order for the amount.*

JOHN GRANT, 25   34 George IV. Bridge, Edinburgh.

Leighton's (Alexander) Mysterious Legends of Edinburgh,
illustrated, crown 8vo, cloth (pub 5s), 2s 6d.
CONTENTS :—Lord Kames' Puzzle, Mrs Corbet's Amputated Toe, The Brownie
of the West Bow, The Ancient Bureau, A Legend of Halkerstone's Wynd, Deacon
Macgillvray's Disappearance, Lord Braxfield's Case of the Red Night-cap, The
Strange Story of Sarah Gowanlock, and John Cameron's Life Policy.

Steven's (Dr William) History of the High School of
Edinburgh, from the beginning of the Sixteenth Century, based
upon Researches of the Town Council Records and other Authentic
Documents, illustrated with view, also facsimile of a School
Exercise by Sir Walter Scott when a pupil in 1783, crown 8vo,
cloth, a handsome volume (pub 7s 6d), 2s.
Appended is a list of the distinguished pupils who have been educated in this
Institution, which has been patronised by Royalty from the days of James VI.

Exquisitely beautiful Works by Sir J. Noel Paton at a remarkably
low price.

Paton's (Noel) Compositions from Shakespeare's Tempest,
a Series of Fifteen Large Outline Engravings illustrating the
Great Drama of our National Poet, with descriptive letterpress,
oblong folio, cloth (pub 21s), 3s. Chapman & Hall, 1845.

Uniform with the above.

Paton's (Noel) Compositions from Shelley's Prometheus
Unbound, a Series of Twelve Large Outline Engravings, oblong
folio, cloth (pub 21s), 3s. Chapman & Hall, 1846.

Pollok's (Robert) The Course of Time, a Poem, beautifully printed edition, with portrait and numerous illustrations,
12mo, cloth, 6d. Blackwood & Sons.
"'The Course of Time' is a very extraordinary poem, vast in its conception,
vast in its plan, vast in its materials, and vast, if very far from perfect, in its
achievement."—D. M. MOIR.

The Authorised Library Edition.

Trial of the Directors of the City of Glasgow Bank, before
the Petition for Bail, reported by Charles Tennant Couper,
Advocate, the Speeches and Opinions, revised by the Council and
Judges, and the Charge by the Lord Justice Clerk, illustrated
with lithographic facsimiles of the famous false Balance-sheets,
one large volume, royal 8vo, cloth (pub 15s), 3s 6d. Edinburgh.

History of the Queen's Edinburgh Rifle Volunteer Brigade,
with an Account of the City of Edinburgh and Midlothian Rifle
Association, the Scottish Twenty Club, &c., by Wm. Stephen,
crown 8vo, cloth (pub 5s), 2s 6d. Blackwood & Sons.
"This opportune volume has far more interest for readers generally than might
have been expected, while to members of the Edinburgh Volunteer Brigade it
cannot fail to be very interesting indeed."—*St James's Gazette.*

Edinburgh University—Account of the Tercentenary Fes-
tival of the University, including the Speeches and Addresses on
the Occasion, edited by R. Sydney Marsden, crown 8vo, cloth
(pub 3s), 1s 6d. Blackwood & Sons.

Sent Carriage Free to any part of the United Kingdom on
receipt of Postal Order for the amount.

JOHN GRANT, 25 & 34 George IV. Bridge, Edinburgh.

Grampian Club Publications, of valuable MSS. and Works of Original Research in Scottish History, Privately printed for the Members :—

The Diocesan Registers of Glasgow—Liber Protocollorum
M. Cuthberti Simonis, notarii et scribæ capituli Glasguensis, A.D.
1499-1513; also, *Rental Book of the Diocese of Glasgow*, A.D.
1509-1570, edited by Joseph Bain and the Rev. Dr Charles
Rogers, with facsimiles, 2 vols, 8vo, cl, 1875 (pub £2 2s), 10s 6d.

Rental Book of the Cistercian Abbey of Coupar-Angus,
with the Breviary of the Register, edited by the Rev. Dr Charles
Rogers, with facsimiles of MSS., 2 vols, 8vo, cloth, 1879-80 (pub
£2 12s 6d), 10s 6d.

———— The same, vol II., comprising the *Register of*
Tacks of the Abbey of Cupar, Rental of St Marie's Monastery, and
Appendix, 8vo, cloth (pub £1 1s), 3s 6d.

Estimate of the Scottish Nobility during the Minority of
James VI., edited, with an Introduction, from the original MS.
in the Public Record Office, by Dr Charles Rogers, 8vo, cloth
(pub 10s 6d), 2s.

The reprint of a manuscript discovered in the Public Record Office. The
details are extremely curious.

Genealogical Memoirs of the Families of Colt and Coutts,
by Dr Charles Rogers, 8vo, cloth (pub 10s 6d), 2s 6d.

An old Scottish family, including the eminent bankers of that name, the
Baroness Burdett-Coutts, &c.

Rogers' (Dr Charles) Memorials of the Earl of Stirling
and of the House of Alexander, portraits, 2 vols, 8vo, cloth (pub ·
£3 3s), 10s 6d, Edinburgh, 1877.

This work embraces not only a history of Sir William Alexander, first Earl of
Stirling, but also a genealogical account of the family of Alexander in all its
branches; many interesting historical details connected with Scottish State affairs
in the seventeenth century; also with the colonisation of America.

Sent Carriage Free to any part of the United Kingdom on
receipt of Postal Order for the amount.

JOHN GRANT, 25 & 34 George IV. Bridge, Edinburgh.

Scott's (Dr Hew) Fasti Ecclesiæ Scoticanæ, Historical and
Biographical Notices of all the Ministers of the Church of Scotland from the Reformation, A.D. 1560, to the Present Time, 6
large vols, demy 4to, cloth, uncut (pub £9), £4 15s, Edinburgh, W. Paterson.

David Laing, the eminent antiquarian, considered this work a valuable and
necessary addition to the Bannatyne, Maitland, or Abbotsford Club Publications.
The work is divided into Synods, and where priced the volumes can be had
separately.

Vol 1.—Embraces Synods of Lothian and Tweeddale.   Not
sold separately.
Vol 2.—Synods of Merse and Teviotdale, Dumfries and Gal-
loway (pub 30s), 15s.
Vol 3.—Synods of Glasgow and Ayr (pub 30s), 15s.
Vol 4.—Synods of Fife, Perth, and Stirling (pub 30s), 15s.
Vol 5.—Synods of Argyll, Glenelg, Moray, Ross, Sutherland,
Caithness, Orkney, and Shetland, not sold separately.
Vol 6.—Synods of Aberdeen, and Angus and Mearns (pub
30s), 15s.

Historical Sketches of the Highland Clans of Scotland,
containing a concise account of the origin, &c., of the Scottish
Clans, with twenty-two illustrative coloured plates of the Tartan
worn by each, post 8vo, cloth, 2s 6d.

"The object of this treatise is to give a concise account of the origin, seat,
and characteristics of the Scottish Clans, together with a representation of the
distinguishing tartan worn by each."—*Preface.*

Historical Geography of the Clans of Scotland, by T. B.
Johnston, F.R.G.S., F.R.S.E., and F.S.A.S., Geographer to
the Queen, and Colonel James A. Robertson, F.S.A.S., demy 4to,
cloth, with a map of Scotland divided into Clans (large folding
map, coloured) (pub 7s 6d), Keith Johnston, 3s. 6d.

"The map bears evidence of careful preparation, and the editor acknowledges
the assistance of Dr William Skene, who is known for eminent services to Highland archæology."—*Athenæum.*

Keltie's (John S.) History of the Scottish Highlands,
Highland Clans, and Highland Regiments, with an account of the
Gaelic Language, Literature, Music, &c., illustrated with portraits,
views, maps, &c., engraved on steel, clan tartans, numerous
woodcuts, including armorial bearings, 2 vols, imperial 8vo, half
morocco (pub £3 10s), £1 17s 6d.

*Sent Carriage Free to any part of the United Kingdom on
receipt of Postal Order for the amount.*

JOHN GRANT, 25 & 34 George IV. Bridge, Edinburgh.

Burt's (Capt.) Letters from the North of Scotland (1754), with an Introduction by R. Jamieson, F.S.A. ; and the History of Donald the Hammerer, from an authentic account of the Family of Invernahyle, a MS. communication by Sir Walter Scott, with facsimiles of all the original engravings, 2 vols, 8vo, cloth (pub 21s), 8s 6d. W. Paterson.

" Captain Burt was one of the first Englishmen who caught a glimpse of the spots which now allure tourists from every part of the civilised world, at a time when London had as little to do with the Grampians as with the Andes. The author was evidently a man of a quick, an observant, and a cultivated mind."— LORD MACAULAY,
" An extremely interesting and curious work."—LOWNDES.

Chambers's (William, of Glenormiston) History of Peebles-shire, its Local Antiquities, Geology, Natural History, &c., with one hundred engravings, vignettes, and coloured map from Ordnance Survey, royal 8vo, cloth (pub £1 11s 6d), 9s. W. Paterson.

" To the early history and antiquities of this district, and to old names and old families connected with the place, Mr Chambers lends a charm which is not often met with in such subjects. He discerns the usefulness of social as well as political history, and is pleasantly aware that the story of manners and morals and customs is as well worth telling as the story of man," &c.—*Athenæum.*

Douglas' (Gavin, Bishop of Dunkeld, 1475-1522) Poetical Works, edited, with Memoir, Notes, and full Glossary, by John Small, M.A., F.S.A. Scot., illustrated with specimens of manuscript, title-page, and woodcuts of the early editions in facsimile, 4 vols, beautifully printed on thick paper, post 8vo, cloth (pub £3 3s), £1 2s 6d. W. Paterson.

" The latter part of the fifteenth and beginning of the sixteenth century, a period almost barren in the annals of English poetry, was marked by a remarkable series of distinguished poets in Scotland. During this period flourished Dunbar, Henryson, Mercier, Harry the Minstrel, Gavin Douglas, Bellenden, Kennedy, and Lyndesay. Of these, although the palm of excellence must beyond all doubt be awarded to Dunbar,—next to Burns probably the greatest poet of his country,—the voice of contemporaries, as well as of the age that immediately followed, pronounced in favour of him who,
' In barbarous age,
Gave rude Scotland Virgil's page,'—
Gavin Douglas. We may confidently predict that this will long remain the standard edition of Gavin Douglas ; and we shall be glad to see the works of other of the old Scottish poets edited with equal sympathy and success."—*Athenæum.*

Lyndsay's (Sir David, of the Mount, 1490-1568) Poetical Works, best edition, edited, with Life, Notes, and Glossary, by David Laing, 3 vols, crown 8vo, cloth (pub 63s), 18s 6d. W. Paterson.

" When it is said that the revision, including Preface, Memoir, and Notes, has been executed by Dr David Laing, it is said that all has been done that is possible by thorough scholarship, good judgment, and conscientiousness."—*Scotsman.*

Sent Carriage Free to any part of the United Kingdom on receipt of Postal Order for the amount.

JOHN GRANT, 25 & 34 George IV. Bridge, Edinburgh.

Crieff: Its Traditions and Characters, with Anecdotes of Strathearn, Reminiscences of Obsolete Customs, Traditions, and Superstitions, Humorous Anecdotes of Schoolmasters, Ministers, and other Public Men, crown 8vo, 1s.

"A book which will have considerable value in the eyes of all collectors of Scottish literature. A gathering up of stories about well-known inhabitants, memorable local occurrences, and descriptions of manners and customs."— *Scotsman.*

Dunfermline—Henderson's Annals of Dunfermline and Vicinity, from the earliest Authentic Period to the Present Time, A.D. 1069-1878, interspersed with Explanatory Notes, Memorabilia, and numerous illustrative engravings, large vol, 4to, half morocco, gilt top (pub 21s), 6s 6d.

The genial Author of " Noctes Ambrosianæ."

Christopher North—A Memoir of Professor John Wilson, compiled from Family Papers and other sources, by his daughter, Mrs Gordon, new edition, with portrait and illustrations, crown 8vo, cloth (pub 6s), 2s 6d.

"A writer of the most ardent and enthusiastic genius."—HENRY HALLAM.

" The whole literature of England does not contain a more brilliant series of articles than those with which Wilson has enriched the pages of *Blackwood's Magazine.*"—Sir ARCHIBALD ALISON.

The Cloud of Witnesses for the Royal Prerogatives of Jesus Christ; or, The Last Speeches and Testimonies of those who have Suffered for the Truth in Scotland since the year 1680, best edition, by the Rev. J. H. Thompson, numerous illustrations, handsome volume, 8vo, cloth gilt (pub 7s 6d), 4s 6d.

" The interest in this remarkable book can never die, and to many we doubt not this new and handsome edition will be welcome."—*Aberdeen Herald.*

"Altogether it is like a resurrection, and the vision of Old Mortality, as it passes over the scenes of his humble but solemn and sternly significant labours, seems transfigured in the bright and embellished pages of the modern reprint."— *Daily Review.*

M'Kerlie's (P. H., F.S.A. Scot.) History of the Lands and their Owners in Galloway, illustrated by woodcuts of Notable Places and Objects, with a Historical Sketch of the District, 5 handsome vols, crown 8vo, roxburghe style (pub £3 15s), 26s 6d. W. Paterson.

Wilson's (Dr Daniel) Memorials of Edinburgh in the Olden Time, with numerous fine engravings and woodcuts, 2 vols, 4to, cloth (pub £2 2s), 16s 6d.

Hamilton's (Lady, the Mistress of Lord Nelson) Attitudes, illustrating in 25 full-page plates the great Heroes and Heroines of Antiquity in their proper Costume, forming a useful study for drawing from correct and chaste models of Grecian and Roman Sculpture, 4to, cloth (pub £1 1s), 3s 6d.

Sent Carriage Free to any part of the United Kingdom on receipt of Postal Order for the amount.

JOHN GRANT, 25 & 34 George IV. Bridge, Edinburgh.

Hay's (*D. R.*) *Science of Beauty*, as Developed in Nature and Applied in Art, 23 full-page illustrations, royal 8vo, cloth (pub 10s 6d), 2s 6d.

Art and Letters, an Illustrated Magazine of Fine Art and Fiction, edited by J. Comyns Carr, complete year 1882-83, handsome volume, folio, neatly bound in bevelled cloth, gilt top, edges uncut, and Parts 1 and 2 of the succeeding year, when the publication ceased, illustrated with many hundred engravings in the highest style of art, including many of the choicest illustrations of "L'Art," published by arrangement with the French proprietors (pub £1 1s), 8s 6d.

The artistic excellence of this truly handsome volume commends itself to all lovers of what is beautiful in nature and art. The illustrations, which are numerous and varied, embrace—Specimens of Sculpture Old and New, Facsimile Drawings of the Old Masters, Examples of Art Furniture, with objects exhibited in the great European Collections, Animals in Art illustrated by Examples in Painting and Sculpture, Art on the Stage, Products of the Keramic Art Ancient and Modern, the various forms of Art Industry, &c. &c., accompanied by interesting articles by men thoroughly acquainted with the various subjects introduced.

Stewart's (*Dugald*) *Collected Works*, best edition, edited by Sir William Hamilton, with numerous Notes and Emendations, 11 handsome vols, 8vo, cloth (pub £6 12s), the few remaining sets for £2 10s. T. & T. Clark.

Sold Separately,

Elements of the Philosophy of the Human Mind, 3 vols, 8vo, cloth (pub £1 16s), 12s.

Philosophy of the Active Powers, 2 vols, 8vo, cloth (pub £1 4s), 10s.

Principles of Political Economy, 2 vols, 8vo, cloth (pub £1 4s), 10s.

Biographical Memoirs of Adam Smith, Principal Robertson, and Thomas Reid, 8vo, cloth (pub 12s), 4s 6d.

Supplementary Volume, with General Index, 8vo, cloth (pub 12s), 5s.

" As the names of Thomas Reid, of Dugald Stewart, and of Sir William Hamilton will be associated hereafter in the history of Philosophy in Scotland, as closely as those of Xenophanes, Parmenides, and Zeno in the School of Elea, it is a singular fortune that Sir William Hamilton should be the collector and editor of the works of his predecessors. . . . The chair which he filled for many years, not otherwise undistinguished, he rendered illustrious."—*Athenæum.*

Sent Carriage Free to any part of the United Kingdom on receipt of Postal Order for the amount.

JOHN GRANT, 25 & 34 George IV. Bridge, Edinburgh.

Campbell *(Colin, Lord Clyde)—Life of,* illustrated by Extracts from his Diary and Correspondence, by Lieut.-Gen. Shadwell, C.B., with portrait, maps, and Plans, 2 vols, 8vo, cloth (pub 36s), 10s 6d, Blackwood & Sons.

"In all the annals of 'Self-Help,' there is not to be found a life more truly worthy of study than that of the gallant old soldier. The simple, self-denying, friend-helping, brave, patriotic soldier stands proclaimed in every line of General Shadwell's admirable memoir."—*Blackwood's Magazine.*

Crime—*Pike's (Luke Owen) History of Crime in England,* illustrating the Changes of the Laws in the Progress of Civilisation from the Roman Invasion to the Present Time, Index, 2 very thick vols, 8vo, cloth (pub 36s) 10s, Smith, Elder, & Co.

Creasy *(Sir Edward S.)—History of England,* from the Earliest Times to the End of the Middle Ages, 2 vols (520 pp each), 8vo, cloth (pub 25s), 6s, Smith, Elder, & Co.

Garibaldi—*The Red Shirt,* Episodes of the Italian War, by Alberto Mario, crown 8vo, cloth (pub 6s), 1s, Smith, Elder, & Co.

"These episodes read like chapters in the 'History of the Seven Champions;' they give vivid pictures of the incidents of that wonderful achievement, the triumphal progress from Sicily to Naples; and the incidental details of the difficulties, dangers, and small reverses which occurred during the progress, remove the event from the region of enchantment to the world of reality and human heroism."—*Athenæum.*

History of the War of Frederick I. against the Communes of Lombardy, by Giovanni B. Testa, translated from the Italian, and dedicated by the Author to the Right Hon. W. E. Gladstone, (466 pages), 8vo, cloth (pub 15s) 2s, Smith, Elder, & Co.

Martineau *(Harriet)—The History of British Rule in India,* foolscap 8vo (356 pages), cloth (pub 2s 6d), 1s, Smith, Elder, & Co.

A concise sketch, which will give the ordinary reader a general notion of what our Indian empire is, how we came by it, and what has gone forward in it since it first became connected with England. The book will be found to state the broad facts of Anglo-Indian history in a clear and enlightening manner; and it cannot fail to give valuable information to those readers who have neither time nor inclination to study the larger works on the subject.

Mathews *(Charles James, the Actor)—Life of,* chiefly Autobiographical, with Selections from his Correspondence and Speeches, edited by Charles Dickens, portraits, 2 vols, 8vo, cloth (pub 25s), 5s, Macmillan, 1879.

"The book is a charming one from first to last, and Mr Dickens deserves a full measure of credit for the care and discrimination he has exercised in the business of editing."—*Globe.*

"Mr Dickens's interesting work, which should be read by all students of the stage."—*Saturday Review.*

Reumont *(Alfred von)—Lorenzo de Medici, the Magnificent,* translated from the German, by Robert Harrison, 2 vols, 8vo, cloth (pub 30s), 6s 6d, Smith, Elder, & Co.

Oliphant (*Laurence*)—The Land of Gilead, with Excursions in the Lebanon, illustrations and maps, 8vo, cloth (pub 21s), 8s 6d, Blackwood & Sons.

. "A most fascinating book."—*Observer*.
"A singularly agreeable narrative of a journey through regions more replete, perhaps, with varied and striking associations than any other in the world. The writing throughout is highly picturesque and effective."—*Athenæum*.
"A most fascinating volume of travel. . . . His remarks on manners, customs, and superstitions are singularly interesting."—*St James's Gazette*.
"The reader will find in this book a vast amount of most curious and valuable information on the strange races and religions scattered about the country."—*Saturday Review*.
"An admirable work, both as a record of travel and as a contribution to physical science."—*Vanity Fair*.

Patterson (*R. H.*)—The New Golden Age, and Influence of the Precious Metals upon the War, 2 vols, 8vo, cloth (pub 31s 6d), 6s, Blackwood & Sons.

CONTENTS.

VOL I.—THE PERIOD OF DISCOVERY AND ROMANCE OF THE NEW GOLDEN AGE, 1848-56.—The First Tidings—Scientific Fears, and General Enthusiasm—The Great Emigration—General Effects of the Gold Discoveries upon Commerce—Position of Great Britain, and First Effects on it of the Gold Discoveries—The Golden Age in California and Australia—Life at the Mines. A RETROSPECT.—History and Influence of the Precious Metals down to the Birth of Modern Europe—The Silver Age in America—Effects of the Silver Age upon Europe—Production of the Precious Metals during the Silver Age (1492-1810)—Effects of the Silver Age upon the Value of Money (1492-1800).
VOL II.—PERIOD OF RENEWED SCARCITY.—Renewed Scarcity of the Precious Metals, A.D. 1800-30—The Period of Scarcity. Part II.—Effects upon Great Britain—The Scarcity lessens—Beginnings of a New Gold Supply—General Distress before the Gold Discoveries. "CHEAP" AND "DEAR" MONEY—On the Effects of Changes in the Quantity and Value of Money. THE NEW GOLDEN AGE.—First Getting of the New Gold—First Diffusion of the New Gold—Industrial Enterprise in Europe—Vast Expansion of Trade with the East (A.D. 1855-75)—Total Amount of the New Gold and Silver—Its Influence upon the World at large—Close of the Golden Age, 1876-80—Total Production of Gold and Silver. PERIOD 1492-1848.—Production of Gold and Silver subsequent to 1848—Changes in the Value of Money subsequent to A.D. 1492. PERIOD A.D. 1848 and subsequently. PERIOD A.D. 1782-1865.—Illusive Character of the Board of Trade Returns since 1853—Growth of our National Wealth.

Richardson and Watts' Complete Practical Treatise on Acids, Alkalies, and Salts, their Manufacture and Application, by Thomas Richardson, Ph.D., F.R.S., &c., and Henry Watts, F.R.S., F.C.S., &c., illustrated with numerous wood engravings, 3 thick 8vo vols, cloth (pub £4 10s), 8s 6d, London.

Tunis, Past and Present, with a Narrative of the French Conquest of the Regency, by A. M. Broadley, Correspondent of the *Times* during the War in Tunis, with numerous illustrations and maps, 2 vols, post 8vo, cloth (pub 25s), 6s, Blackwood & Sons.
"Mr Broadley has had peculiar facilities in collecting materials for his volumes. Possessing a thorough knowledge of Arabic, he has for years acted as confidential adviser to the Bey. . . . The information which he is able to place before the reader is novel and amusing. . . . A standard work on Tunis has been long required. This deficiency has been admirably supplied by the author."—*Morning Post*.

Cervantes—History of the Ingenious Gentleman, Don Quixote of La Mancha, translated from the Spanish by P. A. Motteux, illustrated with a portrait and 36 etchings, by M. A. Laluze, illustrator of the library edition of Moliere's Works, 4 vols, large 8vo, cloth (sells £3 12s), £1 15s.   W. Paterson.

Dyer (Thomas H., LL.D.)—Imitative Art, its Principles and Progress, with Preliminary Remarks on Beauty, Sublimity, and Taste, 8vo, cloth (pub 14s), 2s.   Bell & Sons, 1882.

Junior Etching Club—Passages from Modern English Poets, Illustrated by the Junior Etching Club, 47 beautiful etchings by J. E. Millais, J. Whistler, J. Tenniel, Viscount Bury, J. Lawless, F. Smallfield, A. J. Lewis, C. Rossiter, and other artists, 4to, cloth extra, gilt edges (pub 15s), 4s.

Smith (J. Moyr)—Ancient Greek Female Costume, illustrated by 112 fine outline engravings and numerous smaller illustrations, with Explanatory Letterpress, and Descriptive Passages from the Works of Homer, Hesiod, Herodotus, Æschylus, Euripides, and other Greek Authors, printed in brown, crown 8vo, cloth elegant, red edges (pub 7s 6d), 3s.   Sampson Low.

Strutt's Sylva Britanniæ et Scotiæ; or, Portraits of Forest Trees Distinguished for their Antiquity, Magnitude, or Beauty, drawn from Nature, with 50 highly finished etchings, imp. folio, half morocco extra, gilt top, a handsome volume (pub £9 9s), £2 2s.

Walpole's (Horace) Anecdotes of Painting in England, with some Account of the Principal Artists, enlarged by Rev. James Dallaway ; and Vertue's Catalogue of Engravers who have been born or resided in England, last and best edition, revised with additional notes by Ralph N. Wornum, illustrated with eighty portraits of the principal artists, and woodcut portraits of the minor artists, 3 handsome vols, 8vo, cloth (pub 27s), 14s 6d. Bickers.

———— The same, 3 vols, half morocco, gilt top, by one of the best Edinburgh binders (pub 45s), £1 8s.

Warren's (Samuel) Works—Original and early editions as follows :—

Miscellanies, Critical, Imaginative, and Juridical, contributed to *Blackwood's Magazine,* original edition, 2 vols, post 8vo, cloth (pub 24s), 5s.   Blackwood, 1855.

Now and Then ; Through a Glass Darkly, early edition, crown 8vo, cloth (pub 6s), 1s 6d.   Blackwood, 1853.

Ten Thousand a Year,, early edition, with Notes, 3 vols, 12mo, boards, back paper title (pub 18s), 4s 6d.   Blackwood, 1853.

Wood (Major Herbert, R.E.)—The Shores of Lake Aral,
with large folding maps (352 pages), 8vo, cloth (pub 14s), 2s 6d,
Smith, Elder, & Co.

Arnold's (Cecil) Great Sayings of Shakespeare, a Comprehensive Index to Shakespearian Thought, being a Collection
of Allusions, Reflections, Images, Familiar and Descriptive Passages, and Sentiments from the Poems and Plays of Shakespeare,
Alphabetically Arranged and Classified under Appropriate Head-
ings, one handsome volume of 422 pages, thick 8vo, cloth (pub
7s 6d), 3s. Bickers.

Arranged in a manner similar to Southgate's "Many Thoughts of Many
Minds." This index differs from all other books in being much more comprehensive, while care has been taken to follow the most accurate text, and to
cope, in the best manner possible, with the difficulties of correct classification.

Bacon (Francis, Lord)—Works, both English and Latin,
with an Introductory Essay, Biographical and Critical, and
copious Indices, steel portrait, 2 vols, royal 8vo, cloth (originally
pub £2 2s,) 12s, 1879.

" All his works are, for expression as well as thought, the glory of our nation,
and of all later ages."—SHEFFIELD, Duke of Buckinghamshire.
"Lord Bacon was more and more known, and his books more and more
delighted in; so that those men who had more than ordinary knowledge in
human affairs, esteemed him one of the most capable spirits of that age."

*Burnet (Bishop)—History of the Reformation of the
Church of England,* with numerous Illustrative Notes and copious
Index, 2 vols, royal 8vo, cloth (pub 20s), 10s, Reeves & Turner,
1880.

"Burnet, in his immortal History of the Reformation, has fixed the Protestant
religion in this country as long as any religion remains among us. Burnet is,
without doubt, the English Eusebius."—Dr APTHORPE.

Burnet's History of his Own Time, from the Restoration
of Charles II. to the Treaty of the Peace of Utrecht, with
Historical and Biographical Notes, and a copious Index, complete in 1 thick volume, imperial 8vo, portrait, cloth (pub £1 5s),
5s 6d.

"I am reading Burnet's Own Times. Did you ever read that garrulous
pleasant history? full of scandal, which all true history is; no palliatives, but all
the stark wickedness that actually gave the *momentum* to national actors; none
of that cursed *Humeian* indifference, so cold, and unnatural, and inhuman," &c.
—CHARLES LAMB.

Dante—The Divina Commedia, translated into English
Verse by James Ford, A.M., medallion frontispiece, 430 pages,
crown 8vo, cloth, bevelled boards (pub 12s), 2s 6d. Smith,
Elder, & Co.

"Mr Ford has succeeded better than might have been expected; his rhymes
are good, and his translation deserves praise for its accuracy and fidelity. We
cannot refrain from acknowledging the many good qualities of Mr Ford's translation, and his labour of love will not have been in vain, if he is able to induce
those who enjoy true poetry to study once more the masterpiece of that literature
from whence the great founders of English poetry drew so much of their sweet-
ness and power."—*Athenæum.*

*Sent Carriage Free to any part of the United Kingdom on
receipt of Postal Order for the amount.*

JOHN GRANT, 25 & 34 George IV. Bridge, Edinburgh.

Dobson (W. T.)—The Classic Poets, their Lives and their Times, with the Epics Epitomised, 452 pages, crown 8vo, cloth (pub 9s), 2s 6d.   Smith, Elder, & Co.

CONTENTS.—Homer's Iliad, The Lay of the Nibelungen, Cid Campeador, Dante's Divina Commedia, Ariosto's Orlando Furioso, Camoens' Lusiad, Tasso's Jerusalem Delivered, Spenser's Fairy Queen, Milton's Paradise Lost, Milton's Paradise Regained.

English Literature: A Study of the Prologue and Epilogue in English Literature, from Shakespeare to Dryden, by G. S. B., crown 8vo, cloth (pub 5s), 1s 6d.   Kegan Paul, 1884.

Will no doubt prove useful to writers undertaking more ambitious researches into the wider domains of dramatic or social history.

Johnson (Doctor)—His Friends and his Critics, by George Birkbeck Hill, D.C.L., crown 8vo, cloth (pub 8s), 2s. Smith, Elder, & Co.

"The public now reaps the advantage of Dr Hill's researches in a most readable volume.   Seldom has a pleasanter commentary been written on a literary masterpiece.   .   .   .   Throughout the author of this pleasant volume has spared no pains to enable the present generation to realise more completely the sphere in which Johnson talked and taught."—*Saturday Review.*

Jones' (Rev. Harry) East and West London, being Notes of Common Life and Pastoral Work in St James's, Westminster, and in St George's-in-the-East, crown 8vo, cloth (pub 6s), 2s. Smith, Elder, & Co.

"Mr Jones gives a graphic description of the trades and industries of East London, of the docks and their multifarious populations, of the bonded stores, of Jamrach and his wild animal repository, of Ratcliffe Highway with its homes and its snares for sailors, until the reader finds himself at home with all sorts and conditions of strange life and folk.   .   .   .   A better antidote to recent gloomy forebodings of our national decadence can hardly be found."—*Athenæum.*

Kaye (John William, F.R.S., author of " History of the War in Afghanistan ")—The Essays of an Optimist, crown 8vo, 8vo, cloth extra (pub 6s), 1s 6d.   Smith, Elder, & Co.

"The Essays are seven in number,—Holidays, Work, Success, Toleration, Rest, Growing Old, and the Wrong Side of the Stuff,—themes on which the author discourses with bright and healthy vigour, good sense, and good taste."— *Standard.*
" We most sincerely trust that this book may find its way into many an English household.   It cannot fail to instil lessons of manliness."—*Westminster Review.*

Selkirk (J. B.)—Ethics and Æsthetics of Modern Poetry, crown 8vo, cloth gilt (pub 7s), 2s.   Smith, Elder, & Co.

Sketches from Shady Places, being Sketches from the Criminal and Lower Classes, by Thor Fredur, crown 8vo, cloth (pub 6s), 1s.   Smith, Elder, & Co.

"Descriptions of the criminal and semi-criminal (if such a word may be coined) classes, which are full of power, sometimes of a disagreeable kind."—*Athenæum.*

Sent Carriage Free to any part of the United Kingdom on receipt of Postal Order for the amount.

JOHN GRANT, 25 & 34 George IV. Bridge, Edinburgh.

£ S. D.

By the Authoress of " The Land o' the Leal."

Nairne's (Baroness) Life and Songs, with a
Memoir, and Poems of Caroline Oliphant the Younger, edited
by Dr Charles Rogers, *portrait and other illustrations*, crown
8vo, cloth (pub 5s)   Griffin   0   2   6
" This publication is a good service to the memory of an excellent and gifted
lady, and to all lovers of Scottish Song."—*Scotsman.*

Ossian's Poems, translated by Macpherson,
24mo, best red cloth, gilt (pub 2s 6d)   0   1   6
A dainty pocket edition.

Perthshire—Woods, Forests, and Estates of
Perthshire, with Sketches of the Principal Families of the
County, by Thomas Hunter, Editor of the *Perthshire Consti-
tutional and Journal, illustrated with 30 wood engravings,*
crown 8vo (564 pp.), cloth (pub 12s 6d)   Perth   0   6   0
"Altogether a choice and most valuable addition to the County Histories of
Scotland."—*Glasgow Daily Mail.*

Duncan (John, Scotch Weaver and Botanist)
—Life of, with Sketches of his Friends and Notices of the
Times, by Wm. Jolly, F.R.S.E., H.M. Inspector of Schools,
etched portrait, crown 8vo, cloth (pub 9s)   Kegan Paul   0   4   0
"We must refer the reader to the book itself for the many quaint traits of
character, and the minute personal descriptions, which, taken together, seem to
give a life-like presentation of this humble philosopher. . . . The many incidental notices which the work contains of the weaver caste, the workman's
esprit de corps, and his wanderings about the country, either in the performance
of his work or, when that was slack, taking a hand at the harvest, form an interesting chapter of social history. The completeness of the work is considerably
enhanced by detailed descriptions of the district he lived in, and of his numerous
friends and acquaintance."—*Athenæum.*

Scots (Ancient)—An Examination of the An-
cient History of Ireland and Iceland, in so far as it concerns
the Origin of the Scots; Ireland not the Hibernia of the
Ancients; Interpolations in Bede's Ecclesiastical History and
other Ancient Annals affecting the Early History of Scotland
and Ireland—the three Essays in one volume, crown 8vo, cloth
(pub 4s)   Edinburgh, 1883   0   1   0
The first of the above treatises is mainly taken up with an investigation of the
early History of Ireland and Iceland, in order to ascertain which has the better
claim to be considered the original country of the Scots. In the second and
third an attempt is made to show that Iceland was the ancient Hibernia, and
the country from which the Scots came to Scotland; and further, contain a
review of the evidence furnished by the more genuine of the early British Annals
against the idea that Ireland was the ancient Scotia.

Magic and Astrology—Grant (James)—The
Mysteries of all Nations: Rise and Progress of Superstition,
Laws against and Trials of Witches, Ancient and Modern
Delusions, together with Strange Customs, Fables, and Tales
relating to Mythology, Miracles, Poets, and Superstition,
Demonology, Magic and Astrology, Trials by Ordeal, Super-
stition in the Nineteenth Century, &c., 1 thick vol, 8vo, cloth
(pub 12s 6d)   1880   0   2   6

An interesting work on the subject of Superstition, valuable alike to archæo-
logists and general readers. It is chiefly the result of antiquarian research and
actual observation during a period of nearly forty years.

A Story of the Shetland Isles.·

Saxby (*Jessie M., author of " Daala-Mist," &c.*)—*Rock-Bound*, a Story of the Shetland Isles, second edition, revised, crown 8vo, cloth (pub 2s), 6d.   Edinburgh, 1877.

"The life I have tried to depict is the life I remember twenty years ago, when the islands were far behind the rest of Britain in all that goes to make up modern civilisation."—*Extract from Preface.*

Burn (*R. Scott*)—*The Practical Directory for the Improvement of Landed Property*, Rural and Suburban, and the Economic Cultivation of its Farms (the most valuable work on the subject), plates and woodcuts, 2 vols, 4to, cloth (pub £3 3s), 15s, Paterson.

Burnet's Treatise on Painting, illustrated by 130 Etchings from celebrated pictures of the Italian, Venetian, Flemish, Dutch, and English Schools, also woodcuts, thick 4to, half morocco, gilt top (pub £4 10s), £2 2s.

The Costumes of all Nations, Ancient and Modern, exhibiting the Dresses and Habits of all Classes, Male and Female, from the Earliest Historical Records to the Nineteenth Century, by Albert Kretschmer and Dr Rohrbach, 104 coloured plates displaying nearly 2000 full-length figures, complete in one handsome volume, 4to, half morocco (pub £4 4s), 45s, Sotheran.

Dryden's Dramatic Works, Library Edition, with Notes and Life by Sir Walter Scott, Bart., edited by George Saintsbury, portrait and plates, 8 vols, 8vo, cloth (pub £4 4s), £1 10s, Paterson.

Lessing's (Dr J.) Ancient Oriental Carpet Patterns, after Pictures and Originals of the 15th and 16th Centuries, 35 plates (size 20 × 14 in.), beautifully coloured after the originals, 1 vol, royal folio, in portfolio (pub £3 3s), 21s, Sotheran.

The most beautiful Work on the " Stately Homes of England."

Nash's Mansions of England in the Olden Time, 104 Lithographic Views faithfully reproduced from the originals, with new and complete history of each Mansion, by Anderson, 4 vols in 2, imperial 4to, cloth extra, gilt edges (pub £6 6s), £2 10s, Sotheran.

Richardson's (Samuel) Works, Library Edition, with Biographical Criticism by Leslie Stephen, portrait, 12 vols, 8vo, cloth extra, impression strictly limited to 750 copies (pub £6 6s), £2 5s, London.

Sent Carriage Free to any part of the United Kingdom on receipt of Postal Order for the amount.

JOHN GRANT, 25 & 34 George IV. Bridge, Edinburgh.